T0368355

Lecture Notes of the Institute for Computer Sciences, Social Informatics and Telecommunications Engineering   **600**

The LNICST series publishes ICST's conferences, symposia and workshops.

LNICST reports state-of-the-art results in areas related to the scope of the Institute. The type of material published includes

- Proceedings (published in time for the respective event)
- Other edited monographs (such as project reports or invited volumes)

LNICST topics span the following areas:

- General Computer Science
- E-Economy
- E-Medicine
- Knowledge Management
- Multimedia
- Operations, Management and Policy
- Social Informatics
- Systems

Xiang Li · Yuhong Liu · Fan Wu

Editors

Smart Grid and Innovative Frontiers in Telecommunications

8th EAI International Conference, EAI SmartGIFT 2024a
Santa Clara, United States, March 23–24, 2024
Proceedings

Editors
Xiang Li
Santa Clara University
Santa Clara, CA, USA

Yuhong Liu
Santa Clara University
Santa Clara, CA, USA

Fan Wu
Beijing University of Posts
and Telecommunications
Beijing, China

ISSN 1867-8211   ISSN 1867-822X (electronic)
Lecture Notes of the Institute for Computer Sciences, Social Informatics
and Telecommunications Engineering
ISBN 978-3-031-78805-5   ISBN 978-3-031-78806-2 (eBook)
https://doi.org/10.1007/978-3-031-78806-2

This Springer imprint is published by the registered company Springer Nature Switzerland AG
The registered company address is: Gewerbestrasse 11, 6330 Cham, Switzerland

If disposing of this product, please recycle the paper.

Preface

We are delighted to introduce the proceedings of the 8th European Alliance for Innovation (EAI) International Conference on Smart Grid and Innovative Frontiers in Telecommunications (SmartGIFT 2023). This conference brought together researchers, developers, and practitioners around the world who are leveraging and developing smart grid technology for a smarter and more resilient grid. The theme of SmartGIFT 2023 was "AI and Security for Smart Grid and Wireless Communication".

The technical program of SmartGIFT 2023 consisted of 10 full papers in oral presentation sessions at the main conference tracks. The conference tracks were: Track 1 – Wireless Communication and Distribution Networks; Track 2 – Artificial Intelligence Technologies; Track 3 – Security in Wireless Communication; and Track 4 – System Design for Smart Grid and IoT. Aside from the high-quality technical paper presentations, the technical program also featured one keynote speaker. The keynote speaker was My T. Thai from the Department of Computer & Information Science & Engineering, University of Florida, Gainesville, Florida, USA.

Coordination with the steering chair, Imrich Chlamtac, was essential for the success of the conference. We sincerely appreciate his constant support and guidance. It was also a great pleasure to work with such an excellent organizing committee team for their hard work in organizing and supporting the conference. We are also grateful to the Conference Manager, Patricia Gabajova, for her support and to all the authors who submitted their papers to the SmartGIFT 2023 conference and workshops.

We strongly believe that the SmartGIFT conference provides a good forum for all researchers, developers, and practitioners to discuss all science and technology aspects relevant to smart grids. We also expect that future SmartGIFT conferences will be as successful and stimulating as indicated by the contributions presented in this volume.

Xiang Li
Yuhong Liu
Fan Wu

Organization

Steering Committee

Imrich Chlamtac	University of Trento, Italy
Kun Yang	University of Essex, UK
Victor C. M. Leung	University of British Columbia, Canada

Organizing Committee

General Chair

Xiang Li	Santa Clara University, USA

General Co-chairs

Hongwei Du	Harbin Institute of Technology, China
Haibing Lu	Santa Clara University, USA

TPC Chairs and Co-chairs

Yuhong Liu	Santa Clara University, USA
Fan Wu	Beijing University of Posts and Telecommunications, China

Local Chair

Navid Shaghaghi	Santa Clara University, USA

Workshops Chair

Meng Han	Zhejiang University, China

Publicity and Social Media Chair

Lei Fan	University of Houston, USA

Publications Chair

Kai Pan   Hong Kong Polytechnic University, China

Web Chair

Smita Ghosh   Santa Clara University, USA

Technical Program Committee

Yuheng Cao	Pengcheng Laboratory, China
Thusitha Dayaratne	Monash University, Australia
Yi Fang	Santa Clara University, USA
Mohsen Ghafouri	Concordia University, Canada
Hohyun Lee	Santa Clara University, USA
Lu Li	China Academy of Information and Communications Technology, China
Jiaqi Li	Beijing Institute for General Artificial Intelligence, China
Tao Liu	North China Electric Power University, China
Xin Ma	Monash University, Australia
Sijie Ruan	Beijing Institute of Technology, China
Ferdous Wahid Khan	Airbus Group Innovations, Germany
Chao Wu	National Intelligent Connected Vehicle Quality Inspection and Test Center (Chongqing), China
Jun Yan	Concordia University, Canada
Yang Yang	State Grid Information & Telecommunication Group Co., Ltd., China
Cong Zhang	Beijing University of Posts and Telecommunications, China
Qidong Zhao	North Carolina State University, USA

Contents

Wireless Communication
and Distribution Network

Machine Learning for Ambient Backscatter Channel Estimation and Signal Detection: Opportunities and Challenges

Diancheng Cheng, Fan Wu$^{(\boxtimes)}$, Cong Zhang, Jinjin Sun, and Yuan'an Liu

Beijing University of Posts and Telecommunications, Beijing 100876, China
wufanwww@bupt.edu.cn

Abstract. As a promising low-power connection paradigm in the ubiquitous Internet of Things (IoT), ambient backscatter communication (AmBC) collects energy from ambient radio frequency (RF) signals while using them as carrier signals, which brings ultra-low power consumption and deployment cost. However, it has not been widely applied in practice because of its difficulties in weak signal detection. To overcome these difficulties, machine learning (ML)-based methods have been highlighted recently. ML methods can achieve accurate signal processing under a low receive signal-to-interference-plus-noise ratio (SINR) in unpredictable interference communication scenarios, benefiting from their outstanding inference and classification tools. In this survey, a brief review of AmBC is first introduced and the four-fold signal-receiving challenges of AmBC are discussed. After that, two key signal processing technologies, i.e., AmBC channel estimation and AmBC signal detection, are emphasized. The representative ML-based methods of AmBC channel estimation and AmBC signal detection are summarized, following their advantages and disadvantages. Finally, some valuable research directions on this topic are introduced to guide future research.

Keywords: Ambient Backscatter Communication · Machine Learning · Channel Estimation · Signal Detection

1 Introduction

Backscatter communication, e.g., Radio Frequency IDentification (RFID), introduces an energy-saving connection paradigm to the Internet of Things (IoT), which uses load modulation to re-modulate dedicated or ambient carrier signals in a passive manner instead of generating radio waves actively. Because of no need for bulky and costly components (e.g., mixer, oscillator, ADC, etc.) on backscatter devices (BDs), such a scheme is particularly suitable for ultra-low-power and low-cost IoT scenarios. There exist three architectures of backscatter communication systems, including monostatic backscatter communication (MoBC), bistatic backscatter communication (BiBC), and AmBC [1]. Among

X. Li et al. (Eds.): SmartGift 2024, LNICST 600, pp. 3–19, 2025.
https://doi.org/10.1007/978-3-031-78806-2_1

them, AmBC is regarded as one of the most promising backscatter architectures since it has the potential to be deployed in an existing wireless network arbitrarily and backscatter data in the same frequency band with ambient RF sources, which will significantly reduce deployment costs while increasing spectrum efficiency. However, AmBC has not been widely applied in practice yet because of its crucial technical challenges in signal receiving. As the price of using free RF resources in the air, AmBC needs to work with uncontrollable RF sources and unpredictable carriers. Besides, the backscattered signal from the BDs is generally much weaker than the direct-link signal from the RF sources because the backscattered signal suffers from double path loss. Thus, it is more difficult to recover useful information than traditional wireless communication systems.

To solve signal-receiving challenges, numerous research on AmBC signal processing have been proposed, which mainly focus on two key technologies: AmBC channel estimation and AmBC signal detection. These works were supposed to pave economic and efficient ways for AmBC receivers to estimate channel parameters and distinguish symbols with little prior knowledge (e.g., carriers and channel state knowledge) and little cooperation between ambient RF sources and passive BDs. Many simple and classic methods were extended to AmBC scenarios in the early stages. For example, blind channel estimation [2] and energy detector [3] provided the most intuitive solutions to AmBC channel estimation and signal detection but with limited performance. Differential encoding [4] can release the need for channel estimation, but increase the power consumption of BDs. The classic maximum-likelihood estimation [5] was suitable for AmBC signal detection but needed a complex DLI cancellation design before detection.

Recently, machine learning (ML)-based methods have introduced new solutions to many intractable wireless communication problems without needing exact mathematical models or explicit programming, which can achieve outstanding performance [6]. As for AmBC channel estimation and signal detection, which is difficult to acquire necessary prior knowledge for modeling and is significantly differences from deterministic signal processing, ML-based methods have the potential to overcome the challenge of lacking knowledge of ambient RF source and channel state information (CSI) and reduce costs for canceling direct-link interference (DLI) from the ambient RF sources.

In this paper, we first provide a brief review of AmBC from the perspectives of history, architecture and working paradigms, which explains the advances of AmBC compared to other backscatter communications. Meanwhile, we clarify the crucial backscatter signal receiving problem of AmBC from four aspects and then highlight two key signal processing technologies: AmBC signal estimation and AmBC signal detection. After that, we emphasize ML-based methods for AmBC channel estimation and AmBC signal detection because they often outperform traditional methods benefiting from powerful classification, clustering, and neural network algorithms. We discuss the unique applicability of ML methods for AmBC signal receiving, and introduce ML methods for the two key technologies, respectively. In these sections, we summarize the goals, technique challenges, classical solutions, and current novel ML-based solutions according to different ML algorithms. Specifically, we classify these ML-based solutions into two categories according to whether they conduct feature engineering in advance or not. We discuss their methodology, advantages, and disadvantages. Finally, we propose some future research directions for ML methods on AmBC systems standing in the perspective of technique processes.

2   Brief Overview and Signal Receiving Issues

2.1   History, Architectures and Working Paradigms of AmBC

AmBC was first proposed in 2013 [7], which has been regarded as a promising technology to achieve ultra-low-power and low-cost communication in a passive manner. It can assist existing wireless communication networks (e.g., cognitive radio networks, wireless powered communications networks, etc.) to promote spectrum efficiency as a secondary system or be applied on machine-type communications (e.g., massive IoT networks) as a low-power connective scheme [1]. After the birth of AmBC, various ambient RF signals were explored as potential sources and carriers to realize ambient backscattering, starting with digital television (DTV) signals [7] and then extending to FM [8], Wi-Fi [9], Bluetooth [10], and even long range (LoRa) signals [11] (shown in Table 1). These explorations shaped the prototypes of AmBC systems and proposed many basic enabling technologies, e.g., load modulation, frequency shifting, etc. However, these prototypes can only work in short range and with low data rates limited by their architecture and working paradigms.

Table 1. Prototypes and Achieved Perfomances of AMBC Systems

Systems	Sources	Data Rate	Range	Pow.Consumption
Ambient Backscatter [7]	DTV	1 kbps	0.46 m–0.76 m	0.25μW
FM Backscatter [8]	FM	3.2 kbps	1.5 m–18.3 m	11.07μW
WiFi Backscatter [9]	WiFi	1 kbps	2.1 m	0.65μW
BLE Backscatter [10]	BLE	16.6 kbps	25 m–65 m	37μW
PLoRa [11]	LoRa	1.58 bps–2.23 bps	1.1 km	220μW

AmBC differs from other backscatter communications in architecture and works in three typical paradigms. Among the three architectures of backscatter communications, as shown in Fig. 1 (A), both MoBC and BiBC have dedicated carrier emitters, so they can control the whole process of backscattering autonomously. Especially when acting on signal receiving, their receivers have full prior knowledge of the carrier signal. Differently, AmBC captures ambient RF signals as carriers, which are uncontrollable and unpredictable. Therefore, signal receiving in AmBC is not a determinate signal processing problem anymore. In

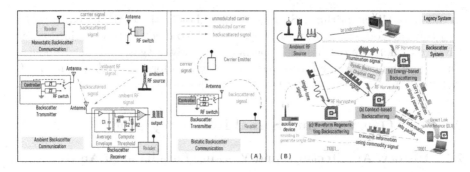

Fig. 1. A: Three architectures of backscatter communication. In MoBC, the carrier emitter and receiver are co-located at the reader. In BiBC, the carrier emitter is physically separated from the reader. In AmBC, the carrier signal is from an ambient RF source and there is no dedicated carrier emitter. **B:** Three working paradigms of AmBC. In energy-based backscattering, the ambient RF signal is regarded as an illumination signal and the BDs carry information on the signal power level. In context-based backscattering, generally, the packet signal is used as a carrier signal to embed information into the packet. In waveform regenerating backscattering, the single-tone signal that is purified from the ambient RF signal or generated by the auxiliary device is exploited to re-generate a waveform that is compatible with commodity devices.

reality, AmBC has three typical working paradigms according to current research work, including energy-based backscattering, context-based backscattering, and waveform regeneration backscattering, as shown in Fig. 1 (B). They carry useful information onto ambient RF signals in different piggyback manners. No matter which kind of working paradigm, however, signal receiving in AmBC faces serious DLI and low receive SINR, which are not so critical in traditional wireless communications and other backscatter communications.

2.2   Signal-Receiving Challenges in AmBC

The architecture and working paradigms make AmBC work at a low data rate (typically from several bps to several kbps) and a short communication range (typically from dozens of centimeters to several meters). Compared with mature backscatter communication, e.g. RFID, there is still a performance gap. We discuss the challenges of AmBC signal receiving from a system perspective and summarize them in the following four aspects.

1. **The Ambient RF Source:** The ambient RF source is uncontrollable, and the ambient carrier is unpredictable. The AmBC systems do not deploy their dedicated carrier emitters but capture and re-modulate RF signals from the surrounding open air. This is the reason why AmBC can cost much less on deployment than other backscatter systems and has the potential to achieve "plug and play" in existing wireless networks. However, these ambient RF sources are intended for legacy systems rather than AmBC systems. They

will not cooperate with AmBC systems and even cannot perceive their existence. Both BDs and ambient receivers have no sufficient knowledge about ambient RF sources used for carrier recovery. Besides, the ambient carrier is unpredictable since it is easily affected by the open environment.

2. **The BDs:** The BDs are limited in function due to strict power constraints and scarce hardware resources. Most BDs are powered by energy harvested from RF signals, which is typically at a μW level. They generally just act with load modulation and limited digital control. Since BDs work in a passive manner, they are not equipped with active RF components, e.g., amplifier, ADC, etc. Therefore, they cannot amplify incident signals, as well as signal processing and control. After energy harvesting and re-modulating at BDs, the modulated backscatter signals become weaker and more difficult to distinguish.

3. **The Backscatter Receivers:** The receivers are complex to design and confronted with an extremely low receiving SINR. With uncooperative ambient RF sources and simply functional BDs, the ambient receivers have to take on almost all the responsibility of communication control, which requires complicated hardware and protocol design. What interests more in this paper is that the ambient receivers are supposed to recover useful information under a very low receiving SINR, because the signal from direct link is generally several orders of magnitude higher than the backscatter signal in an AmBC system [4]. The receivers should adopt efficient DLI cancellation and weak signal-receiving technologies.

4. **The Channel Model:** The backscatter channel in AmBC has deeper fading. The modulation backscatter channel, also called the Dyadic backscatter channel (DBC), has different statistical characteristics from traditional one-way channels, and it has deeper fading [12]. This channel model mainly contains two paths of signals: the ambient RF signal from the direct link and the useful signal from the backscatter link. Since the useful signal travels from an ambient RF source to a BD and then is backscattered to a receiver from the BD, it suffers from double attenuation, which makes backscatter signals fade deeper.

2.3 Key Signal Processing Technologies of AmBC Signal Receiving

To overcome all the aforementioned four-fold challenges in AmBC signal receiving is a systematic problem. It involves a lot of hardware and software technologies, e.g., on-tag circuit designs, DLI cancellation, channel estimation, signal detection, etc. Among them, AmBC channel estimation and signal detection have become hot points these years because they are quite common in AmBC signal receiving and play a key role in signal-receiving challenges.

1. **AmBC Channel Estimation:** Channel estimation is an essential part of signal receiving, which can provide the necessary parameters for signal detection. Further, it can provide key information about instantaneous or statistical channels for transceivers to make communication more efficient and safe. According to the DBC model, there are three individual channel parameters,

which can be seen in Fig. 1 (A), that need to be estimated to obtain full channel state information (CSI). Once the perfect CSI is known, different useful information about BDs can be calculated according to received signal models. More commonly, estimating the partial channel parameters of a direct link and cascaded backscatter link is sufficient to distinguish different backscatter symbols. However, channel estimation is not easy in AmBC, since neither the ambient RF source nor BDs can provide training pilots. Blind channel estimation [2] was proposed naturally, but its performance was poor. Non-blind channel estimations are supposed to provide better estimation performance [13–15], but the cost may not be acceptable in such a power-constrained backscatter system.

2. **AmBC Signal Detection:** Signal detection in AmBC mainly refers to symbol information detection without perfect CSI, as well as knowledge of the ambient RF source. Since ambient channel estimation has been a costly task so far, numerous current studies pave economic ways to directly recover symbol information without estimating channel parameters [16–20]. Despite lacking knowledge of ambient RF source and channel parameters, the backscatter symbols are distinguishable for the receiver because the load modulation at BDs will introduce different link paths. When BDs reflect incident RF signals, there are both a direct link and a backscatter link; but when BDs absorb incident RF signals, there is only the a direct link. The ambient receivers can distinguish different symbol information by exploring power levels or other unintuitive features of the received signals. When it comes to distinguishing different categories with incomplete signal models, unknown prior knowledge, and implicit features, machine learning methods are highlighted.

3   Machine Learning Methods for AmBC Channel Estimation and Signal Detection

3.1   The Trends of Machine Learning Methods

Different from traditional wireless communications that are well-designed to achieve precise system cooperation with perfect prior knowledge, AmBC has difficulties extracting and recovering interested symbol information from a low SINR received signal without CSI due to the aforementioned four-fold challenges. Statistical signal processing technology is favored in AmBC because of lacking key parameters of the received signal. Recently, machine learning methods, which have rich experience in feature extraction and classification, have become a hot research point in AmBC channel estimation and signal detection. Here follows its unique applicability in AmBC.

1. **High fitness for stochastic signal processing tasks in AmBC:** The received signal in AmBC is of great stochasticity for ambient receivers since it comes from an unknown source and experiences unknown re-modulation. The statistical learning methods, e.g., probability analysis and parameter estimation, are often preferred to deal with stochastic signals. As a classical statistical learning method, machine learning can effectively assist AmBC receivers

to obtain channel parameters from the received signal without empirical knowledge [13,15] and distinguish different symbol information [16–20].

2. **Performance improvement on AmBC channel estimation and signal detection:** The existing methods of AmBC channel estimation and signal detection mainly explore the backscattered signals from the perspective of communication and often focus on easily observed intuitive physical quantities (e.g., energy level), which will limit the performance to system design experience. The ML-based method is a data-driven method. It is skilled in dealing with rich and complex signal characteristics in data, not limited to intuitive physical quantities (e.g., signal constellation [19]), which can improve the accuracy of AmBC channel estimation and signal detection. In addition, the deep learning method can often mine more effective features beyond design experience through a specific neural network (e.g., the spatial and temporal correlation of the received pilot signal [15] and the eigenvalue of the sampling correlation matrix [20]), which will significantly improve the performance.

3. **Adaptable to volatile and massive communication scenarios:** AmBC captures carriers from open air, which is vulnerable to the legacy wireless network and surrounding environment. When they change, the methods based on mathematical analysis and specific models cannot be inferred and predicted, which brings serious performance degradation. In addition, when an AmBC system comes to massive IoT scenarios, the channel and signal model becomes quite complicated, which makes it hard to propose an accurate model and obtain a mathematical solution. Fortunately, data-driven ML-based methods have inference and prediction ability. They can adjust the trained model flexibly and timely to improve the performance of AmBC channel estimation and signal detection in these scenarios.

3.2   Machine Learning Methods for AmBC Channel Estimation

In AmBC, many researchers assume perfect CSI is known before signal detection. However, estimating channel parameters in such a low-power backscatter communication system is challenging and unaffordable. This section will discuss specific goals and technical challenges of AmBC channel estimation, and introduce ML-assisted methods, which learn implicit channel parameters from noisy training pilots.

Goals: A typical three-node AmBC system is composed of an ambient RF source, a single-antenna BD, and a single/multi-antenna receiver, as shown in Fig. 2 (A). It usually fits the following channel models:

- There are mainly two links: A direct link from the ambient RF source to the receiver (S-R) and a double attenuated cascade link relayed by the BD (S-BD-R).
- When transmitting symbol '0', the BD absorbs all ambient signals without backscattering, so there is only a direct link. While transmitting '1', the BD backscatters ambient signals introducing the cascade link.

- Since BDs are very close to ambient RF sources for collecting more energy, the channel between them can be usually regarded as a constant.

The goal of AmBC channel estimation is to obtain the individual or combined channel parameters in the above channel model when transmitting different symbols. It is mainly used to recover symbol information since the channel changes with load modulation at BDs.

Technical Challenges: Channel estimation in AmBC is much more difficult than that in traditional wireless communication. The commonly used channel estimation methods in traditional wireless communication include blind estimation, semi-blind estimation, and non-blind estimation. Non-blind estimation algorithms based on pilot training are most commonly used, e.g., least square (LS), linear minimum mean square error (LMMSE), and minimum mean square error (MMSE). They occupy a certain spectrum of resources but have high accuracy. However, they are not applicable in AmBC. The reasons are as follows:

- Since the ambient RF source is not cooperative, it cannot provide necessary training pilots, and BDs cannot transmit pilots actively either due to energy and hardware constraints.
- The channel parameters are not consistent when the BDs transmit different symbols since the channel changes when BDs act load modulation, which increases the complexity of estimation.

Although blind channel estimation methods can be used to avoid the need for pilots, their performance is not appealing. The authors in [13] combined the expectation maximization (EM) algorithm to blind channel estimation in a typical AmBC system. However, it can only obtain the amplitude of the channel parameters, which is far from meeting the requirement of accurately describing AmBC channels. Therefore, non-blind and semi-blind channel estimation is still the research hotspot for AmBC channel estimation [21]. AmBC channel estimation needs to solve the problems of obtaining training pilots and estimating inconsistent channel parameters when BDs transmit different symbols.

Protocol for Passive Pilots Acquirement: To obtain training pilots, a classic communication protocol is widely used in the AmBC system, as shown in Fig. 2(B). In the transmission frame, it utilizes the amount of symbols with known contents as training pilots before transmitting useful data, which replaces the need for necessary pilots from the ambient RF source. Considering transmission synchronization in this protocol, only simple interaction between the receiver and the BD is needed in practice. At the beginning of each frame, the receiver will send a high-level pulse to inform BD of the transmission start [20].

Besides, to solve the problem that channel parameters vary with BD symbols, it is necessary to provide an individual training phase for every symbol in the above transmission frame. In current studies, which prefer simple binary

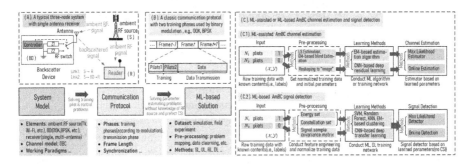

Fig. 2. The structure and process of machine learning method for AmBC channel detection and AmBC signal detection.

modulation (e.g., OOK and BPSK), there are two training phases for estimating inconsistent channel parameters before transmitting useful data. It is worth noting that this popular protocol has a trade-off between training accuracy and data rate since it has to provide more training phases while the BD adopts high-order modulation. However, it is still the mainstream solution because of its simplicity, and we highlight this protocol because it has been widely used in ML-based methods in AmBC channel estimation and signal detection.

Current ML-Assisted AmBC Channel Estimation: After solving pilot problems, non-blind and semi-blind channel estimation methods can be applied in AmBC. The traditional methods make it difficult to achieve accurate and efficient performance in AmBC. For example, LS usually regards channel parameters as deterministic but unknown constants, but the AmBC channel is a random variable affected by the environment, so the estimation is not accurate. Although LMMSE and MMSE regarded the channel parameters as random variables, they need quite a lot of computation to determine a model. In addition, when the channel changes, it is expensive to recalculate a new model. To promote estimation performance and provide a model with inference ability, ML-assisted methods are favored in AmBC channel estimation, which is summarized in Table 2. These methods are introduced to classify channel vectors or matrices into different categories according to different symbols without sufficient prior knowledge.

To apply machine learning methods in AmBC channel estimation, the general process is shown in Fig. 2(C.1). The input raw data is sampled from training phases of the classic communication protocol (generally with unknown content as labels). Before the training task, the raw training data must be pre-processed to obtain initial parameters or get a normalized input format for training the model. Then, appropriate machine learning algorithms are chosen for model training. Finally, the estimated channel parameters are applied to corresponding AmBC systems, and the well-trained model could be deployed in corresponding online transmission.

Table 2. ML-Based Methods for AMBC Channel Estimation

Category	Methods	Advantages	Disadvantages
ML-assisted channel estimation	UL (EM, semi-blind channel estimator) [13]	1. Obtain combined channel parameter 2. More efficient than blind channel estimation	1. Need few pilots from RF source 2. Need rough estimation
DL-based channel estimation	DL (CNN, Residual learning,denoiser) [15]	1. Obtain channel coefficient vectors 2. Hign performance close to optimal MMSE channel estimation	1. Need larger dataset 2. Higher computational complexity

In [13], the authors proposed a semi-blind ML-assisted methods based on the EM algorithm. They used LS estimation to pre-process pilots and obtained rough channel parameters as initial parameters of EM estimation. It achieved more accurate channel state information than blind channel estimation. In the deep learning method, the channel estimation problem can be transformed into an image denoising problem, which has achieved many mature solutions [15,22]. In the pre-processing phases, the training pilots are reshaped into two-dimensional data, and a noisy channel "picture" is obtained. Then the deep learning image denoising method is used to obtain a well-denoised picture. Finally, the picture is recovered to a one-dimensional vector to obtain the AmBC channel parameter. In [15], the authors proposed a deep residual learning method based on the convolutional neural network (CNN) to estimate the AmBC channel. The proposed architecture denoised the channel picture through several denoising units, each of which contained an L-layer network. The method can achieve an accuracy comparable to the optimal MMSE channel estimation under perfect assumption. That is because the temporal and spatial characteristics of the pilots are utilized in the process of denoising the channel picture.

3.3 Machine Learning Methods for AmBC Signal Detection

In most traditional wireless communication, signal detection is a series of signal processes of recovering useful information under demand received SINR after perfect channel estimation. However, the received SINR in AmBC is quite low, and perfect CSI is difficult to obtain. ML-based AmBC signal detection introduces effective and economical manners.

Goal: The goal of AmBC signal detection is to recover different modulated symbols from the received signal under extremely low SINR without perfect CSI. It is worth noting that binary impedance modulation is widely used in current research because of its simplicity. Therefore, the goal of AmBC signal detection is usually to detect two different symbols in the superimposed backscatter signal.

Technical Challenges: AmBC signal detection is significantly different from traditional wireless communication:

- AmBC receivers face weak signal detection problems under ultra-low SINR because the received backscatter signal is generally several orders of magnitude lower than the ambient RF signal from a direct link. DLI is desperately needed.
- The BDs are low-power passive devices, which do not have sufficient energy and hardware resources to support complex signal processing and control. Therefore, they cannot amplify incident signals and act in complex modulating and encoding, which makes the useful backscatter signal hard to distinguish.
- The CSI is absent. AmBC channel estimation is a challenging task. The receiver cannot know the knowledge of ambient signals and channel state, which makes AmBC signal detection more difficult.

Classical Solutions: In the early state after AmBC was proposed, many simple and intuitive non-coherent detectors were proposed, including energy detection (ED) [7] and maximum likelihood detection (MLD) [5].

The ED is based on received signal power levels between different symbols. It is widely used in early prototypes, and it can be implemented only using analog circuits. However, it is merely suitable for a very short distance. In [7], the authors designed a classic analog ED. It averaged and smoothed the envelope of received backscatter signal first, and then detected symbol information by a carefully designed threshold comparing circuit. However, in the superimposed received signal, the useful backscatter signal is often drowned in the strong direct link ambient RF signal, which significantly reduces its detection performance.

The MLD is based on received signal statistical distributions between different symbols, which regards AmBC signal detection as a hypothesis testing problem [5]. Such algorithms often assume that the ambient RF signal follows circularly symmetric complex Gaussian distribution (CSCG) distribution and the superimposed received signal will follow the same statistical distribution model (e.g., Gaussian Mixture Model) with different parameters when BDs backscatter different symbols. By analyzing the received signal, the likelihood or log-likelihood function can be designed to estimate different distribution parameters in the hypothesis space. However, the real statistical distribution model in AmBC is more complex than the assumption above since the surrounding environment is changeful, and the differences between assumed models are usually not significant because the ambient RF source performs a dominant contribution instead of a useful backscatter signal.

Current ML-Based AmBC Signal Detection: Compared to ED and MLD, ML-based AmBC signal detection can conduct more distinguishable features between different symbols, and has powerful classification and clustering tools to put received signals into correct symbol categories. From the perspective of constructing features, ML-based methods for AmBC signal detection can be divided into ML methods based on feature engineering and deep learning (DL) methods based on the artificial neural network (ANN), as summarized in Table 3

Table 3. ML-Based Methods for AMBC Signal Detection

Category	Methods		Advantages	Disadvantages
ML Methods Based on Feature Engineering	Energy based	SL (SVM, random forest) [16]	1. Jointly consider channel estimation and signal detection 2. Directly recover symbol without CSI	1. Difficult to collect labeled dataset 2. Need to cancel DLI
		SL(KNN) [17] UL(EM) [18]		
	Pattern based	UL(EM) [19]	1. Little affected by DLI 2. Fast convergence rate	1. Need to analyze input feature 2. Need remarkable pattern feature
DL Methods Based on ANN	DL (CNN, DNN, transfer learning) [20]		1. More distinguished feature(e.g., temporal and spacial features) 2. Higher detection performance	1. Need larger dataset 2. Hign computational complexity

ML Methods Based on Feature Engineering: These methods need to construct feature engineering according to specific problems before model training. The features describe the individual characteristics of the input data, and feature engineering is generally conducted according to background knowledge and previous experience. In AmBC, the popular features include intuitive physical quantity [16–18] and communication patterns [19] of the signal. At present, a large number of ML algorithms have been applied to AmBC signal detection based on feature engineering. Technically including, supervised learning (SL) methods, e.g., support vector machine (SVM) [16], random forests [16], K-Nearest Neighbors (KNN) [17], and unsupervised learning (UL) methods (e.g., EM algorithm [19]).

The SVM and random forest methods are explored in [16], where a typical AmBC system with BPSK modulation at BD was adopted, and it assumed system deployment and channel states remained unchanged. This work utilized energy sets as input features, which were conducted from the average of N signal samples after data enhancement. Since the contents of signal samples were known as labels, the input feature vectors and labels were used by SVM and random forest algorithms, and binary classifiers were output for direct symbol detection. In re-processing, this work first estimated the ambient RF signal by an MMSE estimator and then eliminated it from the original received signal to enhance the power level of useful backscatter signals. It is worth noting that such pre-processing is a software DLI cancellation. The error rates of the proposed methods were lower than ED and traditional MMSE detection, especially under low SNR.

The KNN method was proposed in [17]. In this study, an AmBC system with a ULA antenna array receiver and adopting BPSK modulation, as well as the protocol in Fig. 2(B), was considered. The samples of training pilot signals were used as input feature vectors directly to calculate distances to their k nearest neighbors. Besides, beamforming technology was utilized to distinguish DLI and backscatter signals, and Hadamard encoding was exploited to correct weak signal transmission. In pre-processing, the receiver estimated the angle of arrival (AoA) of the DLI first to obtain the weight vector. Then according to the weight vector, the useful backscatter signal was shifted to an orthogonal signal space. After that, the samples of clear backscatter signals were regarded as the input vectors of the KNN algorithm, and the output was the classifier. Since the symbols were encoded by Hadamard codeword, the receiver can decode it for error correction, which can promote detection accuracy. The proposed method can achieve non-error receiving in the high SNR region when the distance is not too long.

The UL method based on the energy set and the EM algorithm was introduced in [18]. It studied a typical AmBC system, assuming that the ambient RF source adopted an equal amplitude modulation, and so the average energy levels of the received signal only depended on load modulation at BDs. However, the difference between energy levels was generally very small because of strong DLI. To avoid directly using energy as an input feature, the authors built mixture distributions to describe energy features when BDs transmitted different symbols. Then, the corresponding distribution parameters of different symbols were estimated by using the EM algorithm. This method has good performance when the BD is not far away from the receiver, but when the distance increases or the channel states change, the clustering accuracy will decline.

The above methods are all based on energy feature engineering, which is limited by DLI. To expand alternative features, the authors in [19] explored a UL method based on the pattern of the signal constellation. The authors found that the received superimposed signal can maintain the constellation pattern similar to the ambient RF source signal, and thus they considered constellation pattern as a feature to distinguish different symbols. This work first assumed the received superimposed signal followed the Gaussian Mixture model (GMM) and mined the corresponding relationship between the received signal and constellation patterns. The clustering results were solved by the EM algorithm. Then different symbols were matched with clustering results according to labels. In the above process, DLI did not affect the generation of constellation patterns, so the performance of the proposed method can overcome the technical challenges faced by energy features and achieve better performance than energy-based feature engineering.

DL Methods Based on ANN: The ML method based on feature engineering relies too much on background knowledge and feature engineering experience. Limited by that, the designed training model is not always optimal. Instead, the DL methods based on ANN can extract and analyze the hidden features of the raw input data through the designed neural networks. DL methods have made many achievements in wide fields, e.g., traditional wireless communication, natural language processing, computer vision, etc. In AmBC signal detection, the DL methods are expected to combine with the multi-antenna receiver to explore abundant instinct features (e.g., temporal and spatial features) in raw data to achieve better detection performance [23].

The article [20] designed a deep transfer learning framework suitable for AmBC signal detection. It considered a classical AmBC system using the multi-antenna receiver and adopted the classical communication protocol. The symbol detection problem using OOK modulation was transferred into a binary hypothesis detection problem in this research. To utilize rich temporal and spatial features, the covariance matrix was used as input data to extract features via two convolution layers. The parameters obtained after training can obtain the optimal likelihood ratio test (LRT) performance, which is close to the optimal signal detector with perfect CSI.

4   Future Research Trends

4.1   Enriching Data Sets

At present, the data sets used in ML methods of AmBC channel estimation and signal detection are mainly manually simulated based on the typical three-node AmBC system. There is still a lack of real data in field experiments of actual communication scenarios, let alone standard data sets for scholars to conduct extensive research on ML methods. It is of great significance to enrich AmBC data set generation methods and construct real data sets for AmBC channel estimation and AmBC signal detection.

4.2   Improving Model Accuracy

Both supervised learning and unsupervised learning require a large number of training data to ensure the accuracy of the trained model. However, online training with typical communication protocols cannot provide such a large scale of data. The current research transmits known content pilot symbols to obtain the original training data set with labels for offline training. However, the environment is volatile, and the offline data sets usually cannot accurately describe the real-time channels, and thus the accuracy of the ML method is reduced. To solve this problem, transfer learning can conduct abundant offline training to obtain the basic parameters of AmBC. Few fine-tuning steps are conducted to make the trained model more accurate for real-time channels in online training. It accelerates the training speed in new scenarios. In addition, data enhancement techniques can be adopted to maximize the utilization of limited pilot symbols.

4.3 Reducing Training Costs

The computational complexity of ML methods is generally higher than traditional methods. Both supervised learning and unsupervised learning methods usually require a large of computational resources for model training. Meanwhile, deep learning methods have higher computation requirements because they use multi-layer neural networks. The computational cost of these methods may not be afforded in many AmBC systems. Simplifying training models or neural networks and reducing the training overhead of ML methods are crucial in ultra-low-power IoT scenarios.

4.4 Expanding Application Scopes

The ML methods discussed in this paper are mainly used in the physical layer to handle channel estimation and signal detection challenges in AmBC systems. In the future, AmBC is supposed to be applied in large-scale IoT networks, where it will face more challenges in the MAC layer and network layer. Although ML methods have been used in traditional wireless communications from the physical layer to the application layer, the unique technical challenges discussed in AmBC (e.g., energy constraints, noncooperation of ambient RF source, and lack of perfect CSI) are still major obstacles to ML methods in other layers of AmBC networks. Expanding the application scopes of the ML method AmBC still needs to solve these technical challenges.

5   Conclusion

In this article, we provide a survey on ML-based methods for AmBC channel estimation and signal detection. We first provide a brief overview of AmBC from its brief history, architecture, and working paradigms. Then we summarize signal-receiving issues in AmBC, where we discuss the challenges in different aspects and highlight signal processing key technologies. After that, we focus on machine learning methods for AmBC channel estimation and AmBC signal detection, including the goals, technical challenges, classical solutions, and current ML-based methods. Finally, we introduce many future research trends.

Acknowledgements. This work was supported in part by the Beijing Natural Science Foundation (Grant No. JQ21036), the National Natural Science Foundation of China (Grant No. 62293494, No. 62301078, No. 61821001, No. 62271086), the China Postdoctoral Science Foundation (Grant No. GZB20230086), and the Beijing Key Laboratory of Work SafetyIntelligent Monitoring.

References

1. Van Huynh, N., Hoang, D.T., Lu, X., Niyato, D., Wang, P., Kim, D.I.: Ambient backscatter communications: a contemporary survey. IEEE Commun. Surv. Tutor. **20**(4), 2889–2922 (2018)
2. Ma, S., Wang, G., Fan, R., Tellambura, C.: Blind channel estimation for ambient backscatter communication systems. IEEE Commun. Lett. **22**(6), 1296–1299 (2018)
3. Altuwairgi, K.H., Tota Khel, A.M., Hamdi, K.A.: Energy detection for reflecting surfaces-aided ambient backscatter communications. IEEE Trans. Green Commun. Netw. **8**(1), 279–290 (2024)
4. Wang, G., Gao, F., Fan, R., Tellambura, C.: Ambient backscatter communication systems: detection and performance analysis. IEEE Trans. Commun. **64**(11), 4836–4846 (2016)
5. Jing, F., Zhang, H., Gao, M., Xue, B.: Bayesian-mle signal detection for multi-antenna ambient backscatter communication. IET Commun. **16**(6), 672–684 (2022)
6. Sun, Y., Peng, M., Zhou, Y., Huang, Y., Mao, S.: Application of machine learning in wireless networks: Key techniques and open issues. IEEE Commun. Surv. Tutor. **21**(4), 3072–3108 (2019)
7. Liu, V., Parks, A., Talla, V., Gollakota, S., Wetherall, D., Smith, J.R.: Ambient backscatter: wireless communication out of thin air. ACM SIGCOMM Comput. Commun. Rev. **43**(4), 39–50 (2013)
8. Wang, A., Iyer, V., Talla, V., Smith, J.R., Gollakota, S.: FM backscatter: enabling connected cities and smart fabrics. In: 14th USENIX Symposium on Networked Systems Design and Implementation (NSDI 17), pp. 243–258 (2017)
9. Kellogg, B., Parks, A., Gollakota, S., Smith, J.R., Wetherall, D.: Wi-Fi Backscatter: Internet Connectivity for RF-Powered Devices, pp. 607–618 (2014)
10. Ensworth, J.F., Reynolds, M.S.: Every smart phone is a backscatter reader: modulated backscatter compatibility with Bluetooth 4.0 low energy (BLE) devices. In: 2015 IEEE International Conference on RFID (RFID), pp. 78–85. IEEE (2015)
11. Peng, Y., et al.: PLoRa: a passive long-range data network from ambient lora transmissions. In: Proceedings of the 2018 Conference of the ACM Special Interest Group on Data Communication, pp. 147–160 (2018)
12. Griffin, J.D., Durgin, G.D.: Link envelope correlation in the backscatter channel. IEEE Commun. Lett. **11**(9), 735–737 (2007)
13. Ma, S., Zhu, Y., Wang, G., He, R.: Machine learning aided channel estimation for ambient backscatter communication systems. In: 2018 IEEE International Conference on Communication Systems (ICCS), pp. 67–71. IEEE (2018)
14. Abdallah, S., Verboven, Z., Saad, M., Albreem, M.A.: Channel estimation for full-duplex multi-antenna ambient backscatter communication systems. IEEE Trans. Commun. (2023)
15. Liu, X., Liu, C., Li, Y., Vucetic, B., Ng, D.W.K.: Deep residual learning-assisted channel estimation in ambient backscatter communications. IEEE Wirel. Commun. Lett. **10**(2), 339–343 (2020)
16. Hu, Y., Wang, P., Lin, Z., Ding, M., Liang, Y.-C.: Machine learning based signal detection for ambient backscatter communications. In: ICC 2019-2019 IEEE International Conference on Communications (ICC), pp. 1–6. IEEE (2019)
17. Wang, X., Duan, R., Yigitler, H., Menta, E., Jantti, R.: Machine learning-assisted detection for BPSK-modulated ambient backscatter communication systems. In: 2019 IEEE Global Communications Conference (GLOBECOM), pp. 1–6. IEEE (2019)

18. Zhang, Q., Liang, Y.-C.: Signal detection for ambient backscatter communications using unsupervised learning. In: 2017 IEEE Globecom Workshops (GC Wkshps), pp. 1–6. IEEE (2017)
19. Zhang, Q., Guo, H., Liang, Y.-C., Yuan, X.: Constellation learning-based signal detection for ambient backscatter communication systems. IEEE J. Sel. Areas Commun. 37(2), 452–463 (2018)
20. Liu, C., Wei, Z., Ng, D.W.K., Yuan, J., Liang, Y.-C.: Deep transfer learning for signal detection in ambient backscatter communications. IEEE Trans. Wirel. Commun. 20(3), 1624–1638 (2020)
21. Abdallah, S., Verboven, Z., Saad, M., Albreem, M.A.: Channel estimation for full-duplex multi-antenna ambient backscatter communication systems. IEEE Trans. Commun. (2023)
22. Liu, C., Liu, X., Ng, D.W.K., Yuan, J.: Deep residual learning for channel estimation in intelligent reflecting surface-assisted multi-user communications. IEEE Trans. Wirel. Commun. 21(2), 898–912 (2021)
23. Guo, S., Zhao, X., Zhang, W.: Throughput maximization for RF powered cognitive Noma networks with backscatter communication by deep reinforcement learning. IEEE Trans. Wirel. Commun. (2023)

Phased Array Networking TT&C Relay Terminal with Interference Suppression Technology

Liu Liu[1,2], Tian Liu[2], Yang Li[3], Wensheng Pan[3], and Yan Zhang[1(✉)]

[1] School of Communication Engineering, Xidian University, Xian 710071, China
yanzhang@xidian.edu.cn
[2] Southwest China Institute of Electronic Technology, Chengdu 610036, China
[3] National Key Laboratory of Wireless Communications, University of Electronic Science and Technology of China, Chengdu 611731, China

Abstract. This article aims at the interference suppression problem of full-duplex relay terminals in the telemetry, tracking and command (TT&C) network system, analyzes the interference signal characteristics and the delay expansion of the self-interference signal when the transmitting and receiving antenna arrays are separated, and analyzes the interference in sub-arrays of different sizes. To solve the signal delay expansion, a kind of interference suppression method is proposed after the combination of array antenna reception beamforming. This method expands the delay range according to the layout of the array and the delay expansion of interference signals in sub-arrays of different sizes. All array elements are equivalent to one array element, which greatly reduces the complexity of radio frequency suppression. Theoretical analysis and simulation experimental results show that this method can effectively suppress interference signals. For the scenario of 256 array element transmitting front and 256 array element receiving front, the simulation compared the interference suppression performance under different tap numbers. The simulation results show that using 16 taps can suppress interference with a carrier frequency of 26.8 GHz and a bandwidth of 200 MHz. The signal suppression capability is greater than 47 dB.

Keywords: Phased array · network measurement and control · relay terminal · full-duplex · radio frequency interference suppression

1 Introduction

With the rapid development of unmanned platform technologies, the number of large-scale constellations, star clusters, and formations is constantly increasing, giving rise to an urgent need for a pervasive and all-time TT&C communication network. As the sole channel connecting ground stations with aircraft, the TT&C communication system plays a pivotal role in transmitting flight instructions, equipment status, and reconnaissance data. Its stability and reliability are crucial for maintaining the normal operation of the entire network.

X. Li et al. (Eds.): SmartGift 2024, LNICST 600, pp. 20–35, 2025.
https://doi.org/10.1007/978-3-031-78806-2_2

However, under the conditions of large-scale and wide-area distribution, the varying distances and visible fields of view between aircraft result in significant dynamic variations in wireless link attenuation, leading to high probabilities of measurement and control interruptions and limited durations [1, 2]. To address this issue, the introduction of relay nodes has proven to be an effective solution. By strategically positioning relay nodes, it is possible to forward telemetry and telecommand information, maintain the continuity of tracking and orbit measurement, and establish a distributed networking TT&C communication system based on relay nodes, realizing all-time and pervasive interconnectedness [3–7].

Existing unmanned platform networking TT&C systems typically employ frequency-division duplexing (FDD) or time-division duplexing (TDD) for duplexing. Nevertheless, these approaches are associated with complexities in frequency pairing and limitations in channel capacity. In contrast, co-frequency co-time full-duplex (CCFD) wireless communication technology enables concurrent transmission and reception on the same frequency, facilitating more flexible spectrum allocation and usage, as well as improved channel utilization efficiency and networking access timeliness. Therefore, the application of CCFD technology in large-scale distributed networking TT&C communication systems holds significant promise [9, 10].

The utilization of millimeter-wave signals, characterized by high frequencies, short wavelengths, and miniaturized antenna sizes, has enabled the deployment of millimeter-wave multi-antenna systems on aircraft. While system energy consumption may increase with the expansion of antenna arrays, the directional beamforming capabilities of multiple antennas not only enhance transmission distances but also provide anti-interference and low-intercept characteristics, thereby bolstering network reliability and security [11]. Consequently, millimeter-wave multi-antenna CCFD technology is poised to become a crucial technology for relay nodes in future distributed networking TT&C communication systems.

However, multi-antenna co-frequency transceiver systems face more complex self-interference issues. The self-interference generated by multiple transmit antennas couples and superimposes on the receive antennas [12, 13], potentially leading to saturation and blocking of the receiver's radio frequency (RF) front-end. Furthermore, the analog-to-digital converter (ADC) after receive beamforming is more sensitive compared to the low-noise amplifier (LNA), imposing stricter requirements on the dynamic range of the received signal. This elevates the demand for self-interference suppression in array antennas.

Existing self-interference suppression techniques primarily encompass spatial self-interference suppression [14–21], digital self-interference suppression [22–24], and RF self-interference suppression [25–27]. While these techniques have demonstrated a certain degree of effectiveness in mitigating self-interference, challenges remain. Particularly in phased array systems, the numerous transmit and receive antenna elements give rise to a more intricate self-interference scenario, complicating the task of RF interference suppression. Currently, there is a dearth of research on RF interference suppression techniques specifically tailored for phased arrays, which poses a bottleneck for the practical application of phased array full-duplex technology.

To address this gap, this paper proposes an RF self-interference suppression method tailored for phased array networking TT&C relay terminals. This method is primarily applied after receive beamforming and before the signal enters the receiver's mixing stage. By suppressing the combined self-interference, it aims to prevent saturation of the down-conversion channel and reduce the demand for dynamic range in the receiver channel. Given the vast number of transmit and receive antennas and the varying spatial positions of the array elements, the self-interference signal often contains multiple strong direct paths. To address this, the proposed method leverages the concept of merging self-interferences with different delays within the relevant bandwidth into a single interference. By appropriately grouping antennas with similar delay differences due to their spatial positions and selecting an appropriate number of taps for suppression, the method effectively mitigates self-interference.

2   System Model

2.1   Phased Array Network Measurement and Control Relay Terminal Usage Scenarios

The usage scenario of the phased array network measurement and control relay terminal is shown in Fig. 1. Network 1 and Network 2 are different communication networks at the same operating frequency. Network 1 needs to exchange information with Network 2, due to the long distance between the networks, but direct communication cannot be accomplished, so a relay terminal is required.

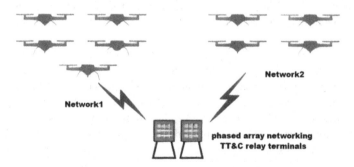

Fig. 1. Usage scenarios of phased array networking TT&C relay terminals

The phased array network measurement and control relay terminal uses the same frequency as Network 1 and Network 2 to receive the information from Network 1 and forward it to Network 2 to complete the relay function. At this time, the transmission and reception of the phased array network measurement and control relay terminal work at the same time, and the transmission and reception work at the same frequency. In order to ensure the normal operation of the relay terminal, the transmitter coupling signal needs to be suppressed at the receiving end.

2.2 Phased Array Network Measurement and Control Relay Terminal System Model

Figure 2 shows the structural block diagram of the phased array network measurement and control terminal. After the signal transmitted from the remote end is received by the receiving antenna, it is sent to the receiving link for processing and digital signal processing. The processed digital signal passes through the transmitting link and the transmitting antenna is sent out to complete the relay. In this system, the same frequency is used for reception and transmission. The receiving antenna not only receives the small signal from the remote end, but also receives the strong radio frequency signal transmitted and forwarded by the terminal itself. The transmitted signal causes strong interference to the received signal, so the receiver needs suppress the received self-interference signal, otherwise the remote signal cannot be correctly demodulated. In order to reduce the impact of co-channel interference on received signals, antenna isolation technology, digital interference cancellation technology and radio frequency interference cancellation technology are usually used. This article studies radio frequency interference suppression technology for phased array array antennas.

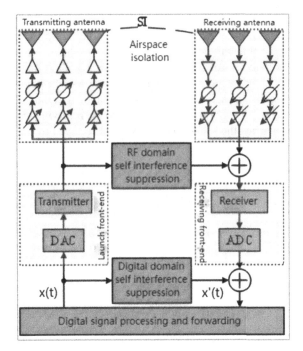

Fig. 2. Structure of phased array networking TT&C terminal architecture

2.3 Phased Array Self-interference Signal Model

For a transceiver antenna using a phased array of $P \times Q$ array elements placed in the same plane, the model is shown in Fig. 3. Suppose the (1,1) lattice element is the reference array element, establish a Cartesian coordinate system based on the reference array element, d_x is the horizontal spacing, d_y is the vertical spacing, for any beam direction (φ, θ), φ is the direction angle, θ is the pitch angle.

The spatial phase difference of other array elements relative to the (1,1) lattice element is

$$\Delta\phi_{i,k} = \frac{2\pi}{\lambda}\left((i-1)d_x \cos\varphi \cos\theta + (k-1)d_y \sin\varphi \sin\theta\right) \tag{1}$$

Among them, λ is the signal wavelength, $i = 1...P$, $k = 1...Q$.

For the channel phase $\phi_{i,k}$ of any radiation array element, it can be expressed as:

$$\phi_{i,k} = \phi_{1,1} + \Delta\phi_{i,k} \tag{2}$$

For the (i,k)th array element of the transmitting antenna, its radiation signal complex radio frequency signal can be expressed as:

$$s_{i,k}(t) = \sqrt{p}x(t)e^{j2\pi f_c t} + d_{i,k}(t) + n_{i,k}(t) \tag{3}$$

Among them, $x(t)$ represents the equivalent baseband signal, $E(x^2) = 1$; f_c is the signal carrier frequency; $d_{i,k}(t)$ represents the nonlinear component of the signal transmitted by the (i, k)th array element; $n_{i,k}(t)$ represents the transmission noise of the (i, k)th array element; p is transmit power.

Due to the large path loss of millimeter waves and the short distance between the transmitting and receiving antennas, the self-interference signal caused by the multipath effect is relatively small. The self-interference signal studied in this article is caused by the direct path from the transmitting array element to the receiving array element.

For the receiving array, the self-interference signal received by the (i,k)th receiving array element can be expressed as:

$$r_s(t)_{m,n} = \sum_{i=0}^{P}\sum_{k=0}^{Q}\left(l_{i,k}^{m,n}s_{i,k}(t - \frac{d_{i,k}^{m,n}}{c})\right) \tag{4}$$

Among them, $l_{i,k}^{m,n}$ is the path loss factor from the (i,k)th transmitting array element to the (m,n)th receiving array element; $d_{i,k}^{m,n}$ is the transmission from the (i,k)th transmitting array element to the (m,n)th receiving array element. The distance, $d_{i,k}^{m,n}$ can be expressed as:

$$d_{i,k}^{m,n} = \sqrt{[D + (P - m + i - 1)d_x]^2 + [(k - n)d_y]^2} \tag{5}$$

Then the self-interference signal synthesized by receiving beamforming can be expressed as:

$$r_s(t) = \sum_{m=1}^{P}\sum_{n=1}^{Q}\sum_{i=1}^{P}\sum_{k=1}^{Q}\left(\omega_{m,n}l_{i,k}^{m,n}s_{i,k}(t - \frac{d_{i,k}^{m,n}}{c})\right) + n_r(t) \tag{6}$$

Among them, $\omega_{m,n}$ is the receiving beamforming factor of the (m,n)th receiving array element; $n_r(t)$ is the thermal noise of the receiving channel.

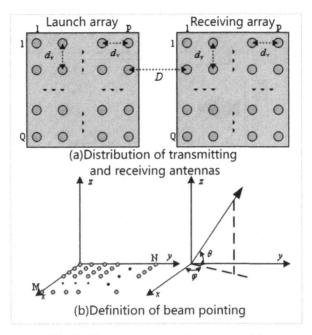

Fig. 3. Phased array transceiver array model

It can be seen from the formula that the self-interference signal synthesized after receiving is composed of P^2Q^2 signals with different amplitudes, delays and phases. The combined self-interference signal has rich multipaths and high power, which affects the dynamic range of the receiver and needs to be canceled in the radio frequency domain so that the receiving channel can normally receive small signals from the far end [13].

2.4 Multi-antenna Self-interference RF Suppression

The radio frequency interference suppression architecture is shown in Fig. 4 [30]. Before the transmit signal is sent to the terminal active phased antenna array, the coupling part of the transmit signal is used as a reference signal for radio frequency interference suppression. The reference signal is adjusted by multi-tap phase amplitude with different delays. Finally, they are combined together as a self-interference reconstructed signal.

The core content of radio frequency self-interference cancellation is radio frequency self-interference reconstruction. To improve the radio frequency self-interference cancellation capability, it is necessary to optimize the channel response of the reconstructed channel, so as to minimize the amplitude-frequency response of the equivalent channel response obtained by superimposing the received signal and the radio frequency self-interference reconstructed signal. The basic parameters of radio frequency self-interference reconstruction include the number of taps, delay, amplitude and phase. By adjusting the parameter values, the construction of different reconstructed channels can be achieved.

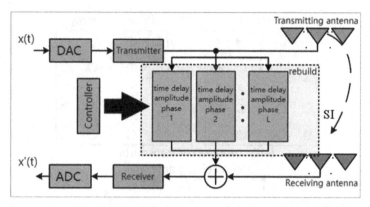

Fig. 4. RF self-interference suppression model

In the radio frequency self-interference suppression model, the reference signal is:

$$s_{ref}(t) = \sqrt{P_{ref}}x(t) + n_{ref}(t) \tag{7}$$

Among them, $n_{ref}(t)$ represents the thermal noise of the reference signal; p_{ref} is the power of the reference signal. Then the signal output by self-interference reconstruction is

$$s_{re}(t) = \sum_{l=1}^{L}\left(\alpha_l s_{ref}(t-\tau_l)e^{j\varphi_l} + n_{re,l}(t)\right) \tag{8}$$

Among them, L represents the number of taps of the reconstructed channel; α_l is the attenuation of the l th reconstructed tap; τ_l is the delay of the l th reconstructed tap; φ_l is the phase of the l th reconstructed tap; $n_{re,l}(t)$ is the noise of the l th reconstructed tap.

Then the signal after cancellation is

$$
\begin{aligned}
r_c(t) &= r_s(t) - s_{re}(t) \\
&= \sum_{m=1}^{P}\sum_{n=1}^{Q}\sum_{i=1}^{P}\sum_{k=1}^{Q}\left(\omega_{m,n}l_{i,k}^{m,n}s_{i,k}(t-\frac{d_{i,k}^{m,n}}{c})\right) + n_r(t) \\
&\quad - \sum_{l=1}^{L}\left(\alpha_l s_{ref}(t-\tau_l)e^{j\varphi_l} + n_{re,l}(t)\right)
\end{aligned} \tag{9}
$$

It can be seen from the equation that it is difficult to complete the reconstruction of the self-interference signal using one or a small number of reconstruction taps and obtain better cancellation performance. If one reconstruction tap is used to correspond to a self-interference signal of a specific amplitude and phase, P^2Q^2 reconstruction taps need to be used. Although better RF cancellation performance can be obtained at this time, the RF cancellation module will be bulky and the cost will increase. It has no practical significance in engineering.

Since the signal coupling between transceiver elements at different locations experiences different delays in space, for the synthesized self-interference signal, the superposition of several signal components with different delays will make the spectrum of the broadband self-interference signal appear frequency selective., this phenomenon is equivalent to the multipath effect. When the reciprocal of the maximum delay difference between the transmitting and receiving array elements is much larger than the signal bandwidth, signals with different delay components can be equivalent to one path.

According to the formula, combined with Fig. 3, in the planar array antenna model, the transmission delay between the array elements in the same row as the P th column of the transmitting array and the 1st column of the receiving array is the smallest, that is, when $m = P, i = 1, k = n$, the minimum signal transmission delay is

$$\tau_{min} = D/c \tag{10}$$

The transmission delay between diagonally diagonal elements of the transceiver array is the largest, that is, when $m = 1, i = P, k - n = Q - 1$, the maximum signal transmission delay is

$$\tau_{max} = \sqrt{[D + (2P - 2)d_x]^2 + [(Q - 1)d_y]^2}\Big/c \tag{11}$$

The maximum delay difference is

$$\tau_{d-max} = \sqrt{[D + (2P - 2)d_x]^2 + [(Q - 1)d_y]^2}\Big/c - D/c \tag{12}$$

When $1/\tau_{d-max}$ is much larger than the signal bandwidth, a path can be used to fit the self-interference signal. However, in large-scale phased array antenna systems, the RF cancellation performance of one tap is limited.

For a sub-array of size $P_t \times Q_t$ in the transmitting array and a sub-array of size $P_r \times Q_r$ in the receiving array element, the minimum delay, maximum delay and maximum delay difference of signal transmission between the sub-arrays are respectively:

$$\tau'_{min} = [(P - P_t - i_0 + m_0 - 1)d_x + D]\Big/c \tag{13}$$

$$\tau'_{max} = \sqrt{[\tau'_{min} \times c + (P_t + P_r - 2)d_x]^2 + [(k_0 + Q_t - n_0 - 1)d_y]^2}\Big/c \tag{14}$$

$$\tau'_{d-max} = \tau'_{max} - \tau'_{min} \tag{15}$$

Among them, (i_0, k_0) is the reference point of the transmitting sub-array, (m_0, n_0) is the reference point of the receiving sub-array, and $n_0 \le k_0$; the reference array element position and the sub-array scale satisfy the following constraint relationship:

$$i_0 + P_t + 1 \le P, m_0 + P_r + 1 \le P$$
$$k_0 + Q_t + 1 \le Q, n_0 + Q_r + 1 \le Q \tag{16}$$

According to this constraint relationship, it is easy to prove that $\tau_{min} \le \tau'_{min}, \tau_{max} \ge \tau'_{max}$, then $\tau'_{d-max} \le \tau_{d-max}$, that is, the delay expansion of any pair of sub-arrays is smaller than the delay expansion of the entire array.

It can be seen from the formula that when the array element spacing is determined, the maximum delay difference of the sub-array has nothing to do with the carrier frequency. Therefore, multiple array elements with a similar distance can be regarded as an antenna unit group. Since the array elements of each antenna unit group are relatively concentrated and the spatial distance difference between the transmitting and receiving array elements is small, the self-interference signal between the transmitting and receiving unit groups can be simplified as It consists of a signal with a delay component, as shown in Fig. 5. The transmitting antenna is converted into $P_{Bt}Q_{Bt}$ transmitting sub-arrays, and the receiving antenna is converted into $P_{Br}Q_{Br}$ receiving sub-arrays.

After regionalizing the antenna array, the formula can be rewritten as:

$$r_c(t) = r_s(t) - s_{re}(t)$$

$$= \sum_{g=1}^{P_{BR}} \sum_{h=1}^{Q_{BR}} \left(\sum_{r=1}^{P_{Bt}} \sum_{z=1}^{Q_{Bt}} l_{r,z}^{g,h} s_{r,z}(t - \tau_{r,z}^{g,h}) \right)$$

$$- \sum_{l=1}^{L'} \left(\alpha_l s_{ref}(t - \tau_l) e^{j\varphi_l} + n_{re,l}(t) \right) + n_r(t) \qquad (17)$$

Among them, L' represents the number of taps of the channel that needs to be reconstructed after the array is regionalized; $\tau_{r,z}^{g,h}$ is the time delay for the signal to be transmitted from the (r, z) th transmitting subarray to the (g, h) th receiving subarray; $l_{r,z}^{g,h}$ is the transmission time from the (r, z) th transmitting subarray to the (g, h) th receiving subarray. The complex gain factor of the array includes the channel response between array elements and the shaping factor of the receiving array element.

It can be seen from the formula that after the model is simplified, the self-interference signal can be canceled by $P_{Br}Q_{Br}P_{Bt}Q_{Bt}$ taps. The number of taps is far less than P^2Q^2, which is easy to implement in engineering.

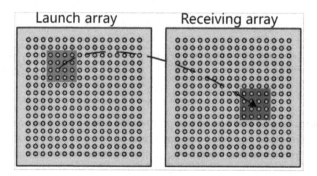

Fig. 5. Equivalent diagram of self-interference between subarrays

3 Verification and Application of RF Self-Interference Cancellation

To verify the research in the previous section, a simulation scenario is set and the performance of the phase control array self-interference and RF self-interference cancellation are simulated. The specific parameter settings of the simulation scenario are shown in Table 1.

Table 1. Simulation scenario parameters

Simulation parameters	Parameter description
Carrier center frequency	26.8 GHz
Signal bandwidth	200 MHz
Transmitter and receiver array scale	16 × 16
Element spacing	5.5 mm
Minimum spacing for transmitting and receiving elements	180 mm
Single element transmission power	6 dBm
Equivalent full-body radiation power of the transmitting array	54 dBm

3.1 The Power Distribution of the Self-interference in the Phase Control Array

Modeling the self-interference channel, and the signal power distribution of the receiver array is shown in Fig. 6 when the transmitting array sends.

-33.3	-31.4	-31.1	-32.1	-32.1	-31.1	-31.4	-33.3
-33.0	-31.6	-31.6	-32.8	-32.8	-31.6	-31.6	-33.0
-32.9	-31.8	-32.2	-33.5	-33.5	-32.2	-31.8	-32.9
-32.8	-32.1	-32.8	-34.2	-34.2	-32.8	-32.1	-32.8
-35.2	-36.9	-38.3	-36.2	-36.2	-38.3	-36.9	-35.2
-35.7	-37.5	-38.6	-36.1	-36.1	-38.6	-37.5	-35.7
-36.2	-38.2	-38.9	-35.9	-35.9	-38.9	-38.2	-36.2
-36.8	-38.8	-39.0	-35.7	-35.7	-39.0	-38.8	-36.8

Fig. 6. Power distribution of receiving array elements

Due to the symmetry relationship between the transmitting and receiving arrays, the received power of each receiver element also has a symmetry relationship. At this point, the received self-interference signals have relatively small power, and it will not cause the front-end low-noise amplifier to saturate.

When keeping the received array beam direction as the normal direction, scan the beam direction and azimuth for the transmitting array, and the power variation trend of

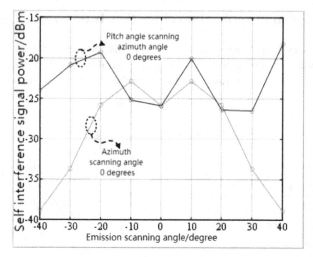

Fig. 7. Self-interference signal power in different directions

the largest self-interference signal in the receiver array is shown in Fig. 7. The maximum self-interference signal power in the receiver element is about −18 dBm.

3.2 Simulation of Frequency Self-interference Cancellation in Array Antennas

According to Eq. (17), divide the receiver and transmitter arrays into regions. Since the time expansion of different receive and transmit sub-arrays is inconsistent, the receive and transmit sub-array with the largest time expansion is selected as the reference sub-array. The maximum time expansion in different sub-array division as shown in Table 2 can be observed. It can be seen that as the number of sub-arrays in the receiver and transmit arrays increases, the time expansion between the receiver and transmit sub-arrays becomes smaller.

Table 2. Delay extension under different region partitioning

Launch array segmentation	Receive array segmentation	Delay extension
1 × 1	1 × 1	0.582 ns
1 × 1	2 × 2	0.441 ns
1 × 1	4 × 4	0.369 ns
2 × 1	2 × 1	0.441 ns
2 × 1	2 × 2	0.440 ns
2 × 2	2 × 2	0.299 ns
4 × 4	4 × 4	0.139 ns

Simulation Model

Figure 8 provides an ADS simulation block diagram for frequency independent interference cancellation based on the different sub-arrays of the transceiver array. The simulation network of the transceiver array simulates the self-interference channel of the transmission antenna to the received antenna with 256×256 channels of delay, phase, and attenuation. The signal reconstruction of the self-interference is simulated through the adjustment of the time delay, amplitude, and phase of each tap, aiming to achieve the minimum amplitude of the reconstructed self-interference signal. The number of tap, L, determines the number of channels in the transceiver array.

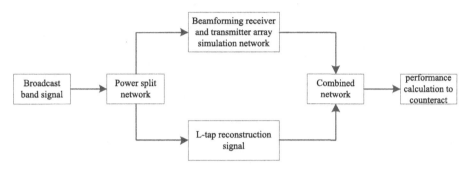

Fig. 8. ADS simulation block diagram

The signal source modulation method is 16QAM, and the simulation is conducted using the pulse-shaping method to optimize the frequency independent interference cancellation performance. According to the actual usage parameters of the device, the time interval of the tap is 10 ns, the phase shifter is $5.625°$, and the attenuation factor is 0.5dB.

The transceiver array is simulated by replacing the transmit and receive arrays with 2×1, 2×1, and 2×2, respectively, and using 4, 8, and 16 taps to reconstruct the interference signal. The simulation of frequency independent interference cancellation performance is conducted.

The Simulation Results

In the direction of the line, the simulation results of the frequency independent interference cancellation performance of the transceiver array with different tap numbers are shown in Fig. 9, and the specific numerical results are presented in Table 3.

From the simulation results, it can be seen that as the number of tap in the transceiver array increases and the number of tap for the reconstruction of the tap increases, the performance of the self-interference cancellation gradually improves. When the 200 MHz bandwidth self-interference signal is reconstructed using 4 taps, the self-interference suppression ability is 21.5 dB; when the 200 MHz bandwidth self-interference signal is reconstructed using 16 taps, the self-interference suppression ability is 47.4 dB. The simulation results prove that the frequency independent self-interference cancellation

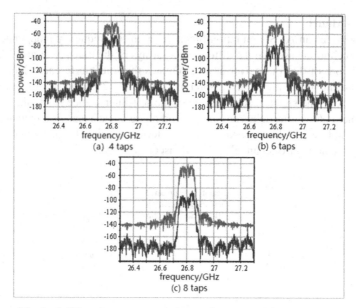

Fig. 9. Self-interference suppression performance with different taps

method with subarray division and a large reduction in the number of tap for the reconstruction of the tap can effectively suppress self-interference signals in the phase control array system.

Table 3. RF self-interference cancellation results with different tap numbers

Tap numbers	Offset before power	Offset after power	Quantum damping factor
4	−33.3 dBm	−54.8 dBm	21.5 dB
8	−33.3 dBm	−64.9 dBm	31.6 dB
16	−33.3 dBm	−81.0 dBm	47.7 dB

Similarly, keeping the beam direction of the receiver array fixed in the direction of the line, the beam scanning of the transceiver array is performed in the azimuth and elevation directions. The simulation results of the frequency independent interference cancellation performance of the transceiver array with different tap numbers are shown in Fig. 10. The results show that when the transceiver array scans in the same beam direction, the frequency independent interference cancellation ability of the transceiver array with the same number of taps in the reconstruction of the interference signal is similar.

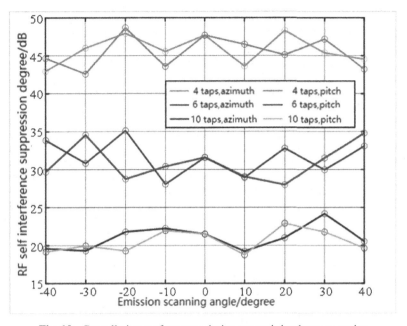

Fig. 10. Cancellation performance during transmitting beam scanning

Conclusion

In conclusion, this paper presents a comprehensive study on the self-interference issue in distributed network communication systems, specifically focusing on millimeter-wave large-scale array antenna scenarios. A simplified model for anti-self-interference suppression in arrays was proposed and validated through simulations, demonstrating its significant effectiveness in suppressing RF self-interference signals. Real-world testing further corroborated these results, achieving a suppression performance of over 47 dB under conditions of a 26.8 GHz central frequency and a 200 MHz self-interference bandwidth. This theoretical and experimental work establishes the foundation for frequency self-interference cancellation in large-scale array antenna network scenarios, paving the way for the application of concurrent frequency reception and transmission in future distributed networked testing and control systems.

References

1. Sivakumar, P., Singh, M., Malhotra J., et al.: Performance analysis of 160Gbit/s single-channel PDM-QPSK based inter-satellite optical wireless communication (IsOWC) system. Wireless Networks, **26**(5), 3579–3590 (2020). https://doi.org/10.1007/s11276-020-02287-2
2. Zhu, Z., Guo, Y., Zhong, C.: Distributed attitude coordination tracking control for spacecraft formation with time-varying delays. Trans. Inst. Measure. Control (2017). https://doi.org/10.1177/0142331217696146
3. El-Ferik, S., Hashim, H.A., Lewis, F.L.: Neuro-adaptive distributed control with prescribed performance for the synchronization of unknown nonlinear networked systems. IEEE Trans. Syst. Man Cybern. Syst. 1–10 (2017). https://doi.org/10.1109/TSMC.2017.2702705

4. Zhao, Z., Xu, G., Zhang, N., Zhang, Q.: Performance analysis of the hybrid satellite-terrestrial relay network with opportunistic scheduling over generalized fading channels. IEEE Trans. Veh. Technol. **71**(3), 2914–2924 (2022)
5. Ei, C.L., Jun, L., Wei, Z.: Distributed relay selection strategy for satellite-terrestrial cooperative system based on fairness. Comput. Eng. (2016)
6. Zeng, Y., Zhang, R.: Throughput maximization for UAV enabled mobile relaying systems. IEEE Trans. Commun. **64**(12), 4983–4996 (2016)
7. Srikanthakumar, S., Liu, C., Chen, W.H.: Optimization-based safety analysis of obstacle avoidance systems for unmanned aerial vehicles. In: International Conference on Unmanned Aircraft Systems (2012)
8. Samara, L., Ozdemir, O., Mokhtar, M., et al.: Analysis of in-band full-duplex OFDM signals affected by phase noise and I/Q imbalance. In: Qatar Foundation Annual Research Conference Proceedings (2016). https://doi.org/10.5339/qfarc.2016.ICTOP2684
9. Liu, Z.S., Zhou, Q.J., Gan, W.S., et al.: Adaptive joint channel estimation of digital self-interference cancelation in co-time co-frequency full-duplex underwater acoustic communication. In: 2019 IEEE International Conference on Signal, Information and Data Processing (ICSIDP). IEEE (2019). https://doi.org/10.1109/ICSIDP47821.2019.9173156
10. Bo-Lun, L.I., Tao, L., Ai-Wei, S.: Physical-layer security performance analysis of cooperative systems with energy harvesting-based relay. Commun. Technol. (2017)
11. Tahseen, H.U., Yang, L., Hongjin, W.: A dual-array antenna system for 5G millimeter-wave applications. Appl. Comput. Electromagn. Soc. J. **2021**(10), 36 (2021)
12. Jiang, H., Yu, Z., Yang, J.: Research on key technology of full duplex cognitive radio network. J. Phys. Conf. Ser. **1920**(1), 012035 (9pp) (2021). https://doi.org/10.1088/1742-6596/1920/1/012035
13. Mura, M.L., Bagolini, A., Lamberti, P., et al.: Extreme value analysis of the impact of the effective gap tolerance on the acoustic transmit and receive performance of reverse-CMUT arrays. In: 2022 IEEE International Ultrasonics Symposium (IUS), pp. 1–4 (2022). https://doi.org/10.1109/IUS54386.2022.9958299
14. Cacciola, R., Holzman, E., Carpenter, L., Gagnon, S.: Impact of transmit interference on receive sensitivity in a bi-static active array system. In: IEEE International Symposium on Phased Array Systems and Technology (PAST), pp. 1–5. Waltham, MA (2016)
15. Narbudowicz, A., Ruvio, G., Ammann, M.J.: Passive self-interference suppression for single-channel full-duplex operation. IEEE Wirel. Commun. **25**(5), 64–69 (2018). https://doi.org/10.1109/MWC.2018.1700236
16. Makar, G., Tran, N., Karacolak: A high isolation monopole array with ring hybrid feeding structure for in-band full-duplex systems. IEEE Antennas Wireless Propagat. Let. **16**, 356–359 (2016)
17. Shi, C., Pan, W., Shen, Y., Shao, S.: Robust transmit beamforming for self-interference cancellation in STAR phased array systems. IEEE Signal Process. Lett. **29**, 2622–2626 (2022)
18. Zhang, J., Zheng, J.: Prototype verification of self-interference suppression for constant-amplitude full-duplex phased array with finite phase shift. Electronics **11**(3), 295 (2022). https://doi.org/10.3390/electronics11030295
19. Liyanaarachchi, S.D., Barneto, C.B., Riihonen, T., et al.: Joint multi-user communication and mimo radar through full-duplex hybrid beamforming. In: 2021 1st IEEE International Online Symposium on Joint Communications & Sensing (JC&S).IEEE (2021). https://doi.org/10.1109/JCS52304.2021.9376319
20. Lopez-Valcarce, R., Gonzalez-Prelcic, N.: Analog beamforming for Full-duplex millimeter wave communication. In: International Symposium on Wireless Communication Systems. IEEE (2019). https://doi.org/10.1109/iswcs.2019.8877288
21. Kolodziej, K.E., Doane, J.P., Perry, B.T., Herd, J.S.: Adaptive beamforming for multi-function in-band full-duplex applications. IEEE Wirel. Commun. **28**(1), 28–35 (2021)

22. Kim, Y.J., Shin, J., Cho, H., et al.: Implementation of self-interference cancellation techniques for full-duplex communication. J. Korean Inst. Inform. Commun. Eng. **20**(3), 484–490 (2016). https://doi.org/10.6109/jkiice.2016.20.3.484

23. Zhang, Z., Shen, Y., Shao, S., et al.: Full duplex 2×2 MIMO radios. In: 2014 Sixth International Conference on Wireless Communications and Signal Processing (WCSP), pp. 1–6. IEEE (2014)

24. Ma, T., Lei, H., Xiang, X.: Digital self-interference cancellation in single channel full-duplex system. Semicond. Optoelectron. (2016). https://doi.org/10.16818/j.issn1001-5868.2016.03.024

25. Tytgat, L., Yaron, O., Pollin, S., et al.: Analysis and experimental verification of frequency-based interference avoidance mechanisms in IEEE 802.15.4. IEEE/ACM Trans. Network. **23**(2), 369–382 (2015). https://doi.org/10.1109/TNET.2014.2300114

26. Pawinee, M., Peerapong, U., Monthippa, U.: Self-interference cancellation-based mutual-coupling model for full-duplex single-channel MIMO systems. Int. J. Anten. Propagat. **2014**, 1 (2014). https://doi.org/10.1155/2014/405487

27. Tamminen J, et al.: Digitally-controlled RF self-interference canceller for full-duplex radios. In: 24th European Signal Processing Conference (EUSIPCO), pp. 783–787. Budapest, HUNGARY (2016)

On IT and OT Cybersecurity Datasets for Machine Learning-Based Intrusion Detection in Industrial Control Systems

Mohammad Pasha Shabanfar, Yiheng Zhao, Jun Yan$^{(\boxtimes)}$, and Mohsen Ghafouri

Concordia University, Montreal, Canada
{mohammadpasha.shabanfar,yiheng.zhao}@mail.concordia.ca,
{jun.yan,mohsen.ghafouri}@concordia.ca

Abstract. Intrusion detection plays a pivotal role in the cybersecurity of industrial control systems (ICS) to safeguard the safety of individuals, communities, and nations. Lately, intrusion detection models based on machine learning have been adopted to improve the detection of cyberattacks. However, there is a lack of a systematic approach to selecting the appropriate dataset for training these models. An appropriately selected dataset should be based on the needed collection environment, i.e., Information Technology (IT) and Operational Technology (OT), and include required specifications of the under-study ICS, e.g., deployed protocols. On this basis, this paper classifies the existing intrusion detection datasets into IT and OT datasets. The IT datasets are investigated from the perspectives of attack/normal traffic inclusion and their anonymity, number of packets, duration, and kind of traffic. On the other hand, the OT datasets are studied based on features such as data protocols, distribution, and data domain. Then, we have discussed the gap between the method of detection and the selection of the appropriate dataset in terms of (i) performance indicators, i.e., detection time and imbalanced distribution of data, and (ii) use case, i.e., summarizing communication layers, protocols, and attack types contained in datasets. Finally, the essential features for constructing an effective cybersecurity dataset are discussed to illustrate how to establish an ideal dataset accordingly.

Keywords: Information Technology · Operational Technology · Datasets · Cybersecurity · Intrusion Detection System

1 Introduction

According to the statistics reported for cybersecurity, the damages caused by cyberattacks are expected to reach up to three trillion by 2021, with the probability of executing zero-day exploits one per day. Moreover, the amount of information stored in private and public clouds operated by data-driven companies, such as Amazon Web Services, Facebook, and Twitter has been increased

© ICST Institute for Computer Sciences, Social Informatics and Telecommunications Engineering 2025
Published by Springer Nature Switzerland AG 2025. All Rights Reserved
X. Li et al. (Eds.): SmartGift 2024, LNICST 600, pp. 36–53, 2025.
https://doi.org/10.1007/978-3-031-78806-2_3

a hundred times by 2022 [1]. As a result, there would be a need for appropriate detection systems.

Machine learning (ML) methods are one of the commonly used solutions that are increasingly popular and effective in detecting malware and cyber attacks; however, selecting an efficient dataset for training them is essential. Knowing the dataset collection environment and their associated use cases would help researchers to choose the most appropriate dataset for training their methods. According to the kind of dataset testbed, we can classify them into two subsets of IT and OT.

Due to the importance of Information Technology (IT) security, much effort has been spent researching intrusion and insider threat detection [2]. Many papers have been published for security-related data, detecting attacks, etc. All of them need a network-based testbed. During these years, some good IT datasets have been published to evaluate the detection methods' power. Given a labeled dataset in which each data point is assigned to the class normal or attack, the number of detected attacks or false alarms may be used as evaluation criteria [2].

On the other hand, Operational Technology (OT), which includes Industrial Control Systems (ICSs), plays an influential role in managing and supervising processes in the industry, such as water, energy, gas, chemical, etc. Although improving technology affected deterring attacks, the risk of cyberattacks is still increasing. To respond to these security threats targeting ICSs, a security technology that reflects the ICS operating environment is needed [3]. Industrial Detection System (IDS) is in charge of detecting suspicious activities and cyberattacks. Generally, IDS monitors the environment and triggers alerts following any suspicious activity. Moreover, IDS adoption in ICS is being influenced by the increasing number of ICS attacks and their consequence. As a result, several ICS datasets have been published in different domains (such as gas pipelines, power systems, etc.) that give us useful information.

The ICS experimental environment generally consists of three levels, which have been shown in Fig. 1 [3]. Devices should be located and set up when building the environment. In addition, a system for collecting various data is arranged during the ICS operation.

OT consists of compassionate information regarding industrial process operations. Unlike the IT domain, industries are reluctant to share their confidential and sensitive operational data for analysis. Therefore, The researchers are forced to utilize the publicly available ICS datasets, which are outdated and lack the right classification of their use cases [4].

In recent years, cyber security solutions have started to deploy big data analytics to correlate security events across multiple data sources, providing, amongst others, early detection of suspicious activities. Methods employed in cyber data analytics are predominantly based on ML, which needs appropriate data used for specific use cases [5].

However, there is a gap between choosing a dataset and using an appropriate method. This gap can be divided in terms of performance indicators and use cases. Detection time and imbalanced datasets are the most important perfor-

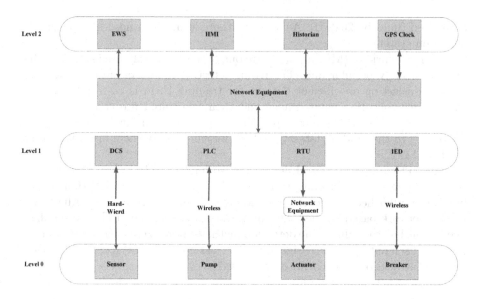

Fig. 1. ICS Environment Rating

mance indicators. Imbalanced data could lead to inefficient results for testing an ML method. On the other hand, a prolonged detection time for a cyber attack might result in overwhelming damage or crashing a big part of a system. In terms of use cases, IT and OT datasets are two different types of datasets. As a result, communication layers, protocols, and attack types contained in different datasets are summarized, which can help researchers more conveniently choose the dataset appropriate for their objectives. Furthermore, performing a detection algorithm for datasets with different mapping OSI layers will yield inaccurate results. Thus, knowing this mapping helps researchers design more effective algorithms for testing their on-target dataset.

In this paper, we introduced the following:

- A new mapping of IT and OT datasets has been introduced that gives better details of each dataset to researchers for designing more effective detection methods for cybersecurity attacks.
- Two performance indicators, i.e., detection time and imbalanced distribution of data, have been studied to assist in selecting suitable ML algorithms for various systems and explore how imbalanced data affects these algorithms' performance.
- Critical features for generating an ideal dataset have been investigated. These features can be useful to generate a real-world dataset that researchers can use to train and evaluate their detection methods in their application systems.

The rest of the paper is organized as follows. In Sect. 2, we discuss the concept of IT and OT first and then compare the IT cybersecurity datasets with OT cybersecurity datasets. After that, we discuss IT security and OT security to classify datasets into two subsets of IT and OT datasets, which will be investigated in Sect. 3. In addition, we analyze some popular ML algorithms to evaluate their performances on the detection time of attacks and evaluate the impact of imbalanced data distribution on the performance of these algorithms in Sect. 4. Moreover, we also delve into additional crucial characteristics of datasets, with the aim of facilitating the selection of the most appropriate dataset tailored to various specific targets in Sect. 4. Then, we introduced how to construct an ideal cybersecurity dataset based on these essential features in Sect. 5. Finally, We have summarized our work in Sect. 6.

2 IT and OT Security in ICS

In this section, first, we discuss the concept of IT and OT and then, compare the IT cybersecurity datasets with OT cybersecurity datasets.

2.1 IT Security in ICS

Security in IT systems is understood conceptually in the academic literature and to a degree in practice in the enterprise environment. IT security measures have evolved over the past two decades from a binary 'secure or not secure' measurement to one based on risk. Since risk management is already a functioning business requirement, the risk management concept has made it easier to integrate security into business decisions. For instance, the CIA triad serves as the foundation for nearly all IT security solutions, which is a description of IT security that goes beyond the scope and focus of this essay [6].

IT security is widely used on the public Internet as well as ICS for many applications, e.g., email, voice-over-IP, in energy, transportation, healthcare, and many other sectors. These networks facilitate internal and external communication for employees, suppliers, and customers. Backend offices of energy companies are another example of maintaining corporate IT networks that handle administrative tasks, finance, human resources, and other business operations. These networks often include servers hosting enterprise applications and databases. For instance, IT networks in the oil and gas industry support exploration, extraction, and production activities. This includes communication between remote drilling sites, data centers, and corporate offices for managing exploration data and production processes.

2.2 OT Security in ICS

Systems employed in manufacturing, transportation, critical infrastructure, cyber-physical systems, and other areas are often referred to as OT systems. These systems are where computers manage operational procedures and make data accessible to the business [6]. OT communications are widely used in ICS right now. Supervisory control and data acquisition (SCADA) systems are used to monitor and control industrial processes and infrastructure. They use various OT communication protocols to gather data from sensors and control equipment. Distributed Control Systems (DCSs) are used in manufacturing and process industries to control and automate production processes. They rely on dedicated communication networks for real-time control [7].

OT systems have two sources of security specification, one for general-purpose deployments and a second set of requirements driven separately by infrastructure segmentation [6]. Regarding specific sector recommendations on security in the context of control systems, many distinct standards may or may not be applicable depending on the business and other variables [6]. Furthermore, Programmable Logic Control (PLC) regulates machinery and equipment in industrial settings. They use OT communication protocols to receive input signals and send control commands. Also, Generic Object-Oriented Substation Events (GOOSE) [8] communication is primarily associated with OT. GOOSE is a part of the International Electrotechnical Commission (IEC) 61850 suite of standards and specifies the communication of electrical substation events. It is a messaging protocol used in electrical power systems, particularly substation automation and protection systems [9].

2.3 Comparing IT Security with OT Security in ICS

The importance of OT security is as well as IT security. While the systems may not be completely developed from technological security capabilities, they are from a regulatory standpoint. The focus of IT security is on protecting information, networks, and computer systems, while OT systems are related to the control and automation of physical processes, such as manufacturing, industrial machinery, and critical infrastructure. Therefore, even though OT systems (i) may not have many technical level controls, such as access control systems and cryptography, and (ii) though they may not have much to no forensic and logging capability, these features are all governed by regulatory decree. OT personnel are put in a cognitive cage where regulatory compliance trumps security considerations when regulatory edict is used instead of serious security functionality. Cognitively, OT employees may confuse security with regulatory compliance, which is difficult to spot before a significant preventable incident. Figure 2 shows some differences between IT and OT regarding priority, risks, networks, and protocols [10].

3 Datasets for IT and OT Security in ICS

The selection of an appropriate dataset for training ML algorithms for intrusion detection is of paramount importance. To assist researchers in better-selecting datasets to train their ML algorithms based on their application environment, i.e., IT and OT, we have categorized the existing significant intrusion detection

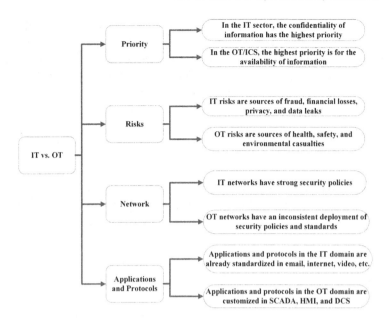

Fig. 2. Differences Between IT and OT

datasets into IT and OT datasets. In this section, we first mention some differences between the IT dataset and the OT dataset. Then, we discuss the existing important IT and OT datasets.

3.1 Comparison of IT Dataset and OT Dataset

The differences between IT and OT security datasets lie in the data collected, the systems and environments they pertain to, and the specific cybersecurity challenges they address. The most significant difference between IT and OT cybersecurity datasets is the environment in which they operate to generate data. OT cybersecurity safeguards industrial environments, typically involving machinery, PLCs, and communication across industrial protocols. OT systems do not run on regular operating systems, often lack traditional security tools, and are usually programmed differently from conventional computers. Conversely, IT cybersecurity protects common devices, such as networks, computers, keyboards, printers, and smartphones. It secures everyday environments like servers using standard solutions, such as antivirus and firewalls, as well as popular communication protocols like Hypertext Transfer Protocol (HTTP).

There are different purposes for IT and OT security based on what they aim to achieve for organizations. The primary objective of OT cybersecurity is to ensure the availability and safety of critical equipment and processes. It maintains physical systems that require meticulous, ongoing control to prevent significant financial damage caused by ceased production. IT cybersecurity focuses more on confidentiality by helping organizations store and transmit data securely.

Another noteworthy difference between OT and IT datasets is the type of security events they defend against. OT cybersecurity datasets are typically generated to put in place to prevent highly-destructive events. OT systems generally have fewer entry points, yet the magnitude of a compromise is comparatively greater-even a minor incident can result in vast financial losses and can affect an entire nation through a power outage or water contamination. IT systems tend to have more gateways and entry points due to the Internet, which a cybercriminal can exploit, which means more security risks and vulnerabilities.

Although IT datasets and OT datasets have some differences, the cyber-attack types of these two types of datasets are similar. There are four general classes of attacks against the integrity, availability, confidentiality, access control, authentication, and non-repudiation security aspects [11]. These attacks include interruption attacks, interception attacks, modification attacks, and fabrication attacks.

An interruption attack includes both hardware-based DoS attacks and software-based DoS attacks [12]. DoS attacks and distributed DoS (DDoS) attacks occur when an attacker hacks several machines (or zombies) and uses up network resources. This overloads the target's bandwidth and causes genuine traffic to be slowed down or dropped. DoS attacks, for example, can result in missed or delayed measurements from EPES devices that rely on real-time measurement data. This leads to incomplete failure of network measurement devices, erroneous forecasts of the transmission system status, and delayed response to power system issues.

Information traveling over the network between devices is accessible to an interception attack. These attacks may take two forms: passive and active. Packet sniffing attacks are a type of interception attack. In which attackers can gain access to the contents of the Phasor measurement unit (PMU) or smart meter Transmission Control Protocol (TCP)/Internet Protocol (IP) packets that are sent across the EPES network using software programs such as Wireshark [11].

Modification attacks use network security flaws to hijack, change, or contaminate a genuine process. Man-in-the-middle (MITM) attacks are one type of modification attack. In MITM attacks, the attacker poses as the legitimate target to both the legitimate client and server during the protocol session [11].

In fabrication attacks, the attacker forges an identity on the IT network and uses it to send fake data that, if improperly verified, could be accepted by other network devices. System spoofing is a type of fabrication attack. System Spoofing: Data accuracy in the IT network is critical for efficient and reliable operation. System spoofing injects fabricated (inaccurate) data into the control centers.

3.2   IT Datasets

An IT dataset can be developed by collecting information from varied sources, such as network traffic flows that contain information about the host, user behavior, and system configurations [13]. This information is required to study various network attack patterns and abnormal activity. The network activity is collected through a router or network switch. After collecting the incoming and outgoing network traffic, network flow analysis is performed to study the traffic. Flow analysis can be described as analyzing the network packet information such as source IP address, destination IP address, source port number, destination port number, and type of network services, to name a few. The network host delivers the system configurations and user information that cannot be extracted from the network flow analysis [14].

According to the categorization, some public IT datasets frequently used for intrusion detection in ICS are:

CICIDS 2017. CICIDS 2017 [15], generated over a span of five days in an emulated environment, encompasses network traffic presented in both packet-based and bidirectional flow-based formats. The dataset comprises extensive attributes, exceeding 80 for each flow, accompanied by supplementary metadata concerning IP addresses and attack details. It encompasses a wide range of attack types, including but not limited to SSH brute force, Heartbleed, botnet, DoS, DDoS, web, and infiltration attacks.

CIC DOS. The CIC DoS datasetcite [16], sourced from the Canadian Institute for Cybersecurity, was developed with the aim of constructing an intrusion detection dataset featuring application layer DoS attacks. To achieve this, the researchers conducted eight distinct application layer DoS attacks. To generate normal user behavior data, they merged the obtained traces with attack-free traffic extracted from the ISCX 2012 dataset.

DARPA, KDD CUP, NSL-KDD. The DARPA 1998/99 datasets [17], widely recognized as the primary datasets for intrusion detection, were crafted at the MIT Lincoln Lab in an emulated network environment. Comprising packet-based network traffic data, the DARPA 1998 dataset spans seven weeks, while the DARPA 1999 dataset covers five weeks.

KDD CUP 99 [18], derived from the DARPA 98 dataset, ranks among the most extensively employed datasets for intrusion detection purposes. This dataset includes fundamental attributes concerning TCP connections and higher-level features, such as the count of unsuccessful login attempts, though it omits IP addresses.

NSL-KDD [2], an evolved dataset, was created as a response to duplicate data concerns within KDD CUP. This dataset, stemming from the original KDD cup99 dataset, was born after Tavallaee et al.'s analysis of the KDD training and test sets, which unveiled duplicate network packets accounting for around 78

DDOS 2016. The DDOS 2016 dataset [19], constructed in 2016 through the utilization of the NS2 network simulator, adopts a packet-based format. Unfortunately, specific details regarding the simulated network environment remain undisclosed. Within the DDoS 2016 dataset, attention is primarily directed toward various categories of DDoS attacks. In addition to normal network traffic, this dataset encompasses four distinct DDoS attack types: UDP flood, smurf, HTTP flood, and SIDDOS.

UNSW-NB 15. The UNSW-NB15 dataset, as outlined in [19], comprises both regular and malicious network traffic, presented in a packet-based format. This dataset was generated within a confined emulated environment over a period of 31 h, utilizing the IXIA Perfect Storm tool. It encompasses a diverse array of attack categories, including but not limited to backdoors, DoS (Denial of Service), exploits, fuzzers, and worms, forming nine distinct attack families. UNSW-NB15 comes equipped with predefined partitions for training and testing purposes, with a total of 45 unique IP addresses included in the dataset.

Table 1. General Information of IT Datasets

Dataset	Normal Traffic	Attack Traffic	Anonymity	Count	Duration	Kind of Traffic
CIC DoS	yes	yes	none	4.6 GB packets	1 day	emulated
CICIDS 2017	yes	yes	none	3.1 M flows	5 days	emulated
DARPA	yes	yes	none	n.s.	7.5 weeks	emulated
DDoS 2016	yes	yes	yes	2.1 M packets	n.s.	synthetic
KDD Cup 99	yes	yes	none	5 M points	none	emulated
NSL-KDD	yes	yes	none	150 K points	n.s.	emulated
UNSW-NB15	yes	yes	none	2 M points	31 h	emulated

A detailed overview of IT data sets is shown in Table 1. According to Table 1, general information on IT datasets, such as normal and attack data, the amount of the datasets, and their kind of traffic, has been shown. Moreover, most datasets have been generated in an emulated environment, and there are fewer datasets with real network environments. The presence of specific attack scenarios is an important aspect when searching for a network-based data set. According to [2], which describes the specific attacks within IT datasets, DoS, DDoS, port scans, and botnets are the most popular attacks used in the datasets to simulate an abnormal situation in the network.

3.3 OT Datasets

This section discusses public OT datasets used in several surveys to detect attacks by implementing different algorithms and methods. ICSs are one of the most effective tools to prevent cyberattacks. The key components of the ICS include SCADA, Human Machine Interface (HMI), PLC, Remote Terminal Unit, and DCS. A SCADA system helps collect data from field sensors, enabling us to control the system through HMI software [10]. OT monitors all industrial systems, and ICS relates to the security of industrial systems. Thus, ICS datasets are a type of subset of OT datasets.

Here are some public OT datasets used frequently for detecting algorithms to compare them based on four categories that we will discuss in the next subsection.

Morris et al. Datasets [3]. For their research on intrusion detection, Morris et al. have made five separate datasets about the production of electricity, gas, and water available. The Morris datasets can be used for ML in creating intrusion detection systems because they all provide labels in common. The Morris-1 dataset includes 37 scenarios for power system events that consider the number of intelligent electronic device (IED) operations and typical and unusual occurrences in the testbed for power systems comprising generators, IEDs, breakers, switches, and routers. The RS-232, or Ethernet interface in the gas pipeline testbed, is connected in the Morris-2, Morris-3, and Morris-4 datasets to enable Modbus protocol connection between the control device and the HMI. Every dataset has network data information that has some header information removed.

SWaT [3]. The SWaT dataset encompasses sensor data, actuators, PLC input/output (I/O) signals, and network traffic, which were recorded over a duration of four days during an assault scenario and seven days under regular operational conditions. It is worth noting that the SWaT datasets represent one of the most extensive data collections within a substantial testbed. SWaT has meticulously crafted a total of 36 attack scenarios, encompassing both field signals and network traffic. Each attack scenario was meticulously designed by specifying the targeted devices and physical points, with each attack being individually structured. These attack scenarios are meticulously aligned with the operational principles of the physical system. Furthermore, the datasets are well-suited for monitoring research, as they are categorized into distinct segments based on the physical layer and the network layer.

Lemay [3]. Lemay et al. have contributed a network traffic dataset focused on covert channel command and control within the SCADA domain. For the creation of the testing environment, a SCADA network was established utilizing the publicly available SCADA Sandbox tool. Additionally, two master terminal units were implemented through SCADA BR. The dataset encompasses Modbus/TCP communication, involving the connection of three controllers and four field devices per controller.

Rodofile et a. Dataset [3]. It comprises two elevated reservoir tanks, six consumer tanks, two raw water tanks, and a return tank. It contains chemical dosing systems, booster pumps, valves, instrumentation, and analyzers. WADI is controlled by 3 PLCs that operate over 100 network sensors. Moreover, the testbed is equipped with a SCADA system. WADI consists of three main processes: (i) P1 (Primary supply and analysis), (ii) P2 (Elevated reservoir with Domestic grid and leak detection), and (iii) P3 (Return process). Its use cases are to show that the detection mechanism applies to real-world ICS data and to see whether any attack methodology is transferable from a scenario in which simulated data are used to another scenario in which real data are used.

WADI [20]. The WADI testbed comprises a comprehensive facility encompassing two elevated reservoir tanks, six consumer tanks, two raw water tanks, and a return tank. Within this setup, you'll find an array of essential components, including chemical dosing systems, booster pumps, valves, instrumentation, and analyzers. The control of WADI is managed by three PLCs, each communicating with over 100 network sensors. Additionally, the testbed is equipped with a SCADA system to facilitate monitoring and control. WADI's operations revolve around three primary processes: P1 (Primary supply and analysis), P2 (Elevated reservoir with Domestic grid and leak detection), and P3 (Return process). The primary objectives of this testbed are twofold: firstly, to demonstrate the applicability of the detection mechanism in real-world ICS data, and secondly, to explore the transferability of attack methodologies from scenarios involving simulated data to scenarios employing real data.

EPIC [21]. Data from the EPIC testbed encompasses eight distinct scenarios during normal operation, each scenario spanning approximately 30 min. The data collected includes sensor and actuator information, meticulously recorded in an Excel spreadsheet, and network traffic data, which has been archived in *.pcap* files. EPIC represents a power testbed that faithfully replicates a compact real-world smart grid system, encompassing four essential stages: generation, transmission, microgrid, and smart home. Each stage is under the control of its dedicated PLC/controller. Additionally, communication channels are established between the SCADA system, the DCS, the energy management system (EMS), and each PLC/controller.

WUSTL [22]. This dataset encompasses network data derived from the Industrial Internet of Things (IIoT) for the purpose of cybersecurity research. The primary objective of this testbed is to replicate real-world industrial systems with maximum fidelity, enabling the execution of genuine cyber-attacks for research purposes. A substantial volume of data, totaling 2.7 GB, was accumulated over a period of approximately 53 h. Prior to its release, the dataset underwent thorough preprocessing and cleaning procedures.

Here, we briefly compare the OT datasets. We compare datasets based on their public information, data domain, and size of normal and attack data. Each dataset is collected from its own experimental environment in a specific or complex domain. To specify our analysis target, we limited our study to the ICS-related datasets that can be accessed publicly. Table 2 describes the data domain and size of the normal and attack of some of the datasets as an example.

Table 2. Data Domain and Dimensions of Normal and Attack of OT Datasets

Dataset	Data Domain	Num. of Normal Traffic (%)	Num. of Attack Traffic (%)
Morris5	EMS	16,362(92.09)	1,405(7.91)
Lemay	SCADA	395,298(87.86)	54,321(12.14)
Rodofile	Mining Refinery	1,137,294(63.09)	665,463(36.91)

4 Gaps in Developing ML-Based Algorithms with Existing IT and OT Security Datasets for Diverse Use Cases

Nowadays, the use of ML methods for intrusion detection in cybersecurity has become increasingly important and effective. However, there is a gap between choosing a dataset and using an appropriate method in terms of performance indicators and use cases. This is the point that we will discuss in this section.

4.1 Performance Indicators

In this section, we first evaluated the detection time of various ML algorithms on NSL-KDD and UNSBW-NB15 datasets to choose a suitable algorithm for use cases from different collection environments. This is due to the varied detection time requirements imposed by diverse use cases originating from different collection environments. Then, to illustrate the adverse impact of imbalanced datasets on the intrusion detection performance of the algorithm, we evaluated the intrusion detection performance of the CNN-LSTM algorithm on the original imbalanced Morris Power and CICIDS 2017 datasets, as well as on the Morris Power and CICIDS 2017 datasets that had been preprocessed to achieve balance.

Detection Time. The detection time of different ML algorithms on NSL-KDD and UNSBW-NB15 datasets is shown in Table 3 [23]. According to Table 3, the detection time of different algorithms in descending order is Support Vector Machine (SVM), K-nearest Neighbors (KNN), Gradient Boosting Tree (GBT), Logistic Regression (LG), and Gaussian Naive Bayes (GNB) on these two datasets and the same algorithm has a longer detection time on UNSBW-NB15 dataset since UNSBW-NB15 dataset has more features than NSL-KDD dataset. Therefore, these algorithms, except SVM, can be used for use cases in information system environments that do not require short detection time. However, GNB is an appropriate choice for use cases in operational system environments with high real-time algorithm requirements [23].

Table 3. Detection Time Models Comparison on NSL-KDD and UNSBW-NB15 Datasets

Models	Detection Time(s)	
	NSL-KDD	UNSBW-NB15
Gradient Boosting Tree (GBT)	0.41	0.96
K-nearest Neighbors (KNN)	1.79	5.55
Logistic Regression (LG)	0.24	0.81
Gaussian Naive Bayes (GNB)	0.06	0.21
Support Vector Machine (SVM)	67.26	634.11

Imbalanced Distribution of Data. To compare the intrusion detection results of ML algorithms on imbalanced and balanced datasets, we first need to process the imbalanced dataset into the balanced dataset. Therefore, we used undersampling and oversampling techniques to process two common imbalanced datasets, Morris Power and CICIDS 2017, into balanced datasets. Undersampling is a technique for lowering the proportion of the majority class [24]. This method is adopted when the number of elements belonging to the majority class is rather high. Oversampling, on the other hand, increases the minority class's percentage by randomly reproducing it [24]. Table 4 shows the number of normal and attack data before and after implementing these two technologies on Morris power and CICIDS 2017 datasets. It can be observed that after using undersampling and oversampling techniques, the imbalance of the dataset has been greatly alleviated.

Secondly, to evaluate the impact of imbalanced datasets on algorithm intrusion detection performance, We trained the CNN-LSTM algorithm on imbalanced Morris power, balanced Morris power obtained through undersampling, and balanced Morris power obtained through oversampling datasets, and then evaluated their F1-SCORE performance on the test set of the original Morris Power dataset. We also used the same experimental method on the CICIDS 2017 dataset.

The experimental results are shown in Table 5. The authors of [24] used the CNN-LSTM model to experiment with these balanced datasets. According to that, the CNN-LSTM achieves higher F1-Score results on both undersampled and oversampled balanced datasets compared to the original imbalanced dataset. Specifically, when using the undersampling technique to train the CNN-LSTM on the balanced Morris power dataset, compared to training on the original imbalanced Morris power dataset, this F1-Score was improved by 8.03 on the test set of the original Morris power dataset. Therefore, the dataset should be well-balanced regarding the number of malicious data samples vs. benign traffic samples to achieve adequate results when we use an ML method. However, [25] suggests that resampling to full balance is generally not the optimal resampling rate, at least when the test set is balanced. Furthermore, the optimal resampling rate varies from domain to domain and resampling strategy to resampling strategy.

Table 4. Data Distribution of Morris Power and CICIDS 2017 Datasets

Technique	Morris power		CICIDS 2017	
	Normal	Attack	Normal	Attack
Unbalanced	15,471	38,583	625,757	218,251
Undersampling	15,471	19,338	291,001	218,251
Oversampling	32,425	38,583	625,757	457,547

Table 5. Intrusion Detection Results on Imbalanced and Balanced Morris Power and CICIDS 2017 Datasets

Datasets	Technique	F1-Score
Morris Power	Unbalanced	58.06
	Undersampling	66.09
	Oversampling	64.18
CICIDS2017	Unbalanced	98.44
	Undersampling	99.34
	Oversampling	99.46

4.2   Use Cases

Using the right dataset that results in better accuracy of results comes from being aware of the complete use cases of each cybersecurity dataset. This is part of the gap that we discussed before. Apart from discerning the categorization of this dataset as either IT or OT, this section explains other essential features of the datasets that can be considered when choosing the closest dataset to different targets.

In order to select an appropriate dataset for training an ML algorithm to achieve the desired intrusion detection performance, it is essential not only to determine the system in which the algorithm will be employed, i.e., IT or OT, but also to identify the specific communication layer that the algorithm is intended to monitor for intrusion detection. This is crucial because cyber intrusions are typically executed by exploiting vulnerabilities within a specific layer of communication. We also need to determine which specific protocols and attack types of intrusions the algorithm needs to detect, as multiple protocols may also be included in the same communication layer, and various attacks may also be implemented based on a single protocol. Therefore, communication layers, protocols, and types of attacks on the datasets need to be considered to choose the closest dataset to the researcher's target. To help researchers select datasets based on their goals, we have summarized communication layers, protocols, and types of attack contained in the existing important datasets, and the results are shown in Table 6.

5   How to Build and Use Datasets for Combined IT-OT Security in ICS

In this section, we first discuss the limitations of existing important datasets and then discuss how to establish an ideal dataset based on these essential features.

As shown in Table 6, we have shown the essential features that can determine the applicable scenarios of existing important datasets. First, it can be found that the collection environment of these datasets comes from a single system,

Table 6. Essential Features Determining the Applicability Scenarios of Existing Datasets

Datasets	Systems	OSI Layers	Protocols	Attack Types
CIC DoS	IT	Application	HTTP	DoS
CICIDS 2017	IT	Transport Network	TCP IP	Brute Force DoS DDoS Heartbleed Web Infiltration Botnet
DARPA	IT	Transport Network	TCP IP	DoS Privilege escalation Probing
DDoS 2016	IT	Application Network	TCP UDP ICMP HTTP	DDoS
KDD Cup 99	IT	Transport Network	TCP IP	DoS Privilege Escalation Probing
NSL-KDD	IT	Transpor Network	TCP IP	DoS Privilege Escalation Probing
UNSW-NB15	IT	Transport Network	TCP IP	Backdoors DoS Exploits Fuzzers Worms
Morris	OT	Application	MODBUS	Malicious Response Injection DoS
Lemay	OT	Application	MODBUS	Exploits Fingerprinting Unauthorized Command
SWAT	OT	Application Session Network	CIP Ethernet IP	False Data Injection
Rodofile	OT	Application Presentation Session	S7Comm	Reconnaissance
WuSTL	OT	Transport Application	TCP IP	Port scanner Address scanner Device identification Aggressive model device Exploit
EPIC	OT	Data Link	GOOSE MMS	False Data Injection
WADI	OT	Application Session Network	CIP Ethernet IP HSPA	False Data Injection

i.e., IT or OT. Then, these datasets contain limited communication layers, protocols, and types of attacks. For example, algorithms trained on the CIS DOS dataset can only be used to detect DoS attacks against the HTTP protocol at the application layer on IT systems. Therefore, it is necessary to establish an ideal dataset on which algorithms trained can detect as many different cyber intrusions as possible on both IT and OT.

According to the essential characteristics in Table 6, the ML algorithm developed can be applied in the IT system or the OT system based on the goal of the method. We need enough data in both the normal and attack categories. To do this, the researchers should capture necessary network packets from the host and destination for flow analysis and dataset generation. Then, To record realistic attack scenarios, the data collector should have a thorough understanding of the network topology and how networking devices are configured in the testing environment. Collecting all network packets is sometimes not essential. In some cases, we only need to get particular traffic between hosts such as GOOSE or packets that are transmitted to honeynets. Then, the dataset samples should be mapped to various layers of the OSI layers to ensure that algorithms trained on the ideal dataset can detect attacks against different OSI layers. In ML, labels and annotations are essential for supervised learning. Each data point in the dataset should have well-documented labels that specify the type of attack, whether it is benign or malicious, and other pertinent details such as metadata. Thus, labelling the dataset can be an efficient way to train the ML methods well. Also, the data samples should include as many different protocols as possible, as network intrusions may be based on various protocols. Finally, data samples based on different protocols should also strive to include a wide variety of attack types, ensuring that algorithms trained on the ideal dataset can detect different types of attacks.

6   Conclusion

In this work, we classified cybersecurity datasets into two subsets, IT and OT datasets, and investigated them. Then, we discussed the most applicable existing datasets in both subsets of IT and OT and explained their related features and methods for their generation. In addition, we analyzed some popular ML algorithms to assess their performance in detecting anomalies in two different datasets and explore the impact of imbalanced data distribution on the performance of these algorithms. In addition, we have summarized the essential features of existing datasets that can assist researchers in choosing the closest dataset to their target. Furthermore, we also introduce how to build an ideal dataset based on these essential features.

References

1. Gómez, Á.L.P., et al.: On the generation of anomaly detection datasets in industrial control systems. IEEE Access **7**, 177460–177473 (2019)
2. Ring, M., Wunderlich, S., Scheuring, D., Landes, D., Hotho, A.: A survey of network-based intrusion detection data sets. Comput. Secur. **86**, 147–167 (2019)
3. Choi, S., Yun, J.-H., Kim, S.-K.: A comparison of ICS datasets for security research based on attack paths. In: Critical Information Infrastructures Security: 13th International Conference, CRITIS: Kaunas, 24–26 September 2018, Revised Selected Papers 13, vol. 2019, pp. 154–166. Springer (2018)

4. Mubarak, S., Habaebi, M.H., Islam, M.R., Khan, S.: ICS cyber attack detection with ensemble machine learning and dpi using cyber-kit datasets. In: 8th International Conference on Computer and Communication Engineering (ICCCE), vol. 2021, pp. 349–354. IEEE (2021)
5. Lin, Q., Verwer, S., Kooij, R., Mathur, A.: Using datasets from industrial control systems for cyber security research and education. In: Critical Information Infrastructures Security: 14th International Conference, CRITIS: Linköping, 23–25 September 2019, Revised Selected Papers 14, vol. 2020, pp. 122–133. Springer (2019)
6. Conklin, W.A.: It vs. OT security: a time to consider a change in CIA to include resilience. In: 2016 49th Hawaii International Conference on System Sciences (HICSS), pp. 2642–2647. IEEE (2016)
7. Murray, G., Johnstone, M.N., Valli, C.: The convergence of IT and OT in critical infrastructure (2017)
8. Kush, N.S., Ahmed, E., Branagan, M., Foo, E.: Poisoned goose: exploiting the goose protocol. In: Proceedings of the Twelfth Australasian Information Security Conference (AISC 2014) [Conferences in Research and Practice in Information Technology, vol. 149, pp. 17–22]. Australian Computer Society (2014)
9. Hoyos, J., Dehus, M., Brown, T.X.: Exploiting the goose protocol: a practical attack on cyber-infrastructure. In: IEEE Globecom Workshops, vol. 2012, pp. 1508–1513. IEEE (2012)
10. Mubarak, S., Habaebi, M.H., Islam, M.R., Rahman, F.D.A., Tahir, M.: Anomaly detection in ICS datasets with machine learning algorithms. Comput. Syst. Sci. Eng. **37**(1) (2021)
11. Bedi, G., Venayagamoorthy, G.K., Singh, R., Brooks, R.R., Wang, K.-C.: Review of internet of things (IoT) in electric power and energy systems. IEEE Internet Things J. **5**(2), 847–870 (2018)
12. Beasley, C., Zhong, X., Deng, J., Brooks, R., Venayagamoorthy, G.K.: A survey of electric power synchrophasor network cyber security. In: IEEE PES Innovative Smart Grid Technologies, Europe, pp. 1–5. IEEE (2014)
13. Koch, R.: Towards next-generation intrusion detection. In: 2011 3rd International Conference on Cyber Conflict, pp. 1–18. IEEE (2011)
14. Thakkar, A., Lohiya, R.: A review of the advancement in intrusion detection datasets. Procedia Comput. Sci. **167**, 636–645 (2020)
15. Sharafaldin, I., Lashkari, A.H., Ghorbani, A.A.: Toward generating a new intrusion detection dataset and intrusion traffic characterization. ICISSp **1**, 108–116 (2018)
16. Jazi, H.H., Gonzalez, H., Stakhanova, N., Ghorbani, A.A.: Detecting http-based application layer dos attacks on web servers in the presence of sampling. Comput. Netw. **121**, 25–36 (2017)
17. Lippmann, R.P., et al.: Evaluating intrusion detection systems: the 1998 Darpa off-line intrusion detection evaluation. In: Proceedings DARPA Information Survivability Conference and Exposition (DISCEX 2000), vol. 2, pp. 12–26. IEEE (2000)
18. Lippmann, R., Haines, J.W., Fried, D.J., Korba, J., Das, K.: The 1999 darpa off-line intrusion detection evaluation. Comput. Netw. **34**(4), 579–595 (2000)
19. Moustafa, N., Slay, J.: Unsw-nb15: a comprehensive data set for network intrusion detection systems (unsw-nb15 network data set). In: Military Communications and Information Systems Conference (MilCIS), vol. 2015, pp. 1–6. IEEE (2015)
20. Erba, A., et al.: Constrained concealment attacks against reconstruction-based anomaly detectors in industrial control systems. In: Annual Computer Security Applications Conference, pp. 480–495 (2020)

21. Shen, G., Wang, W., Mu, Q., Pu, Y., Qin, Y., Yu, M.: Data-driven cybersecurity knowledge graph construction for industrial control system security. Wirel. Commun. Mob. Comput. **2020**, 1–13 (2020)
22. Diaba, S.Y., et al.: Scada securing system using deep learning to prevent cyber infiltration. Neural Networks (2023)
23. Zhou, Y., Han, M., Liu, L., He, J.S., Wang, Y.: Deep learning approach for cyber-attack detection. In: IEEE INFOCOM 2018-IEEE Conference on Computer Communications Workshops (INFOCOM WKSHPS), pp. 262–267. IEEE (2018)
24. Balla, A., Habaebi, M.H., Elsheikh, E.A., Islam, M.R., Suliman, F.: The effect of dataset imbalance on the performance of Scada intrusion detection systems. Sensors **23**(2), 758 (2023)
25. Estabrooks, A., Jo, T., Japkowicz, N.: A multiple resampling method for learning from imbalanced data sets. Comput. Intell. **20**(1), 18–36 (2004)

Rate Distortion Analysis of Wavefield Coding in Wireless Geophone Networks

Hamood ur Rehman Khan[1] and Farhan Khan[2]($\boxtimes$)

[1] Sir Syed Center for Advanced Studies in Engineering, Islamabad, Pakistan
hamood.rehman@carepvtltd.com
[2] Electrical and Computer Engineering Program, Habib University,
Karachi, Pakistan
farhan.khan@sse.habib.edu.pk

Abstract. Current and future trends in seismic acquisition point towards higher geophone densities (forecasted to be 1M nodes per survey). The geophones' high operating precision and a sampling rate of a few milliseconds leads to a huge aggregate data rate in the geophone array. To handle this large data rate a hierarchy of multiplexed lines (including fiber optic cables) are used, resulting in substantial deployment costs. This work considers wireless geophone networks to mitigate these costs. Because of limited bandwidth of the wireless medium, compression of acquired data is needed. We assess lossy source coding (signal compression) performance using a rate-distortion tradeoff based on a physical model of the earth. The distortion criterion used is mean squared error. The earth's physical model considered here consists of a randomly layered subsurface structure where the acoustic impedance of the earth varies as a homogeneous spatial random process. The rate distortion performance is assessed in terms of the parameters of this physical model e.g., the speed of sound underground and correlation length of acoustic impedance process. In comparison with previous work, this paper derives a closed form expression for the autocorrelation function for the reflection process for the 3D subsurface volume. We also show from the resulting rate-distortion curves that the compression performance improves both as the coding bock length increases and as the correlation length of the medium properties increases. The rate-distortion surface as a function of normalized MSE and sound of speed underground is also computed and validated through extensive simulations.

Keywords: Wireless Sensor Networks · Seismic Data Compression · Rate Distortion · Wave Equation · Green's Function · Random Differential Equation · Randomly Layered Medium

1 Introduction

In exploration seismology acquisition is the first stage of the signal processing pipeline. It consists of laying out a large number of acoustic sensors (geophones)

X. Li et al. (Eds.): SmartGift 2024, LNICST 600, pp. 54–77, 2025.
https://doi.org/10.1007/978-3-031-78806-2_4

in a network and injecting the ground with energy from an energy source (e.g. Vibroseis). The injected energy is reflected from subsurface layers of differing acoustic impedance as a seismic wave and is sensed at the geophones and converted into an electrical voltage that is digitized and transferred to a central fusion center. In this way, subsurface structures are mapped to investigate the occurrence of natural resources. Wavefield coding entails the use of data compression on the digitized amplitudes of the seismic wavefield and decompression of the data at the recorder unit.

Currently there is a shift towards large scale data acquisition. A 10 to 100-fold increase in sensor node count for a given area is underway [5]. Future node densities are forecasted to be even higher, with some surveys aiming to achieve a density of 1 million nodes [6]. The projected shift is from accurate acquisition to better statistical sampling of seismic data. A second trend is towards completely wireless data acquisition—which is the scenario considered in this paper. This presents a huge increase in the handled data rate. To get an idea of the problem, consider the following: A typical survey might cover an area of 2500 sq km. The line separation between geophone rows is typically on the order of 50 to 100 meters, while the receiver interval is around 10–25 m. This gives a total number of about $50 - 100K$ geophones per survey. Given that the geophones operate at 2 ms sampling interval with a bit depth of usually 24 bits, with shot measurements lasting for 6 s, the total aggregate rate of the network is on the order of 1 Gbps. This is the data traffic of medium-sized city.

Since the wireless channel has limited bandwidth and the nodes have limited power owing to working on batteries or on solar power, there needs to be a careful tradeoff analysis between bandwidth (rate) and reproduction accuracy (alternatively known as distortion incurred in compression). Compression involves discretizing the field's continuous valued amplitude at each spatial location. Information is lost during this process. The problem is known as lossy source coding for sensor networks in information theory parlance.

In geoscience and remote sensing, rate-distortion analysis in the formualtion of compression and coding of signal fields has been done in a number of works (see [1–4] for recent contributions). Previous work done in relation to our problem includes the study of [13,14]. [13] studies the problem when the excitation signal (sound) is a two-dimensional random field emanating from a line source embedded in a stationary fluid in thermodynamic equilibrium supporting acoustic propagation of waves that is free from reflecting and/or scattering interfaces. The work done in [14] corresponds to the case of temperature fields instead of acoustic fields and is done for the geometry of rods and rings instead of a slab of layers (as in our subsurface model). In our work the propagation medium is randomly layered. The area of wave propagation in random media has been very actively researched during the last four decades [23, 26] and is a thorough field as of now. The main motivation for studying wave phenomenon in random media is ostensibly to generate strategies for seismic inversion for complex media [23] whereas here we are concerned with obtaining a statistical model for seismic image sources so that they can be compressed.

In this work we carry out a performance analysis of possible compression algorithms employed in a wireless geophone networks. This paper analyzes the opposite scenario than that considered in [13]. In our case the exciting signal is a known pulse located at the surface (as opposed to being buried in the subsurface as in [13]) and the recorded wavefield is the result of interaction of the excitation signal with a layered medium, which is the case in seismic exploration experiments. As pointed out earlier, sensor nodes have limited resources including computational power, limited energy, memory and bandwidth. Source coding involves finding the optimal tradeoff between the use of these scarce resources and the quality of the reconstructed data at the central recording unit. The main tool we use to characterize this tradeoff is R(D) theory for random fields. We assume the existence of a distortion measure or measure of dissimilarity between the original source wavefield and the reconstructed wavefield at the decoder. Specifically, rate-distortion provides us with the answer to the following question: What is the minimum number of bits per sample that are needed to describe a source (the seismic image) at distortion level D, determined by the distortion measure. In our treatment, the distortion measure D is the squared error per digitized letter of the source wavefield. The theory assumes that a statistical description of the source to be coded is available for analysis.

Unfortunately for the seismic acquisition problem the exact statistics of the source are not known. To date there are no detailed statistical models for seismic images. To overcome this difficulty, we make use of the physics of the seismic acquisition process. That is, the seismic source is modelled through the process of injecting a known signal into a randomly layered medium in which the acoustic wave equation holds to a first order of approximation. The output signal measured at the surface through the sensors is then a random field. The Green's function for the random wave equation is obtained and its power spectrum is computed. The power spectrum for the output random field at the surface is then expressed in terms of the Green's function's spectrum. The output field is sampled in space and time along a line of geophones using periodic spatio-temporal sampling scheme, i.e., a sampling lattice. The sampled field is then coded (quantized) and R(D) bounds are obtained through the use of well-known parametrized formulas of the rate-distortion curves for a process with a known correlation structure [7].

To analyze the compression performance, we consider three source coding schemes. The first scheme is centralized coding in which all the data from all sensors is available at a single spatial location, free of communication costs. The second scheme is independent coding in which all sensors independently code their respective data streams and are independently decoded at the fusion center without paying regard to the correlation of information among different sensors. The third scheme is what is known as distributed coding scheme [9] in which all geophones independently (without internode communication) encode their data streams but are jointly decoded at the fusion center, exploiting the correlation within the data of the entire field. The distributed or multi-terminal coding scheme has historically been of much interest in sensor network engineering as its performance is guaranteed to be as good as when the nodes can communicate with each other, without actual internode communication, thus alleviating the need for internode communication and freeing up precious resources. Recent advances [10] have given realizable (non-asymptotic) source codes that achieve the performance of distributed source coding as promised by theoretical consideration for asymptotically long block length regime. Together, these three coding schemes correspond to the best case, the worst case and a middle ground scenario respectively, in terms of rate-distortion performance. Thus, they in a sense, bound the compression performance achievable for coding of wavefields through a wireless network of geophones. One more point to be considered in our problem formulation is that we treat the channel coding and source coding aspects for the wireless channel as separate. Although it is well known that channel and source separation does not hold in general sensor networks [11], here we treat the two problems as separate, assuming that the wireless channel introduces no errors into the data stream or that at least that the errors introduced by the wireless channel are handled by separate channel coding block independent of the source code without any loss of optimality in performance. This assumption can be justified in light of wireless sensor network models considered in [12] (which are approximated by high geohpone-count networks), where the source-channel separation theorem holds as the number of sensor nodes goes to infinity.

The paper is organized as follows. In Sect. 2 we describe the randomly layered earth model and the governing wave equation that describes propagation of acoustic pressure in the subsurface. The Green function for random wave equation is constructed and the spectral measure for this Green's function is obtained. In Sect. 3 we consider the spatio-temporal sampling of the Green's function. In Sect. 4 the finite order R(D) function is considered. The three cases of centralized, independent and distributed coding are handled. In Sect. 5 the previous analysis is simplified to the case of a one dimensional medium and the R(D) analysis for it carried is out using numerical techniques for non-stationary wavefields. In Sect. 6 numerical analysis and simulations are presented as results. In Sect. 7 conclusions are drawn.

2   The Random Medium Model and Wave Equation

In this section we develop the basic model that is used to analyze wave propagation in a randomly layered earth. A wave equation for the random medium is described and its Green's function is obtained. We express the action of this Green's function on the propagating wave as a random integral operator. The autocorrelation for this operator is obtained at the end. This autocorrelation function is required for the calculation of the R(D) function.

We are interested in assessing the compression performance tradeoff for seismic images generated by reflection seismology. This assessment requires a statistical model for general seismic images. To obtain such a statistical description we model the earth as a randomly layered semi-infinite medium, with the reflectivity varying randomly in the vertical direction. This formulation then effectively allows us to perform information theoretic analysis on the resulting setup. In seismic inversion modelling, the reflectivity function, $\rho(x)$ has a step variation which we approximate by a smoothly varying curve that jumps along the discontinuities in $\rho(x)$ and is flat where the reflectivity is constant (between the random layers). The acoustic approximation for the medium is assumed where the subsurface obeys a scalar wave equation and elasticity of the medium is ignored (i.e., there is no shear wave propagation and the dominant waves are compressional or P waves).

The setting shown in Fig. 1 is considered. A receiver line at the surface measures the sensed field $V(x,t)$. The inverted triangles or wedges are the geophones. The Vibroseis source is to the left of the sensor line and is the original cause of excitation in the subsurface structure. Sound waves travel from the subsurface reflecting layers and travel to the receiver line while satisfying the following acoustic wave equation.

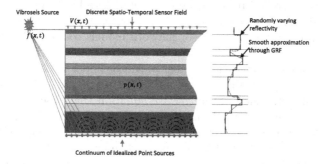

Fig. 1. The physical model of randomly layered earth being considered for the seismic acquistion process

$$\Delta p(t, \mathbf{x}) - \frac{1}{c^2(\mathbf{x})} \frac{\partial^2}{\partial t^2} p(t, \mathbf{x}) = f(t, \mathbf{x}) \tag{1}$$

where the subsurface structure is characterized by position dependent slowness $\frac{1}{c(\mathbf{x})}$, $p(t, \mathbf{x})$ is the acoustic pressure term and $f(t, \mathbf{x})$ is the source field at spatial location $\mathbf{x} = (x_1, x_2, x_3) \in \mathbb{R}^3$ and time $t \in [0, +\infty)$. Δ is the Laplacian operator, defined by $\Delta := \partial^2/\partial^2 x_1 + \partial^2/\partial^2 x_2 + \partial^2/\partial^2 x_3$. In our model the slowness is given by

$$\frac{1}{c^2(\boldsymbol{x})} \rightsquigarrow \frac{1}{c_0^2} \left(n_0^2(\boldsymbol{x}) + \rho(\boldsymbol{x}) \right) \tag{2}$$

where c_0 is the reference wave speed in the medium, $n_0^2(\boldsymbol{x})$ is a smooth background index of refraction taken to be unity throughout the medium and $\rho(\boldsymbol{x})$ is the unknown reflectivity. We assume that $\rho(\boldsymbol{x})$ is a homogenous Gaussian random field. This is a key assumption that leads to the solution of the R(D) problem in later analysis. The condition of homogeneity or shift-invariance is needed because calculation of the R(D) tradeoff for general random fields with arbitrary correlation structure or memory is not possible with current methods. Homogeneous Gaussian random fields enable the application of asymptotic distribution of eigenvalues of Toeplitz forms [15], which is a powerful tool for R(D) computation.

With the slowness thus modelled, the wave equation now reads as:

$$\Delta p(t, \boldsymbol{x}) - \frac{1}{c_0^2}(1 + \rho(\boldsymbol{x}))\frac{\partial^2}{\partial t^2}p(t, \boldsymbol{x}) = f(t, \boldsymbol{x}) \tag{3}$$

together with the following initial conditions:

$$p(0, \boldsymbol{x}) = 0 \tag{4a}$$

$$\left.\frac{\partial p(t, \boldsymbol{x})}{\partial t}\right|_{t=0} = 0 \tag{4b}$$

The initial conditions ensure that the solution obtained to the above Cauchy problem is unique. To retrieve the solution to the hyperbolic PDE that relies only on the effect of the external seismic source initial conditions are assumed to be identically zero.

When the source field is modelled as an impulse at spatial location $\mathbf{y}$ and at time zero, the Green's function for our partial differential equation satisfies,

$$\Delta G(t, \boldsymbol{x}, \boldsymbol{y}) - \frac{1}{c_0^2}(1 + \rho(\boldsymbol{x}))\frac{\partial^2}{\partial t^2}G(t, \boldsymbol{x}, \boldsymbol{y}) = \delta(\boldsymbol{x} - \boldsymbol{y})\delta(t) \tag{5}$$

where δ is the Dirac distribution. Equation (5) is a random differential equation because of the random term $\rho(x)$ as a co-efficient. If the medium is homogeneous ($\rho(\boldsymbol{x}) = 0$) the free space time-dependent Green's function is given by

$$G_0(t, \boldsymbol{x}, \boldsymbol{y}) = \frac{1}{4\pi\|\boldsymbol{x} - \boldsymbol{y}\|}\delta\left(t - \frac{\|\boldsymbol{x} - \boldsymbol{y}\|}{c_0}\right) \tag{6}$$

The above is a spherical wave propagating at speed c_0 outward from the point $\boldsymbol{y}$. Define the temporal Fourier transform of the Green's function as

$$\hat{G}(\omega, \boldsymbol{x}, \boldsymbol{y}) = \int G(t, \boldsymbol{x}, \boldsymbol{y})e^{-i\omega t}dt \tag{7}$$

The free space Green's function in the frequency domain, corresponding to (6) is given by

$$\hat{G}_0(\omega, \boldsymbol{x}, \boldsymbol{y}) = \frac{1}{4\pi\|\boldsymbol{x} - \boldsymbol{y}\|}e^{-ik\|\boldsymbol{x} - \boldsymbol{y}\|} \tag{8}$$

where $k = \omega/c_0$ is the spatial frequency or the wavenumber. Taking the Fourier transform of (5) we get:

$$\Delta \hat{G} + \frac{\omega^2}{c_0^2}\left(1 + \rho(\boldsymbol{x})\right)\hat{G} = \delta(\boldsymbol{x} - \boldsymbol{y}) \tag{9}$$

The free space Green's function satisfies the equation:

$$\Delta \hat{G}_0 + \frac{\omega^2}{c_0^2}\hat{G}_0 = \delta(\boldsymbol{x} - \boldsymbol{y}) \tag{10}$$

It can be shown that under the Born approximation (holds when the reflectivity $\rho(x)$ is either small or has small support), we can write the overall Green's function as:

$$\hat{G}(\omega, \boldsymbol{x}, \boldsymbol{y}) = \hat{G}_0(\omega, \boldsymbol{x}, \boldsymbol{y}) + \frac{\omega^2}{c_0^2}\int \rho(\boldsymbol{z})\hat{G}_0(\omega, \boldsymbol{x}, \boldsymbol{z})\hat{G}_0(\omega, \boldsymbol{z}, \boldsymbol{y})dz \tag{11}$$

The first term in (10) is the direct wave emanating from the source and that reaches the geophone array without interacting with subsurface layers, while the second term accounts for the single scattered waves from source located at $\boldsymbol{y}$ to a subsurface point $\boldsymbol{z}$ and then back to the surface point $\boldsymbol{x}$ inside the geophone array. In usual seismic processing the term $\hat{G}_0(\omega, \boldsymbol{x}, \boldsymbol{y})$ is windowed and removed from the seismogram. We will from now on only consider the second term in our data model. The time domain Green's function is thus given as (with the direct wave removed):

$$G(t, \boldsymbol{x}, \boldsymbol{y}) = -\frac{1}{c_0^2}\frac{\partial^2}{\partial^2 t}\iint \rho(\boldsymbol{z})G_0(t - s, \boldsymbol{x}, \boldsymbol{z})G_0(s, \boldsymbol{z}, \boldsymbol{y})dsdz \tag{12}$$

Assuming a source located at the origin and considering the shift-invariance of the free space Green's function, the expression for the overall Green's function becomes

$$\begin{aligned}
G(t, \boldsymbol{x}, \boldsymbol{0}) &= G(t, \boldsymbol{x} - \boldsymbol{0}) \\
&= -\frac{1}{c_0^2}\frac{\partial^2}{\partial^2 t}\iint \rho(\boldsymbol{z})G_0(t - s, \boldsymbol{z})G_0(s, \boldsymbol{z} - \boldsymbol{0})dsz \\
&= -\frac{1}{c_0^2}\frac{\partial^2}{\partial^2 t}\iint \rho(\boldsymbol{z})G_0(t - s, \boldsymbol{x} - \boldsymbol{z})G_0(s, \boldsymbol{z})dsdz \\
&= G(t, \boldsymbol{x})
\end{aligned} \tag{13}$$

For a general source $f(t, \boldsymbol{x})$ the resultant wavefield is given in terms of this Green's function by the linear superposition and time invariance.

$$\begin{aligned}
p(t, \boldsymbol{x}) &= \iint G(t - s, \boldsymbol{x}, \boldsymbol{y})f(s, \boldsymbol{y})dsd\boldsymbol{y} \\
&= \int G(t, \boldsymbol{x}, \boldsymbol{y}) *_t f(t, \boldsymbol{y})dsd\boldsymbol{y}
\end{aligned} \tag{14}$$

where $*_t$ is the time convolution operator. Define the operator H by as the action of this convolution operator

$$Hf(t, \boldsymbol{x}) = \int G(t, \boldsymbol{x}, \boldsymbol{y}) *_t f(t, \boldsymbol{y}) ds d\boldsymbol{y} \tag{15}$$

Of course for a Dirac distribution source at the origin, i.e., $f(t, \boldsymbol{x}) = \delta(\boldsymbol{x})\delta(t)$, the action of H is given by

$$H \cdot \delta = G(t, \boldsymbol{x}, \boldsymbol{0}) = G(t, \boldsymbol{x}) \tag{16}$$

Note that H is a random operator because of the sctochastic Green's function that corresponds to the random differential equation (5). In fact the valuation of H is Gaussian random field that it inherits from the Gaussianity of the reflectivity function ρ which is involved in the convolution expression (13) that gives rise to $G(t, \boldsymbol{x})$. We are interested in the ensemble averaged autocorrelation function of H. The autocorrelation function of H corresponds to the autocorrelation of the Green function field $G(t, \boldsymbol{x})$. This autocorrelation (which is equal to $G(t, \boldsymbol{x})$'s autocovariance) is needed in the calculation of the rate-distortion tradeoff. The source term used in the analysis is a Dirac distribution. Using (14) we get:

$$\begin{aligned}
R_{Hf}(\tau, \boldsymbol{u}) &= \mathbb{E}[Hf(t, \boldsymbol{r})H^* f(t + \tau, \boldsymbol{r} + \boldsymbol{u})] \\
&= \mathbb{E}[H\delta(t, \boldsymbol{r})H^* \delta(t + \tau, \boldsymbol{r} + \boldsymbol{u})] \\
&= \mathbb{E}[G(t, \boldsymbol{r})G^*(t + \tau, \boldsymbol{r} + \boldsymbol{u})]
\end{aligned} \tag{17}$$

Thus obtaining

$$\begin{aligned}
R_{Hf}(\tau, \boldsymbol{u}) &= \mathbb{E}[-\frac{1}{c_0^2}\frac{\partial^2}{\partial^2 t}\iint \rho(\boldsymbol{z}_1)G_0(t - s_1, \boldsymbol{r} - \boldsymbol{z}_1)G_0(s_1, \boldsymbol{z}_1)ds_1 d\boldsymbol{z}_1 \\
&\quad \times -\frac{1}{c_0^2}\frac{\partial^2}{\partial^2 t}\iint \rho(\boldsymbol{z}_2)G_0^*(t + \tau - s_2, \boldsymbol{r} + \boldsymbol{u} - \boldsymbol{z}_2)G_0^*(s_2, \boldsymbol{z}_2)ds_2 d\boldsymbol{z}_2] \\
&= \frac{1}{c_0^4}\iiiint \frac{\partial^2}{\partial^2 t}G_0(t - s_1, \boldsymbol{r} - \boldsymbol{z}_1)G_0(s_1, \boldsymbol{z}_1) \\
&\quad \times \frac{\partial^2}{\partial^2 t}G_0^*(t + \tau - s_2, \boldsymbol{r} + \boldsymbol{u} - \boldsymbol{z}_2)G_0^*(s_2, \boldsymbol{z}_2)\mathbb{E}[\rho(\boldsymbol{z}_1)\rho(\boldsymbol{z}_2)]ds_1 ds_2 d\boldsymbol{z}_1 d\boldsymbol{z}_2
\end{aligned} \tag{18}$$

Clearly $C(\boldsymbol{z}_1, \boldsymbol{z}_2) = \mathbb{E}[\rho(\boldsymbol{z}_2)\rho(\boldsymbol{z}_1)]$ in the last expression is an autocorrelation function. Since we assume homogeneity for the random field $\rho(\boldsymbol{z})$, $C(\boldsymbol{z}_1, \boldsymbol{z}_2)$ depends only on the difference of $\boldsymbol{z}_1$ and $\boldsymbol{z}_2$. We consider Gaussian correlation for ρ:

$$C(\boldsymbol{z}_1, \boldsymbol{z}_2) = C(\|\boldsymbol{z}_1 - \boldsymbol{z}_2\|) = \sigma^2 e^{-\frac{\|\boldsymbol{z}_1 - \boldsymbol{z}_2\|^2}{a^2}} \tag{19}$$

where σ^2 is the variance of the fluctuation in the reflectivity and a is the correlation length. We define the spectral measure of H via the Weiner-Kinchin theorem:

$$S_H(\Omega, \boldsymbol{\Phi}) = \frac{1}{(2\pi)^4}\int_{\mathbb{R}^4} e^{-j(\Omega\tau + \boldsymbol{\Phi}\cdot\boldsymbol{u})}R_{Hf}(\tau, \boldsymbol{u})d\tau d\boldsymbol{u} \tag{20}$$

where Ω is the temporal frequency, $\boldsymbol{\Phi} = (\Phi_x, \Phi_y, \Phi_z)$ is the three-dimensional spatial frequency and $\boldsymbol{\Phi} \cdot \boldsymbol{u} = \Phi_x u_x + \Phi_y u_y + \Phi_z u_z$ is the dot product between the wave vector $\boldsymbol{\Phi}$ and the space vector $\boldsymbol{u}$. We now turn to sampling of this random field in time and space.

3   Sampling the Green's Function

In this section we consider the sampling of the Green's function obtained in Sect.2. As described before, the geophone array consists of lines of acoustic sensors that are more or less regularly spaced and that acquire the seismic wavefield reflected/scattered off the subsurface structure. The main objective is to temporally and spatially sample and then encode (quantize) the random wavefield generated by the impulsive source. This corresponds to sampling of the stochastic Green's function given by (13). Since in the setting discussed in this paper the geophone array is a one-dimensional linear array this corresponds to a spatio-temporal sampling of the following 2D Green function:

$$(G_1(t, x_1) = G(t, x_1, 0, 0) \tag{21}$$

where G is the Green's function in (13). To avoid cumbersome notation, we drop the subscript of G_1 in the following discussion. The sampling scheme considered is periodic sampling through a lattice in the space-time plane $\{(x, t) \in \mathbb{R}^2\}$. $G(t, x)$ is an analog field which is digitized in space, time and amplitude. The spatio-temporally discretized field is Gaussian, as is $G(t, x)$. The discrete Gaussian field is then quantized using source coding and its Gaussianity facilitates the application of results from information theory for Gaussian random fields to obtain the R(D) tradeoff. We proceed along the lines of [16] which gives the analysis of multidimensional sampling for the case of deterministic signals and arbitrary geometries of the sampling lattice and which is extended in [13] to the case of random fields.

3.1   Spectral Measure of the Sampled Field

Since for bandlimited random process, sampling in time domain implies replication in the spectral domain, we derive the spectral measure of the sampled field in this subsection. A sampling lattice is characterized by sampling matrix V [16] whose columns form the basis which generates the lattice. The set of points $\Lambda_V = \{Vn : n = (n_1, n_2)^T \in \mathbb{Z}^2\}$ form the vertices of the lattice where the analog field $G(t, \boldsymbol{x})$ is sampled to form a discrete parameter random field. The discrete parameter field or the sampled Green's function is given by

$$\tilde{G}[\boldsymbol{n}] = G(\boldsymbol{V}\boldsymbol{n}) = G(v_{11}n_1 + v_{12}n_2, v_{21}n_1 + v_{22}n_2) \tag{22}$$

where $\boldsymbol{v}_1 = (v_{11}, v_{21})^T$ and $\boldsymbol{v}_2 = (v_{12}, v_{22})^T$ are the first and second columns of the sampling matrix V respectively.

Under appropriate conditions (chiefly that the spectrum S_H [$= S_G$ for the case of an impulse source] in (20) has compact support) it is guaranteed by the spectral representation theorem [19] that the spectral measure $S_{\tilde{G}}$ of the discrete parameter random field $\tilde{G}$ is given by

$$S_{\tilde{G}}(\boldsymbol{\omega}) = \frac{1}{|\det \boldsymbol{V}|} \sum_{\boldsymbol{k} \in \mathbb{Z}^2} S_G(\boldsymbol{V}^{-T}(\boldsymbol{\omega} - 2\pi \boldsymbol{k})) \qquad (23)$$

where $\boldsymbol{\omega} = \boldsymbol{V}^T \cdot (\Omega, \Phi)^T$, with Ω being the temporal frequency, Φ the spatial frequency and $\boldsymbol{V}^{-T}$ the transpose inverse of $\boldsymbol{V}$.

4 Finite Order Rate Distortion Analysis

In this setion we give the R(D) analysis. We begin with the finite order R(D) function. By finite order we mean that the block length of the symbols that are jointly encoded is finite and not in the asymptotic regime. The asymptotic R(D) function is considered in Setion V. Finite order allows us to use parametric formulas for the rate-distortion function that are independent of whether the wavefield is stationary or not. W using reverse water filling [24] to compute the R(D) function. We consider the three basic source coding schemes to arrive at three bounds for the R(D) function as is done in the analysis of [13]. The first is the centralized coding scheme. In the centralized scheme it is assumed that there is zero cost of communication between sensors: every sensor knows the entire data of every other sensor and encodes its data accordingly. In effect we have all the data available at a single "super" sensor. This is the best possible performance that can be achieved and thus forms a lower bound for the R(D) function. The second scheme is the one where all sensors encode their data independently without regard to the correlation between adjacent sensors. This forms an upper bound on the R(D) performance as this is the worst possible that can be done. The third scheme is a multi-terminal source doing scheme in which the sensors do not communicate with each directly, but inter-sensor correlation is exploited jointly by the decoder at the fusion center or recorder unit. This forms a tighter lower bound and is known is the Berger-Tung inner bound. It is known to be tight for some cases.

4.1 Simplification of the Autocorrelation Function for the Green's Function Field

In order to obtain the R(D) tradeoff for the wireless geophone network the autocorrelation function of the Green field $G(t, x)$ is needed. To that end, the expression for $G(t, x)$ as given in Eq. (13) is analyzed and simplified first.

$$G(t, x) = -\frac{1}{c_0^2}\frac{\partial^2}{\partial^2 t}\iint \rho(z)G_0(t - s, x - z)G_0(s, z)dsdz$$

$$= -\frac{1}{c_0^2}\frac{\partial^2}{\partial^2 t}\iint \frac{\rho(z)}{\|z\|\|x - z\|}\delta\left(t - s - \frac{\|x - z\|}{c}\right)\delta\left(s - \frac{\|z\|}{c}\right)dsdz \quad (24)$$

$$= -\frac{1}{c_0^2}\frac{\partial^2}{\partial^2 t}\int \frac{\rho(z)}{\|z\|\|x - z\|}\delta\left(t - \frac{\|z\| + \|x - z\|}{c}\right)dz$$

Considering that the Green's Function Field is only two dimensional according to Eq. (21) and also that the reflectivity function ρ is one dimensional (constant over a given layer at a given depth), we see that the above expression becomes

$$G(t, x) = -\frac{1}{c_0^2}\frac{\partial^2}{\partial^2 t}\iiint \frac{\rho(z_1)}{\sqrt{z_1^2 + z_2^2 + z_3^2}\sqrt{(x - z_1)^2 + z_2^2 + z_3^2}}$$

$$\times \delta\left(t - \frac{\sqrt{z_1^2 + z_2^2 + z_3^2} + \sqrt{(x - z_1)^2 + z_2^2 + z_3^2}}{c}\right)dz_1 dz_2 dz_3 \quad (25)$$

Equation (25) can be simplified to:

$$G(t, x) = \frac{4\pi}{x^2}\left[\rho\left(\frac{ct + x}{2}\right) + ct\dot\rho\left(\frac{ct + x}{2}\right)\right] \quad (26)$$

Since ρ is a Gaussian random process by assumption, the time derivative of ρ is also Gaussian owing to the fact that differentiation is a linear operation. The linear combination of two terms involving ρ and $\dot\rho$ is thus Gaussian, and hence so is $G(t, x)$.

The non-stationary autocovariance function for the Green Function field is given by:

$$R_G(t_1, x_1; t_2, x_2) := \mathbb{E}[G(t_1, x_1)G(t_2, x_2)]$$

$$= \frac{\sigma^2 e^{-\frac{(c\Delta t + \Delta x)^2}{4a^2}}(64a^4\pi^2 + 2a^2c^2(c^2 t_1 t_2 - 4c\pi\Delta t^2 - 4\pi\Delta t\Delta x) - c^4 t_1 t_2(c\Delta t + \Delta x)^2)}{4a^4 x_1^2 x_2^2}$$

$$(27)$$

where $\Delta t = t_1 - t_2$, $\Delta x = x_1 - x_2$, a is the correlation length and σ^2 is the variation of the fluctuation in the reflectivity ρ. Obtaining the autocovariance function enables the construction of the autocovariance matrix Γ_G for the sampled field $\hat{G}$. Γ_G is used to compute the finite order R(D) tradeoff for a Gaussian random field as given in the work of Kolmogorov [17]:

$$R_n(\theta) = \frac{1}{n}\sum_{k=0}^{n-1}\max\left(0, \frac{1}{2}\log_2\frac{\lambda_k^{(n)}}{\theta}\right)$$

$$D_n(\theta) = \frac{1}{n}\sum_{k=0}^{n-1}\min\left(\theta, \lambda_k^{(n)}\right) \quad (28)$$

where n is the block length of the source symbol string that is being coded. $\lambda_k^{(n)}$ is the kth eigenvalue of the $n \times n$-dimensional autocovariance matrix whos $(l,m)^{\text{th}}$ position is given by $\Gamma_G[l,m] := R_G(z_l; z_m)$ where $z_i \in \{jT_0 : j \in \mathbb{N}\} \times \{kX_0 : k \in \mathbb{N}\}$, for $i = 1, 2, \ldots, n$, with T_0 and X_0 being the temporal and spatial sampling intervals respectively. The advantage of using a finite order R(D) formulation is that it gives a lower bound to the optimal asymptotic performance of any code (bounds the R(D) curve from above). In practice the code length is always finite, so it makes sense to make use of finite order R(D) functions.

4.2   Centralized Compression

As discussed before the geophone array samples the analog field spatio-temporally and then performs data compression (quantization) on the sampled field. The analog field amplitudes are converted into binary data and transmitted over a digital wireless channel. In centralized compression all the field's sample are available at a single spatial location or equivalently the communication cost among sensors is zero. This effectively becomes a point-to-point compression problem. The analog field $G(t,x)$ is first discretized on its support as $\tilde{G}[m,n]$, $(m,n) \in \mathbb{Z}^2$, quantized and then reconstructed as $\tilde{G}_r[m,n]$ at the fusion center. The reconstructed analog field. $G_r(t,x)$ can be obtained from $\tilde{G}_r[m,n]$ using sampling representation given in [3]. The distortion criteria used is mean square error (MSE) as formulated in ([3], Sect. 4.6.3), extended here to the case of a 2D random field:

$$
\begin{aligned}
D &= \lim_{\substack{T \to \infty \\ X \to \infty}} \int_{-T}^{T} \int_{-X}^{X} [G(t,x) - G_r(t,x)]^2 dt dx \\
&= \lim_{\substack{N \to \infty \\ K \to \infty}} \frac{1}{2N+1} \frac{1}{2K+1} \sum_{m=-K}^{K} \sum_{n=-N}^{N} [\tilde{G}[m.n] - \tilde{G}_r[m,n]]^2
\end{aligned}
\tag{29}
$$

As pointed out in [13], [3], this is equivalent to finding the distortion normalized by unit time and unit length of the geophone sensor array.

The field to be compressed $\tilde{G}[m,n]$ is a homogeneous Gaussian random field. By simple transposition of the results of Sect. 4.6.3 in [3] for stationary, bandlimited sources to the case of homogeneous random fields, one obtains the following parametric form for the R(D) curve. The main tool used to obtain these expression is the Toeplitz distribution theorem of Szego [15].

$$
D_\gamma = \left(\frac{1}{2\pi}\right)^2 \int_{-\pi}^{\pi} \int_{-\pi}^{\pi} \min[\gamma, S_{\tilde{G}}(\omega, \phi)] d\omega d\phi
\tag{30}
$$

and

$$
R_\gamma = K \left(\frac{1}{2\pi}\right)^2 \int_{-\pi}^{\pi} \int_{-\pi}^{\pi} \max\left[0, \frac{1}{2} \log \frac{S_{\tilde{G}}(\omega, \phi)}{\gamma}\right] d\omega d\phi
\tag{31}
$$

where $S_{\tilde{G}}(\omega, \phi)$ is determined from Eqs. (18), (20) and (23), γ is a parameter of Eqs. (30) and (31) and K is a normalization constant that depends on the

temporal and spatial cutoff frequency in the support of $S_{\tilde{G}}$ and on the geometry
of the sampling lattice.

4.3 Independent Coding

In independent coding all geophones encode and send their data streams directly
to the fusion center without communicating with each other and without taking
into consideration the correlation among data stream of neighboring sensors.
Similarly, the data sent by each individual geophone is decoded/reconstructed
separately by the fusion center. In the independent coding case, all geophones
observe the same spectral measure of the underlying field $\tilde{G}[m, n]$ given by [13]:

$$S(\omega) = \frac{1}{2\pi} \int_{-\pi}^{\pi} S_{\tilde{G}}(\omega, \phi)d\phi \tag{32}$$

while the R(D) function is now given by

$$D_{\gamma} = \frac{1}{2\pi} \int_{-\pi}^{\pi} \min[\gamma, S_{\tilde{G}}(\omega]d\omega \tag{33}$$

$$R_{\gamma} = K\frac{1}{2\pi} \int_{-\pi}^{\pi} \max\left[0, \frac{1}{2}\log\frac{S_{\tilde{G}}(\omega, \phi)}{\gamma}\right] d\omega \tag{34}$$

4.4 Distributed Coding

In distributed source coding the correlation among data streams from different
sensors is taken into account while encoding the source and also while performing
centralized decoding. All this is done while there is no inter-sensor communication among the geophone network nodes, which makes it of high value for wireless
sensor network applications as there is no internode communication cost. The
complete rate-distortion region for distributed source coding has not been found
to date, however several special cases and bounds for the rate region are known.
For nearly lossless coding, the condition of no inter-sensor communication while
encoding places no extra cost on the required rate [28]. In the lossy compression
case, there is an incurred cost in terms of rate for not communicating between
sensors [29]. In [29] a complete characterization of the rate region is also obtained
under the assumption of high-resolution quantization. In [31] the rate-distortion
region for the two-terminal case with Gaussian source is given. The case for arbitrary number of sources is yet unknown. Since the exact rate-distortion region
for distributed source coding remains an open and difficult problem, we evaluate
in this paper the inner bound developed by Tung in her PhD thesis, [30]. Under
that formulation, the parametric form of rate-distortion function is given by

$$D_P = \left(\frac{1}{2\pi}\right)^2 \int_{-\pi}^{\pi}\int_{-\pi}^{\pi} \frac{S_{\tilde{G}}(\omega, \phi)P(\omega)}{S_{\tilde{G}}(\omega, \phi) + P(\omega)}d\omega d\phi \tag{35}$$

and

$$R_P = K \left(\frac{1}{2\pi}\right)^2 \int_{-\pi}^{\pi} \int_{-\pi}^{\pi} \frac{1}{2} \log\left(1 + \frac{S_{\tilde{G}}(\omega,\phi)}{P(\omega)}\right) d\omega d\phi \qquad (36)$$

The fucntion $P(\omega)$ is a parameter of optimization (the minimum rate R_P subject to distortion level D_P) and can be found using Lagrangian optimization.

5 Analysis for a Plane Wave Scenario

In what follows we analyze a specialized, one dimensional version of the model presented in Sect. 2. A plane wave impinging on a one dimensional slab of length L consisting of randomly layered medium is considered. We focus on this simplified model for illustrative purposes, as the analysis is more straightforward and the results more elucidating. The plane wave analysis also allows us to obtain the asymptotic R(D) function as opposed to the finite order R(D) function obtained in Sect. 4. The model and its various generalizations have been extensively considered in [23] for seismic analysis. The main idea used in [23] is to split the total propagation into upward going and downward going waves and represent the total wave as their sum. Using stochastic calculus, the reflected wave from the random medium interface can be shown to be a locally stationary Gaussian process, whose time-varying power spectral density can be calculated in closed form, provided the medium has a constant background density and bulk modulus. This reflected Gaussian process is an asymptotic limit for the case of infinite number of layers in the slab, that is, this "ϵ"-process converges to a Gaussian process, as $\epsilon \to 0$, where ϵ is the width of the plane-wave pulse propagating from the source into the medium. The pulse width is assumed to be large compared to the width of the layers yet small with repsect to L, the width of the slab. The width of layers is taken to be on the order of ϵ^2.

We consider the anlaysis given in [32]. Let $\mathbf{u}(t, \mathbf{x})$ denote the velocity and $p(t, \mathbf{x})$ denote the pressure wiithing the subsurface. The linearized acoustic wave equations are then given by

$$\rho(z)\frac{\partial \mathbf{u}}{\partial t} + \nabla p = \mathbf{F}(t, \mathbf{x})$$
$$\frac{1}{K(z)}\frac{\partial p}{\partial t} + \nabla \cdot \mathbf{u} = 0 \qquad (37)$$

where $\rho(z)$ is the density and $K(z)$ is the bulk modulus. $\mathbf{F}(t, \mathbf{x})$ is the forcing term due to source at the surface. For simplicity we assume that in the one dimensional case the source term is a plane wave given by

$$\mathbf{F}(t, \mathbf{x}) = f(t)\delta(x)\delta(y)\delta(z)\mathbf{e} \qquad (38)$$

where $\mathbf{e} = (0,0,1)$ is a unit directivity vector, $(0,0,0)$ is the position of the source and $f(t)$ is a pulse function with compact support. The random medium occupies a slab of thickness L in the lower half space $z \leq 0$. The parameters ρ and K are constant throughout this half space region. We specify the boundary conditions for the system (24) and rewrite it as (in the 1-D case)

$$\rho(z)\frac{\partial u}{\partial t} + \frac{\partial p}{\partial z} = 0$$
$$\frac{1}{K(z)}\frac{\partial p}{\partial t} + \frac{\partial u}{\partial z} = 0 \tag{39}$$

The material properties $\rho(z)$ and $K(z)$ fluctuate randomly around background smooth functions $\rho_0(z)$ and $K_0(z)$ governed by following relationship

$$\rho(z) = \rho_0(z)\left(1 + \eta(\frac{z}{\epsilon^2})\right)$$
$$K(z) = K_0(z)\left(1 + \nu(\frac{z}{\epsilon^2})\right) \tag{40}$$

where $\eta(\frac{z}{\epsilon^2})$ and $\nu(\frac{z}{\epsilon^2})$ are zero-mean ergodic processes whose fluctuations are the scale ϵ^2. The effective medium assumption [23] is in force within the random medium so that $\rho_0(z) = \rho_0$ and $K_0(z) = K_0$ are constant background material properties. Continuity conditions at $x = 0$ and $x = L$ are imposed. The boundary conditions that are needed to completely specify the system (24) are given by

$$A_\epsilon(z,t) = u(z,t) + \frac{p(z,t)}{\sqrt{\rho_0 K_0}}$$
$$B_\epsilon(z,t) = u(z,t) - \frac{p(z,t)}{\sqrt{\rho_0 K_0}}$$
$$A_\epsilon(0,t) = \frac{1}{\sqrt{\epsilon}}f\left(\frac{t}{\epsilon}\right) \tag{41}$$
$$B_\epsilon(L,t) = 0$$

where A_ϵ is the wave traveling into the ground and B_ϵ is the reflected wave. We are primarily interested in the random process $B_\epsilon(0,t)$. It can be shown [32] that $B_\epsilon(0,t + \epsilon\sigma)$ converges in distribution, to a zero-mean, locally stationary Gaussian process $R_{f,t}(\sigma)$ as $\epsilon \to 0$. We are interested in the correlation function of this reflected process. Accordingly, we carry out the following analysis. The windowed correlation function is given by

$$C_f^\epsilon(t,\sigma) = \mathbb{E}[B_\epsilon(0,t - \frac{\epsilon}{2}\sigma)B_\epsilon(0,t + \frac{\epsilon}{2}\sigma)]$$

Then as discussed, we have the result that

$$C_f^\epsilon(t,\sigma) = \lim_{\epsilon \to 0} C_f^\epsilon(t,\sigma) = \frac{1}{\sqrt{2\pi}}\int_{-\infty}^{\infty} e^{i\omega\sigma}|\hat{f}(\omega)|^2\Lambda(\omega,t)d\omega \tag{42}$$

where $\hat{f}(\omega)$ is the Fourier transform of the source pulse $f(t)$ and $\Lambda(\omega,t)$ is the local power spectral density of the reflected (Gaussian) process from the randomly layered medium. In our case of constant background material properties, it is given by [32]

$$\Lambda(\omega,t) = \frac{\alpha\omega^2}{(1 + \alpha\omega^2 t)^2} \tag{43}$$

where α depends on the matrial properties and on the speed of sound $c_0 = \sqrt{\frac{K_0}{\rho_0}}$ in the subsurface. It is given by the following expression [32],

$$\alpha = \frac{1}{4}\int_0^\infty \mathbb{E}[(\eta(0) - \nu(0))(\eta(z) - \nu(z)]dx \tag{44}$$

We consider a Dirac impulse as the source so that $\hat{f}(\omega) = 1$. The autocorrelation function of the process can be obtained in closed form from the local power spectral density $\Lambda(\omega,t)$by Fourier inverting it with respect to the ω variable and treat t as the center of the time window with edges at $-\frac{\sigma}{2}.\frac{\sigma}{2}$. The expression thus obtained for the non-stationary autocorrelation function is thus given as

$$R(t_1,t_2) = \mathbb{E}[B(0,t_1)B(0,t_2)] = \frac{e^{-\frac{\sqrt{2}|t_1-t_2|}{\sqrt{\alpha(t_1+t_2)}}}\left(\sqrt{2\alpha}(t_1+t_2) - 2|t_1-t_2|\sqrt{t_1+t+2}\right)}{2\alpha(t_1+t_2)^{5/2}} \tag{45}$$

This autocorrelation function can be used to find the R(D) function for the process. To that end, we used the approach of [8] in which the R(D) pair given parametrically by [17] is extended to the non-stationary case. Accordingly, we have

$$D_\gamma = \int_0^\infty \min[\gamma, \lambda(f)]df$$

$$R(D_\gamma)) = \int_0^\infty \max[0, \log(\sqrt{\lambda(f)/\gamma})]df \tag{46}$$

where $\lambda(f)$ is the power spectrum given by defined as [8]

$$\lambda(f) = \lim_{\substack{k\to\infty, b-a\to\infty \\ k/(b-a)\to f}} \lambda_k(a,b) \tag{47}$$

where $\lambda_k(a,b)$ is the kth eigenvale of the Karhunen-Loeve (KL) integral equation

$$\lambda g(t) = \int_a^b R(t,s)g(s)ds \tag{48}$$

Up till now we have assumed an infinite receiver line with an infinite number of geophones on it. In practical seismic surveys this is not valid. To model this scenario, we iintroduce the use of a windowing function on the sensed field. A rectangular window in the spatial domain is applied to the green function. In this way the spectrum of the green function is a convolution of the original spectrum and the sinc function. This is computed numerically and then the computations are carried out for the R(D) function, the results of which follow in the next section.

6   Numerical Analysis and Simulations

The results obtained through our analysis are presented next. The results are a result of numerical analysis and simulations of the equationns of rate distortion function and autocorrelation functions of the reflected random field at the suface that is sampled by the sensor network in space and time.

In Fig. 2, the time varying power spectral density of the reflected Gaussian process emanating from the randomly layered medium is plotted. Different snapshots are given, it is seen as that time progresses, or as the center of window of the spectral density moves forward, the power decays. The value of the parameter α that is used is equal to 1.

Figure 3 gives the autocorrelation function of the reflected random process. This autocorrelation function is given in closed form by Eq. (45) and is derived from the power spectral density given by Eq. (43). The autocorrelation function is symmetric in both of its arguments and has a singularity at the origin.

The power spectrum as the solution of the eigenvalue problem for the Karhunen-Loeve equation is plotted in Fig. 4. The frequency variable f is the ratio of the eigenvalue index to the length of the interval on which the KL expansion is sought.

In Fig. 5, the asymptotic R(D) curve is given for $\alpha = 1$. Complete finite order R(D) tradeoff is obtained for a scenario where the wave propagation speed underground is 400 m/s and the correlation length a is 10 m.

It can be seen from Fig. 6 that in the limit of very low bit rate compression (on the order of 0.05 bits per sample) the distortion is practically infinite. However, for moderate compression ratios (12 bits per sample) the distortion is in the order of .001 MSE. While these results seem pessimistic somewhat, it should be noted that they are for a moderate block length of 625. In actual compression larger block lengths are to be expected.

In Fig. 7, the three bounds of independent, centralized and distributed source coding are given. The bounds have an intersection at a certain point along the distortion axis. Figure 8 gives the effect of finite aperture length on coding performance. The number of sensors are now limited and the sensor density increases with the number of total sensors as the receiver line is of finite length. We see that as we reduce the number of sensors the rate-distortion tradeoff detiorates.

The effect on compression performance for different block lengths can be seen in Fig. 9. Here there is a marked improved in compression performance as

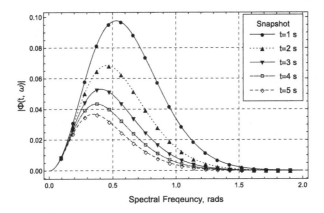

Fig. 2. Locally stationary windowed power spectral density of the reflected Gaussian process with $\alpha = 1$ at various time snapshots t which index the center the of the window. The excitation function is a Gaussian pulse

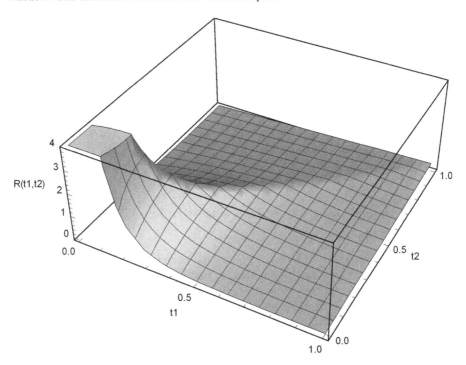

Fig. 3. Plot of the autorcorrelation surface of the reflected process with time indices t_1 and t_2 as argument, plotted for $\alpha = 1$

the block length increases with a distortion of .0001 MSE with 5 bits/sample allocation for a block length of 2401, which is quite good.

In Fig. 10 there is a plot of R(D) function for various correlation lengths between the random layers. The rate disotortion curves for a 100th order $R(D)$

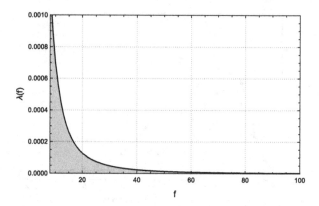

Fig. 4. Plot of the power spectrum $\lambda(f)$ for the reflected Gaussian process. The power spectrum is the eigen-solution to the KL equation

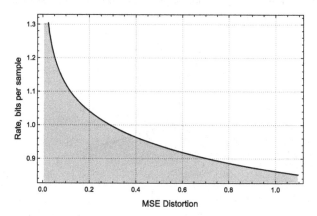

Fig. 5. Complete asymptotic R(D) curve for the reflected Gaussian process

function are given. The curves corresponds to a correlation length ranging from 10m (highly uncorrelate) to 1000m (highly correlated case). It is seen that as correlation increases the R(D) performance improves by a factor of almost 4 across the range for correlation lengths.

Figure 11 plots the R(D) surface as a function of sound speed under ground. Two surfaces are given, one for centralized coding and the other for distributed coding. As the sound speed increases the R(D) tradeoff improves.

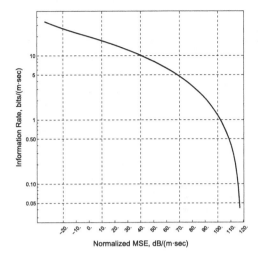

Fig. 6. Complete finite-order R(D) tradeoff for wavespeed $c_0 = 400$ m/s, correlation length $a = 10$ m and $\sigma^2 = 1$. The order of the R(D) function n, is 625.

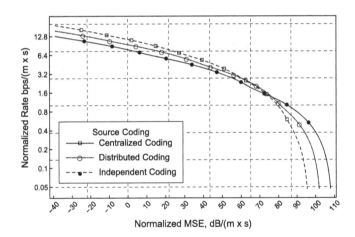

Fig. 7. R(D) bounds for indepdent, centralied and distributed source coding, the sensor line is assumed to be infinte, sound speed is c_0 is 1000 m/s

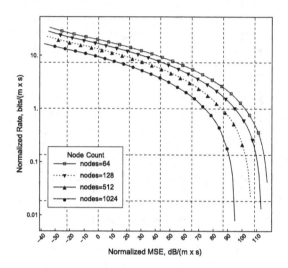

Fig. 8. R(D) for a finite receiver line. The node counts are given and vary between 64 to 1024 nodes.

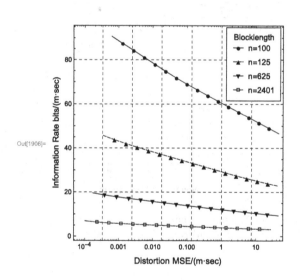

Fig. 9. Rate-distortion functions for various orders n or block lengths, $c_0 = 1000$ m/s, $a = 10$m

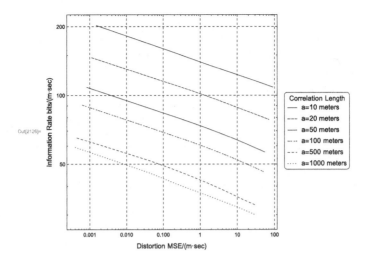

Fig. 10. Rate-distortion functions for various correlation lengths with a block length of 100m and $c_0 = 1000$m/s

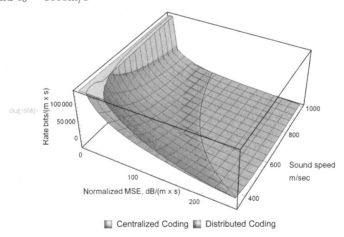

Centralized Coding   Distributed Coding

Fig. 11. R(D) surface as function of sound speed under ground

7   Conclusion

In this work we developed a detailed R(D) analysis for signal compression of seismic wavefields in a wireless geophone network. The analysis was based on a physical model of a randomly layered subsurface earth. The acoustic impedance of in the subsurface was assumed to vary according to a homogeneous Gaussian random field, with a given autocorrelation structure. Energy propagation in the earth was governed by a random wave equation involving the acoustic pressure. The Green's function was obtained for this random wave equation and its action on an impulse was seen to be a result of a random integral operator.

The R(D) analysis was built upon the autocorrelation function of this random operator. A finite order R(D) analysis for a two-dimensional subsurface medium and an asymptotic R(D) analysis for a one-dimensional medium (plane wave case) was carried out. The finite order R(D) analysis gives an indication of the of the compression performance for finite source code block lengths, whereas the asymptotic R(D) curve describes the absolute optimum performance achievable by any source code. We have presented and compared both. The final results obtained consisted of the R(D) function on an infinite receiver line, the R(D) function on a finite line (fixed number of nodes), R(D) function variation vs. the length of the coded block and the R(D) function vs. the physical model parameters like correlation length of the acoustic impedance process and the speed of sound underground. It is see that the compression performance improves as the coding block length increases and as the correlation length of the underlying random process that describes the earth's impedance increases. The rate distortion performance also improves as the speed of the sound in the subsurface increases. The study has particular significance as a guideline to the design of practical signal compression algorithms for seismic acquisition.

References

1. Gleich, D., Planinsic, P., Gergic, B., Cucej, Z.: Progressive space frequency quantization for SAR data compression. IEEE Trans. Geosci. Remote Sens. **40**(1), 3–10 (2002)
2. Gueguen, L., Datcu, M.: Image time-series data mining based on the information-bottleneck principle. IEEE Trans. Geosci. Remote Sens. **45**(4), 827–838 (2007)
3. Valsesia, D., Magli, E.: A novel rate control algorithm for onboard predictive coding of multispectral and hyperspectral images. IEEE Trans. Geosci. Remote Sens. **52**(10), 6341–6355 (2014)
4. Huang, K., Dai, D.: A new on-board image codec based on binary tree with adaptive scanning order in scan-based mode. IEEE Trans. Geosci. Remote Sens. **50**(10), 3737–3750 (2012)
5. Savazzi, S., Spagnolini, U., Goratti, L., Molteni, D., Latva-aho, M., Nicoli, M.: Ultra-wide band sensor networks in oil and gas explorations. IEEE Commun. Mag. **51**(4), 150–160 (2013)
6. Savazzi, S., Spagnolini, U.: Compression and coding for cable-free land acquisition systems. Geophysics **76**(5) (2011)
7. Berger, T.: Rate Distortion Theory: A Mathematical Basis for Data Compression, 1st edn. Prentice-Hall, Englewood Cliffs (1971)
8. Burger, T.: Information rates of Wiener processes. IEEE Trans. Inf. Theory **16**(2), 134–139 (1970)
9. Dragotti, P., Gastpar, M.: Distributed Source Coding: Theory, Algorithms, and Applications, 1st edn. Elsevier Inc., Burligton (2009)
10. Pradhan, S., Ramachandran, K.: Distributed source coding using syndromes (DISCUS): design and construction. In: Proceedings of the 1999 IEEE Data Compression Conference, Snowbird (1999)
11. Gastpar, M., Rimoldi, B., Vetterli, M.: To code, or not to code: lossy source-channel communication revisited. IEEE Trans. Inf. Theory **49**(5), 1147–1158 (2003)

12. Gastpar, M., Dragotti, P., Vetterli, M.: The distributed Karhunen-Loève transform. IEEE Trans. Inf. Theory **52**(12), 5177–5196 (2006)
13. Konsbruck, R., Telatar, E., Vetterli, M.: On sampling and coding for distributed acoustic sensing. IEEE Trans. Inf. Theory **58**(5), 3198–3214 (2012)
14. Beferull-Lozano, B., Konsbruck, R.: On source coding for distributed temperature sensing with shift-invariant geometries. IEEE Trans. Commun. **59**(4), 1053–1065 (2011)
15. Grenander, U., Szego, G.: Toeplitz Forms and Their Applications, 1st edn. UC Berkley Press, Berkeley and Los Angeles (1958)
16. Dudgeon, D., Mersereau, R.: Multidimensional Digital Signal Processing, 1st edn. Prentice-Hall, Upper Saddle River (1984)
17. Kolmogorov, A.: On the Shannon theory of information transmission in the case of continuous signals. IRE Trans. Inf. Theory **2**(4), 102–108 (1956)
18. Adler, R.: The Geometry of Random Fields, 1st edn. Wiley, Chichester (1981)
19. Doob, J.: Stochastic Processes, 1st edn. Wiley, Chichester (1953)
20. Grigoriu, M.: Evaluation of Karhunen-Loeve, spectral, and sampling representations for stochastic processes. J. Eng. Mech. **132**(2), 179–189 (2006)
21. Gersho, A., Gray, R.: Vector Quantization and Signal Compression. Kluwer, Boston (1992)
22. Gray, R., Neuhoff, D.: Quantization. IEEE Trans. Inf. Theory **44**(6), 2325–2383 (1998)
23. Fouque, J.-P., Garnier, J., Papanicolaou, G., Solna, K.: Wave Propagation and Time Reversal in Randomly Layered Media. Springer, New York (2007)
24. Cover, T.M.: Elements of Information Theory. Wiley-Interscience, Hoboken (2006)
25. Lippmann, B.A., Schwinger, J.: Variational principles for scattering processes. I. Phys. Rev. **79**(3), 469–480 (1950)
26. Bellman, R.: Stochastic process in mathematical physics and engineering. In: Proceedings of Symposia in Applied Mathematics, American Mathematical Society, Providence (1963)
27. Evans, L.C.: Partial Differential Equations. American Mathematical Society, Providence (2002)
28. Slepian, D., Wolf, J.K.: Noiseless coding of correlated information sources. IEEE Trans. Inf. Theory **19**(4), 471–480 (1973)
29. Zamir, R., Berger, T.: Multiterminal source coding with high resolution. IEEE Trans. Inf. Theory **45**(1), 106–117 (1999)
30. Tung, S. Y.: Multiterminal Source Coding. Ph.D. thesis Cornell University, Ithaca (1978)
31. Wagner, A.B., Tavildar, S., Viswanath, P.: Rate region of the quadratic Gaussian two-encoder source-coding problem. IEEE Trans. Inf. Theory **54**(5), 1938–1961 (2008)
32. Asch, M., Kohler, W., Papanicolaou, G., Postel, M., White. B.: Frequency content of randomly scattered signals. SIAM Rev. **33**, 526–629 (1991)

Artificial Intelligence Technologies

ECIC: A Content and Context Integrated Data Acquisition Method for Artificial Internet of Things

Donglong Zhang[1], Wang Cong[2], Xiong Zhang[3], Chao Wu[3(✉)], Chengjun Feng[3], Zhenyan Chen[3], and Peng Zhou[3]

[1] Technical Research Institute, Beijing Foton AUV New Energy Auto Co., Ltd., Beijing 102206, China

[2] China National Accreditation Service for Conformity Assessment (CNAS), Beijing 100062, China

[3] China Merchants Testing Vehicle Technology Research Institute Co., Ltd., Chongqing 401329, China
cjwuchao@cmhk.com

Abstract. The Artificial Internet of Things (AIoT) is considered to reshape future business models and provide accurate services for multi-source, heterogeneous, massive, low-value density IoT data, which is vital to deepening the application of IoT. Aiming at the existing data collection mechanism's low accuracy, limited latency performance, underutilization of edge computing resources, and neglect of user data collection context, a content and context integrated data acquisition method is proposed. First, an edge entity observation content prediction method is proposed to precisely assess the entity observation based on the edge computing. Second, a cloud context-aware approach is designed that considers the user's explicit and implicit data acquisition context to select appropriate entity data according to user preferences. Finally, an intelligent data collection mechanism that integrates edge resources and cloud resources is presented to improve the performance of AIoT data collection services. Simulation results show that the proposed method can enhance 7% of the precision and lower 16% of the delay performance in comparison with traditional methods.

Keywords: Artificial Internet of Things · Edge-cloud collaborative · Data acquisition · Context perception

1 Introduction

As the era of the Internet of Everything is approaching, the Internet of Things (IoT) and artificial intelligence (AI) are regarded as the key to reshaping future business models and even changing human living models. The integration of new technologies such as artificial intelligence, cloud computing, and edge computing is an efficient way to achieve high-level and intelligent applications of AIoT [1,2].

X. Li et al. (Eds.): SmartGift 2024, LNICST 600, pp. 81–99, 2025.
https://doi.org/10.1007/978-3-031-78806-2_5

Currently, there is no consensus in the academia and industry on the concept of AIoT. The AIoT has been implemented in various actual fields such as intelligent home, smart city, smart medical care, unmanned driving, and smart industrial control.

The upgrade of communication technologies just solve the interconnection problem of things. Intelligent and personalized service is the bottleneck of IoT development [3]. To this end, researchers apply cloud computing [4] technology to the Internet of Things to effectively alleviate the conflict of limited computing, communication and storage capabilities of IoT devices. However, the restricted bandwidth and ultra-long distance between devices and cloud servers, the high load, large delay, privacy leakage and other problems are brought about by the long communication link. Researchers further proposed the edge computing [5] architecture. The characteristics of edge servers close to users are able to effectively alleviate the problems of cloud computing models. However, edge computing only grasps partial data rather than all the data, and the resources of edge are relatively limited. The cloud-edge collaborative computing model can make full use of the rich communication, computing and storage re-sources of the cloud, and the advantages of the edge being close to the user and being able to respond rapidly, thus the cloud-edge collaboration model has attracted a lot of attentions of researchers [6,7]. The cloud can conduct in-depth analysis of the global data, which is suitable for non-real-time data processing scenarios; the edge server focuses on local areas and is suitable for small-scale, real-time intelligent analysis tasks and the cloud can remove its own unloadable components migrate to multiple edges or clouds to minimize service latency in parallel processing.

Data acquisition service is based on the user's submitted desired entity content to select appropriate entity data via searching in massive entity-attached sensors deployed in the AIoT, and return the matched entity data to the user [8–10]. The concept of data acquisition originated from Internet search engines which are mainly oriented to virtual information resources in the cyberspace [11,12]. The data acquisition technology can accurately match the interest information according to the user's intention, greatly reduce the unnecessary communication burden, and make the user's access to information resources more intelligent, convenient, and personalized. On-demand efficient multi-source data acquisition of AIoT is the core service content of AIoT, and it is the data base that supports AIoT third-party service applications [7]. The data acquisition function of Internet data acquisition engine is implemented by establishing a static index of virtual information resources. However, the status of physical entities is extremely dynamical, and traditional Internet data acquisition methods fail to present the accurate status information of physical entities in real time. Therefore, traditional Internet data acquisition methods perform poorly when solving the problem of data acquisition in the AIoT. How to achieve real-time and efficient data acquisition, so as to rapidly and accurately select entities that meet users' needs is a key scientific issue of great research and application value.

Currently, research on data acquisition in the AIoT is at an early stage. In [13], a data acquisition engine, WOTS2E, for semantic AIoT to discover web device resources in real time was designed. A novel type of sensor network data acquisition engine based on natural language processing and semantic Web technologies was proposed in [14]. In [15], a data acquisition framework for AIoT was presented. Furthermore, ViSAIoT was designed in [16] to provide a solution of data acquisition service via virtual sensors distributed on a wide area public cloud platform.

There are huge number of diverse sensors in the AIoT, which generate the state information of the physical world entities all the time. Therefore, data acquisition ser-vice, which selects sensor data based on their observation contents will become one of the most extensive and core services in future AIoT applications [17]. For the existing research on data acquisition mechanism, most of them ignore the communication and computing resources of edge, and concentrate all the tasks of entity state prediction in the cloud, which brings a large amount of computing load to the cloud, making the data acquisition efficiency unsatisfied. Moreover, existing entity content forecasting methods are based on shallow learning theory to predict the observation content, and select the data based on the predicted content, leading to inaccurate data acquisition results and large data acquisition delay. It was pointed out in [18] that the deployed sensors continuously generated a large amount of data about physical world entities. How to understand these data was a crucial issue. Context-aware computing would be an effective way to alleviate this problem and thus promoted the deep application of the AIoT. Context-aware computing technology [19] can filter out the required data re-sources from the AIoT massive information space by analyzing the user's preferences and the current context state. The current data acquisition mechanisms are just based on observation content to match desired sensors and neglect to consider the user's data acquisition context, which further leads to the lower accuracy and poor real-time performances of data acquisition processes.

Aiming at those above problems, an edge-cloud intelligent collaborative data acquisition mechanism, ECIC, is presented. The contributions are listed as follows.

- An Edge content prediction method is proposed. Based on the idea of edge computing and deep learning theory, a prediction method of entity observation con-tent is designed and adopted in the edge, and the temporal correlation of quantitative observation content is analyzed in depth, and the evolution trend of the quantitative observation content is sensed, thereby realizing high-precision prediction of the quantitative observation content and reducing the computing over-load of the cloud;
- A cloud context perception approach is devised. The idea of context-aware computing is introduced. Considering the user interest in terms of sensor attributes in the data acquisition context, the explicit and implicit context awareness methods are designed respectively. The explicit context allows the user to specify the sensor's attribute according to individual preferences.

For the implicit context, the user's potential preference for sensor attributes is dynamically sensed by mining the user's historical data acquisition records;
– An Intelligent data acquisition mechanism is designed. The data acquisition mechanism is presented based on the combination of content prediction and context perception methods, which integrates cloud and edge communication and computing resources to match entity data for enhancing the data acquisition ac-curacy and delay performances.

The following contents are organized as follows. Section 2 lists the related works. Section 3 proposes the edge content prediction method. Section 4 presents the cloud context perception method. Section 5 designs the intelligent data acquisition method. Section 6 verifies the proposed methods. Section 7 summarizes this paper in the end.

2   Related Works

2.1   Content-Based Data Acquisition

There are tremendous number of diverse sensors applied in the AIoT which observe the state content of the physical world entities continuously. Therefore, the selection of sensor data according to their observation contents is one of the most vital services in future AIoT applications [20]. It was pointed out in [21] that in most AIoT application scenarios, the output of sensor that senses the state of the entity is the original measurement value. Therefore, how to select the sensors associated with physical entities that meet the user's requirements based on the content of the sensor's original measurement value is a hot topic in the field of data acquisition.

In order to realize the data acquisition based on the original sensor observation content in the AIoT, a content-based data acquisition system, CSS [22], was designed and implemented. Based on fuzzy logic theory, the historical measurement information output from the sensor was utilized to construct a lightweight observation content prediction model, which estimated the probability that the observation con-tents of the sensor matched with the request, and returned the data acquisition results in descending order of matching probability. In [23], authors elaborated that in most AIoT data acquisition scenarios, users were insensitive to the content of the raw data sensed by associated sensors, and paid more attention to the advanced observation content of the sensors after fusion processing. Based on the assumption that the sensor output was advanced observation contents, a data acquisition system was designed in [23], Dyser, which adopted the existing Web architecture for the data acquisition. A predictive model for periodic conversion of perceptible sensor observation content was constructed. By calculating the probability that the sensor observation content matched with the dynamic attributes requested by the user, a set of physical entities that might match with the user request was acquired.

In [24], a time-correlated data acquisition method, CSME, was proposed, including a matching prediction approach and an ordered verification approach. The matching prediction approach was presented based on the Least Squares

Support Vector Ma-chine (LSSVM) to estimate the short-term entity state to find candidate objects by mining the time correlation between the sequence of observation content and sensing the change trend of the observation content, so that the future observation contents would be accurately predicted, and entities could be further selected based on the predicted content. The ordered verification approach was designed to verify the actual state of candidate sensors, so as to ensure the reliability of search results. In [25], a low-overhead and high-precision data acquisition mechanism, HESPM, was proposed, which designed a multi-step prediction method and ranking method. The high-accuracy entity state prediction method (HESPM) was proposed based on deep belief network (DBN) theory for accurately perceiving the dynamic evolution trend of entity state and precisely predicting the future entity state, thus the match entities would be rapidly selected according to the predicted observation content while reducing communication and computing overhead.

However, the entity content prediction method adopted by the above method adopts a shallow learning model, or the adopted deep learning model fail to accurately mine the temporal correlation information of the entity observation content. Therefore, the prediction accuracy of the observation content of the entity is limited, which further leads to the inaccuracy of the data service content provided to the user. Moreover, the above methods overlook the context state of the user, resulting in limited performance of the user's data acquisition service.

2.2   Context-Aware Computing

In [26], it was elaborated that the introduction of context-aware technology into the data acquisition issue would greatly reduce the data acquisition space, and thus fast found the subset of entities that were most relevant to users' needs. The current context-aware technology in the IoT was summarized in [27], which indicated that the context-aware technology effectively improved the efficiency of data acquisition. Thus a context-aware data acquisition, selection and ranking model, CASSARAM, was designed in [28] to solve the problem of selecting the most relevant sensor subset from massive sensors with same property. In [29], a hypergraph that represented the context information of human-object interaction was constructed, and then a data acquisition method for the IoT, ThingsNavi, was proposed. Given a target entity, other related entities could be searched by mining multi-dimensional context information of human-object interaction. However, it focuses on searching for similar entities, not the state-given data acquisition described above. Authors discussed in [30] that existing context-aware methods neglected to take the intrinsic properties of sensors into consideration. According to sensor semantic overlay networks (SSONs), a meta-heuristic method was presented to raise the efficiency of context aware method. A hierarchical context model was designed and implemented in [31]. Based on the ontology technology, a hierarchical semantic model describing the physical characteristics and contextual relationships of IoT entities was presented, and a Hidden Markov model of con-text was established, combined with the daily habits of users, behavior models, and geographical location, etc.

At present, in the research of data acquisition mechanism based on observation content, most of the methods neglect the edge resources, adopt the shallow learning models, and fails to consider the context factors, severely affecting the data acquisition precision and delay performances of data acquisition. For solving the above problems, ECIC data acquisition mechanism is proposed in this paper.

3   Edge Content Prediction Method

As mentioned above, traversing all edge servers and entities to locate the required entity content will bring huge communication overhead. Thus we adopt content prediction method to match candidate entities as detailed in Sect. 3. However, concentrating all physical observation content prediction tasks in the cloud will bring serious computing overhead to the cloud and waste computing resources in the edge. Besides, most existing entity content assessing algorithms are derived from shallow learning methods, whose precisions are relatively low, resulting in poor accuracy per-formance for data acquisition. Based on the idea of edge computing [32] and deep learning [33], we design an entity content edge prediction method based on GRU (Gate Recurrent Unit) [34], via constructing an observation content prediction model in the edge, to analyze the temporal correlations of quantitative observations in depth, and then perceive the evolutionary trend of quantitative observations, thereby realizing high-precision content prediction and reducing the overhead of cloud.

GRU is one of the many variants of LSTM that is very effective. It has a simpler structure than LSTM network and works well. Whereas in GRU, there are only two gates: update gate and reset gate. The deep non-linear structure of GRU owns a strong ability of approximating complex functions, which can solve the long-term learning problem of relying on information and has high prediction accuracy for quantitative time series data.

Due to the time evolution characteristics of observation data, the observation data prediction model designed in this paper is shown in Fig. 1 below, which is a convolutional network that deforms one-dimensional convolution so that it can deal with time series problems. The model adopts a one-dimensional fully convolutional net-work structure where each hidden layer length is identical to that of the input layer, and a zero-padding length is added to maintain the relationship between the subsequent layer and the previous layer, so that the output generated by the network is the same as the input length. In addition, causal convolution is added, and the output of the t period is only related to the elements of the current time and the elements before the period, so as to ensure that historical information or future data will not be missed in the prediction process.

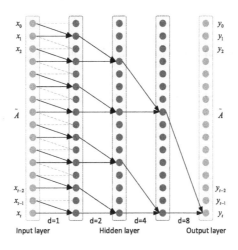

Fig. 1. Data prediction model based on GRU

In general, the observed data is a discrete series, and the predicted value is the value predicted at a certain time in the future using the stored historical data. In the data service system, the content of the observed data at a specific moment is defined as m_t. The historical observation data sequence before time $t+1$ is $M = (m_1, m_2, ..., m_t)$. Use a GRU neural network to predict observations at time $t+1$.

a. Reset gate.

Send the last observed data h_{t-1}, and the current time input m_t to reset gate for deciding which one of the historical information should discard.

$$r_t = \sigma(W_r \cdot [h_{t-1}, m_t] + b_r), \tag{1}$$

where r_t is the output of the reset gate, W_r is the weight of the reset gate, and b_r is the offset term of the reset gate. Activation function is $\sigma = 1/(e^{-x})$.

b. Update gate.

The last state content h_{t-1}, and the current time input m_t are connected to the update gate to determine which information will be updated last time.
The update stage is

$$Z_t = \sigma(W_z \cdot [h_{t-1}, m_t] + b_z), \tag{2}$$

Among them, Z_t, W_Z, b_Z respectively are the output, weight, and offset of the update gate.

c. Candidate stage.

Apply activation functions $tanh(*)$ and m_t to generate candidate states $\tilde{h}_t$ and threshold them down to [-1,1] as

$$\tilde{h}_t = tanh(W_h \cdot [r_{t-1}, m_t] + b_h), \tag{3}$$

$$tanh(x) = \frac{e^x - e^{-x}}{e^x + e^{-x}}, \tag{4}$$

d. Current state.

Discard h_{t-1} and keep $\tilde{h}_t$ to generate new state content h_t.

$$h_t = (1 - Z_t) * h_{t-1} + Z_t * \tilde{h}_t, \tag{5}$$

e. Spatiotemporal feature.

Through sigmoid function activation, the time-dependent character of the task sequence is extracted. The extracted temporal features are considered as the input into support vector regression for prediction, and the final predicted value is computed.

$$y_t = \sigma(W_0 \cdot h_t), \tag{6}$$

$$f(m) = \sum_t^{t-1} (\alpha_t^* - \alpha_i)\mathrm{k}(m_i, m) + b, \tag{7}$$

4   Cloud Context Perception Method

Perceiving the data acquisition context of users in the cloud can better provide users with excellent data acquisition experience and improve data acquisition accuracy. The entity-attached sensor owns diverse attribute functions, such as accuracy, power, security, response time, etc. Different users have diversified preferences for them, even the same user has diverse preferences in various data acquisition scenarios. To accurately sense the change of the user's data acquisition context, we first design an explicit context aware method. Before the user selects the entity, the attribute preferences are first explicitly specified by the user. Then, for perceiving the change of the user's data acquisition context, we further propose an implicit context aware method. By mining the user's historical data acquisition behavior, the user's dynamic preferences towards the sensor attributes is accurately perceived, then the matched results can be further found as described in Sect. 3.

4.1   Explicit Context Aware

The user's preference for the multi-dimensional properties of the sensor reflects the evolution of the data acquisition context. In this subsection, we establish a weighted vector space model for the multi-dimensional attributes of sensors in the cloud. Users manually set the multi-dimensional attributes of sensors according to users' needs.

The user data acquisition interface provides all or part of the sensor's attribute in-formation, and the user can customize the weight of different attribute types according to personal preferences, as shown in Fig. 2. Assume the list of sensor properties is $P = [p_1, p_2, ..., p_n]$ which defines various attributes of sensor, such as accuracy, power, security, response time, etc. p_i represents the $i - th$ attribute of sensor, $i = 1, 2, ..., n$. The weight vector $\omega = [\omega_1, \omega_2, ..., \omega_n]$ is the user's preference for various attributes where ω_i is the user's preference value for the $i - th$ attribute, $\sum_n^{t-1} \omega_i = 1$. Users can freely assign the weight of each attribute.

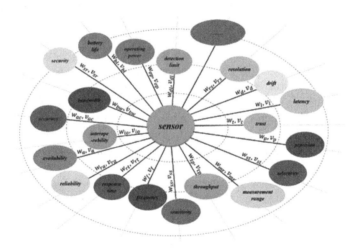

Fig. 2. Data prediction model based on GRU.

After the user defines the preferences and weights for sensor attributes, the cloud needs to determine the degree to which the sensors meet the requirements of the user's data acquisition context based on the actual capabilities of the sensor for each at-tribute. It is assumed that the value of each attribute of the sensor m is defined as $V^m = [v_1^m, v_2^m, ..., v_n^m]$ where v_i^m is the $i - th$ attribute value of sensor m. Due to the various attribute types of sensors, the dimension of each attribute is quite different, and it is impossible to judge the degree to which they match with user needs based on the value of the attribute. In this subsection, the Z-score algorithm is adopted to normalize the sensor attribute values, and the attribute values of different dimensions are converted into a unified metric Z-score value for comparison, which is defined as

$$\mu = \frac{\sum_{m-1}^{n} \sum_{i-1}^{N} v_i^m}{N \times n},$$

(8)

$$\sigma = \sqrt{\frac{1}{N \times n} \sum_{m-1}^{n} \sum_{i-1}^{N} (v_i^m - \mu)^2},$$

(9)

$$\bar{v}_i^m = \frac{v_i^m - \mu}{\sigma}, m = 1, 2, ..., N, i = 1, 2, ..., n,$$

(10)

where N is the number of sensors, μ is the average of all sensor attribute values, σ is the standard deviation of all sensor attribute values, and $\bar{v}_i^m$ is the normalized value of the $i - th$ attribute of sensor m.

4.2   Implicit Context Aware

Explicit context defines the user's relatively fixed preference for the sensor attributes. However, since the user needs to manually set the sensor's attribute preference list, which affects the user's data acquisition experience. Besides, the user's preference for the sensor will change with the data acquisition task varying. Therefore, in this subsection we further design implicit context aware method for users' potential inter-est preferences for sensors.

The implicit user interest is mainly obtained by systematically mining the interrelationships between the user's context information, behavior information, content in-formation, thereby making up for the weakness of the explicit inter-est information that cannot reflect the user's immediacy and dynamic characteristics. Obtaining implicit information is inseparable from the user's context information, that is, request context, environmental context, device context, etc. User behavior and operations are the key to directly reflecting user interests. To calculate the user's implicit interest preference, it is necessary to mine effective information from the user's context that affects the user's behavior and the specific content accessed, and establish an effective implicit user interest model to better reflect the user's personalized preference.

The data acquisition task and the behavior action rely on the user's interest, the core is to reflect the user's data acquisition needs during a specific period, which implicitly indicates the user's interest. Define the set $A = (A_1, A_2, ..., A_n)$ as all the behavioral characteristics of the user. The user behavior contains many aspects, such as the accessed sensor attributes, the accessed frequency, and the length of accessing time.

In the user's historical data acquisition behavior, the common attribute characteristics of all sensing devices that provide users with data acquisition services are the most direct reflection of user interests, and relatively more important attributes should be given higher weight values. The user's individual preference is defined as the user's request probability distribution for data, and the user personalized preference aware model is designed according to the idea of deep learning to analyze the user's individual needs. Define

$q_{u_n} = (q_{f_1,u_n}, ..., q_{f_k,u_n}, ..., q_{f_K,u_n})$ as the probability distribution of the $n-th$ user request, where q_{f_k,u_n} denotes the probability that the $n-th$ user needs the $k-th$ data item, $\sum_{k-1}^{K} q_{f_k,u_n} = 1$, $q_{f_k,u_n} \in [0,1]$, $1 \le k \le K$, $1 \le n \le N$. Denote $Q = (q_{f_k,u_n})^{N \times K}$ as the user's preference matrix, the model design and user implicit preference analysis are as follows.

a. Implicit preference model.

Condition Restricted Boltzmann Machine (CRBM) is often used in the field of recommendation system, which adds comment and uncomment behavior information on the basis of restricted Boltzmann machine as $r \in \{0,1\}^K$ (0 means not commented, 1 means commented). And through the reconstruction of the user's rating data, the implicit information of the user is learned, and the user's predicted rating for the unrated items is obtained, so as to realize the personalized content recommendation, which is suitable for the analysis of the user's potential demand.

In this paper, a user implicit preference perception model is designed in combination with CRBM, and the user's scoring of the acquired data is taken as the user's preference for the content. The higher the preference, the larger the corresponding request probability. Combined with CRBM, a user implicit preference perception model (IP2M) for data collaborative filtering is designed, which predicts the rating of unrequested data according to the user's historical rating information. Each softmax neuron in the visible layer of IP2M is directly related with a user's rating of the data. Assuming that there are a total of N users, of which there are users who have comments on the data, then use softmax neurons and missing neurons to construct the visible layer of IP2M. The IP2M network structure is defined as presented in Fig. 3 below.

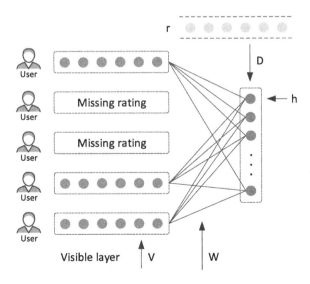

Fig. 3. The network structure of the IP2M model.

b. Implicit preference analysis.

Define $G_{N \times K}$ as the historical rating information of a user for a certain type of data. According to the historical scores, based on IP2M, predict the score of the $n - th$ user on the $k - th$ data, and finally get the reconstructed user's score on all data. The predicted score $\hat{x}_{n,k}$ is the user's preference degree towards the given data. The higher the score, the greater the user's preference for the data and the higher the request probability.

Considering that the same user usually does not request the requested data again, according to the historical score records, reset the user's requested data $\hat{x}_{n,k}$ in the re-constructed preference matrix to 0, that is

$$x_{n,k} = \begin{cases} \hat{x}_{n,k}, & \text{not requested} \\ 0, & \text{requested} \end{cases}, \tag{11}$$

According to $x_{n,k}$, the interested probability of the $m - th$ user towards the $k - th$ data, q_{f_k,u_n}, can be assessed, which is the ratio of the preference of user u_n for the data f_k to the sum of all data preferences. Finally, we can obtain the context score of user m for the sensor attributes $Context(m)$.

$$q_{f_i,u_m} = \frac{x_{m,k}}{\sum_{k=1}^{K} x_{m,k}}, \tag{12}$$

$$Context(m) = \begin{cases} \sum_{i=1}^{n} \omega_i p_i \bar{v}_i^m, & \text{if explicit} \\ \sum_{i=1}^{\phi} \omega_i p_i' q_{f_i,u_m}, & \text{if implicit} \end{cases} \tag{13}$$

5　Intelligent Data Acquisition Method

5.1　System Model

Physical entities in the AIoT own strong dynamic state-varying characteristics, thus traditional Internet data acquisition technologies are inapplicable. Existing data acquisition mechanisms need to traverse entities when performing data acquisition tasks in response to user data acquisition requests, which lead to lower selection accuracy and higher latency. In the latest research results, the prediction value of the entity observation content is stored in the database in advance, and the content-based data acquisition is performed based on the pre-stored prediction contents for effectively in-creasing the accuracy of data acquisition. However, the existing entity observation content prediction methods are concentrated on the cloud to execute, which brings serious computing overhead to the cloud. Besides, current content prediction algorithms are based on shallow learning models which have limited content prediction accuracy. Moreover, the adaptability of the entity to the current data acquisition context is not taken into account when performing the data acquisition task, which further results in the unsatisfied performances of data acquisition precision and time convergence. Targeting at this issue, an intelligent data acquisition method is designed which

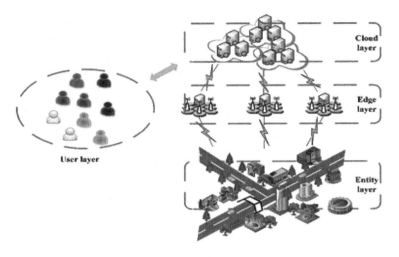

Fig. 4. System architecture.

is based on the idea of edge cloud collaboration and the deep learning theory and fully considers the data acquisition context.

As can be seen in Fig. 4, the data acquisition system is formed by cloud layer, edge layer, entity layer, and the user layer. The cloud layer consists of many cloud servers rich in communication, computing and storage resources. It responds to the user's data acquisition task request and perceiving the user's data acquisition context. The cloud server manages edge servers and interact with edge servers for entity con-tent status information. The edge layer is composed of a large number of edge servers. There are many deployment methods for edge servers, such as geographic location and resource distribution, which is not the focus of this paper. Therefore, we only assume that the edge server is deployed according to geographical location, and each edge server only covers a certain geographical area. Edge servers are only responsible for managing smart entities within their coverage and run the proposed content prediction method for entity content predicting. The entity layer is formed by a large number of physical world entities. Every intelligent entity in the physical world is associated with a sensor, and the attached sensor periodically collects its state data and transmits the observation content to the edge server.

6   Simulation Verification and Analysis

In this paper, we use the real-world dataset IntelLab [36] and NOAA [37] to verify the effectiveness of the proposed ECIC via comparing with the aforementioned mechanisms, CSME [24], HESPM [25], and CASSARAM [28]. IntelLab dataset is composed of the temperature and humidity data observed by 52 sensors and the NOAA dataset includes 98 sensors that sense the water level, water temperature, and other data along the North American coastline. We randomly choose the temperature and humidity data of 45 sensors in IntelLab and select the water level and water temperature data from 80 stations in NOAA. The main comparison performance indicators are the accuracy and delay of data acquisition. The range of sensor observation content is $[a, b]$ which is randomly selected within the interval $[x_{Min}, x_{Max}]$ where x_{Min} and x_{Max} respectively represents the minimum value and maximum value observed by all sensors. The observation period of IntelLab is 20 min and that of NOAA is 60 min. The time when the user initiates the data acquisition request for the sensing service is randomly generated. The simulation software environment is Matlab R2019a. The operating platform is ThinkPad X1 Carbon 2019 with CPU i5-10210U, memory LPDDR3 8GB, and hard disk 512G PCIe SSD. All the simulation results are average values after 100 runs. The prediction step size for entity observations is from 1 to 10. Simulation verifications are based on results within 10 days.

6.1   Content Prediction Performance Validations

Here the MAPE(Mean Absolute Percentage Error) is introduced to validate the precision of the proposed method, which is defined as

$$MAPE = \frac{\sum_{i=1}^{n} |\frac{\hat{f}(m)-f(m)}{f(m)}|}{n} \times 100 \tag{14}$$

where $\hat{f}(m)$ is the predicted value, $f(m)$ denotes the actual value. In Fig. 5, with the rise of the predictive step, the MAPE values of ECIC, CSME, and HESPM, gradually increase, indicating that the growing predictive steps lower the prediction accuracy of the three methods. This is because with the expansion of the predictive step, the prediction errors of the three gradually accumulate, causing the prediction errors of the sensor observation content to gradually enlarge. It is also obvious in Fig. 5 that compared with CSME and HESPM, the ECIC can reduce MAPE by about 15% and 27%, respectively.

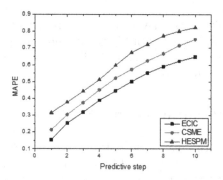

Fig. 5. Validations of prediction accuracy at different predictive steps.

6.2 Context Aware Performance Simulations

As shown in Fig. 6, with the expansion of the query range, the accuracy of data acquisition for ECIC with context, ECIC without context, and CASSARAM is gradu-ally improved. This is due to the reason that as the expansion of the query range, users are becoming less sensitive to the errors of the sensor's observations, which eventually leads to an increasing number of sensors that meet user needs. It can also be found from Fig. 8 that compared with CASSARAM, the proposed ECIC can achieve better data acquisition accuracy in consideration of the data acquisition context. In addition, considering the data acquisition context ECIC with context can improve the selection accuracy by 9% and 13%, respectively.

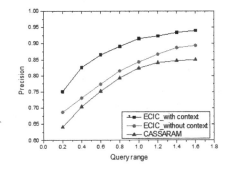

Fig. 6. Validations of prediction accuracy at different predictive steps.

As shown in Fig. 6, the data acquisition delays of the three methods at different simulation time tend to be stable. This is because the three methods are stable in the prediction performance of sensor observations. Therefore, the data acquisition process can rapidly converge and the performance tends to be stable. From Fig. 6 we also find that ECIC_with context can enhance the latency performance by 16% and 22% respectively compared with the other two. It is because ECIC_with context takes into account the user's explicit and implicit data acquisition context factors, and can fast converge when selecting sensors that provide sensing services.

6.3 Data Acquisition Mechanism Verifications

Figure 7 shows the verification results on data acquisition accuracy of ECIC, CSME, and HESPM under different query range. With the expansion of the query range, the selection accuracy of the three gradually increases. This is because the accuracy of data acquisition increases with the query range increasing, which becomes less sensitive to the selection errors. From Fig. 7, we also deduce that compared with CSME and HESPM, ECIC can improve the accuracy of data acquisition by about 7% and 12%, respectively.

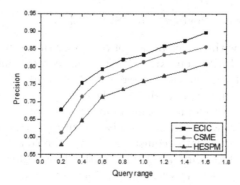

Fig. 7. Verifications on accuracy performances under different query range.

In Fig. 8, we find that with the increase of the query range, the delays of the three mechanisms are roughly stable, manifesting that the prediction accuracy of the three mechanisms towards the observation contents has stable characteristics. Besides, all the three consider the user's data acquisition context to select sensors, so that the data acquisition process can converge fast and smoothly. We can also find in Fig. 8 that the proposed ECIC mechanism can reduce the average selection delay by about 16% and 21%, respectively, in comparison with CSME and HESPM.

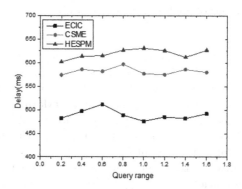

Fig. 8. Verifications on delay performances under different query range.

7   Conclusion

A content and context joint perception data acquisition mechanism is proposed in this paper, including edge content prediction method and cloud context perception method, so as to enhance the efficiency of data acquisition service. Validation results present the rationality of the proposed mechanism. In the future, it is planned to further study the sensing service incentive mechanism in the field of data acquisition service, through rewarding the sensing services and punishing the malicious behaviors, thereby promoting the deep applications of data acquisition service.

References

1. Wu, D., Han, X., Yang, Z., Wang, R.: Exploiting transfer learning for emotion recognition under cloud-edge-client collaborations. IEEE J. Sel. Areas Commun. **17**, 6906–6915 (2021)
2. Zhang, P., Li, X., Wu, D., Wang, R.: Edge-cloud collaborative entity state data caching strategy toward networking search service in CPSs. IEEE Trans. Indust. Inform. **39**, 479–490 (2021)
3. Al-Qarafi, A., et al.: Optimal machine learning based privacy preserving blockchain assisted internet of things with smart cities environment. Appl. Sci. **12**, 479–490 (2022)
4. Lu, H., He, X., Du, M., Ruan, X., Sun, Y., Wang, K.: Edge QoE: computation offloading with deep reinforcement learning for Internet of Things. IEEE Internet Things J. **7**, 9255–9265 (2020)
5. Navarro-Alamán, J., Lacuesta, R., García-Magariño, I., Lloret, J.: EmotIoT: an IoT system to improve users' wellbeing. Appl. Sci. **12**, 5804–5818 (2022)
6. Nilsen, J.M., Park, J.-H., Yun, S., Kang, J.-M., Jung, H.: Competing miners: a synergetic solution for combining blockchain and edge computing in unmanned aerial vehicle networks. Appl. Sci. **12**, 2581–2597 (2022)
7. Zhu, S., Ota, K., Dong, M.: Energy efficient artificial intelligence of things with intelligent edge. IEEE Internet Things J. **9**, 7525–7532 (2022)
8. Wu, D., Si, S., Wu, S., Wang, R.: Dynamic trust relationships aware data privacy protection in mobile crowd-sensing. IEEE Internet Things J. **5**, 2958–2970 (2018)
9. Zhang, P., Chui, Y., Liu, H., Yang, Z., Wu, D., Wang, R.: Efficient and privacy-preserving search over edge-cloud collaborative entity in IoT. IEEE Internet. Things J. https://doi.org/10.1109/JIOT.2021.3132910
10. Zhang, Z.F., Wang, L.S.: Social tie-driven content priority scheme for D2D communications. Inf. Sci. **480**, 160–173 (2019)
11. Wu, D.P., Yang, Z.G., Yang, B.R., Wang, R.Y., Zhang, P.N.: From centralized management to edge collaboration: a privacy-preserving task assignment framework for mobile crowd sensing. IEEE Internet Things J. **8**, 4579–4589 (2020)
12. Wu, D.P., Yan, J.J., Wang, H.G., Wang, R.Y.: User-centric edge sharing mechanism in software-defined ultra-dense networks. IEEE J. Sel. Areas Commun. **38**, 1531–1541 (2020)
13. Kamilaris, A., Yumusak, S., Ali, M.I.: WOTS2E: a search engine for a Semantic web of things. In: Proceedings of the 2016 IEEE World Forum on Internet of Things (WF-AIoT), Reston. **12**, 436–441 (2016)
14. Zhang, K., Marchiori, A.: Natural language search of sensor data. In: Proceedings of the 2016 IEEE International Conference on Pervasive Computing and Communication Workshops (PerCom Workshops), Sydney, pp. 1–6 (2016)
15. Younan, M., Khattab, S., Bahgat, R.: WoTSF: a framework for searching in the web of things. In: Proceedings of the 10th International Conference on Informatics and Systems, New York, pp. 278–285 (2016)

16. Nunes, L., et al.: A distributed sensor data search platform for Internet of Things environments. Int. J. Serv. Comput. **4**, 1–12 (2016)
17. Pattar, S., Buyya, R., Venugopal, K.R., Iyengar, S.S., Patnaik, L.M.: Searching for the AIoT resources: fundamentals, requirements, comprehensive review, and future directions. IEEE Commun. Surv. Tut. **20**, 2101–2132 (2018)
18. Chen, Y., Nevat, I., Zhang, P., Nagarajan, S.G., Wei, H.: Query-based sensors selection for collaborative wireless sensor networks with stochastic energy harvesting. IEEE Internet Things J. **6**, 3031–3043 (2019)
19. Charith, P., Arkady, Z., Peter, C., Dimitrios, G.: Context aware computing for the internet of things: a survey. IEEE Commun. Surv. Tutor. **16**, 414–454 (2014)
20. An, J.W., et al.: Toward global AIoT-enabled smart cities interworking using adaptive semantic adapter. IEEE Internet Things J. **6**, 5753–5765 (2019)
21. Zhang, P.N., Liu, Y.A., Wu, F., Liu, S.Y., Tang, B.H.: Low-overhead and high-precision prediction model for content-based sensor search in the internet of things. IEEE Commun. Lett. **20**, 720–723 (2016)
22. Truong, C., Römer, K.: Content-based sensor search for the web of things. In: Proceedings of the 2013 IEEE Global Communications Conference (GLOBECOM), Atlanta, pp. 2654–2660 (2023)
23. Römer, K., Ostermaier, B., Mattern, F., Fahrmair, M., Kellerer, W.: Real-time search for real-world entities: a survey. Proc. IEEE **98**, 1887–1902 (2010)
24. Zhang, P.N., Liu, Y.A., Wu, F., Fan, W.H., Tang, B.H.: Content-based sensor search with a matching estimation mechanism. IEICE Trans. Inf. Syst. **99**, 1949–1957 (2016)
25. Zhang, P., Kang, X., Wu, D., Wang, R.: High-accuracy entity state prediction method based on deep belief network toward AIoT search. IEEE Wirel. Commun. Lett. **8**, 492–495 (2019)
26. Kertiou, I., et al.: A dynamic skyline technique for a context-aware selection of the best sensors in an AIoT architecture. Ad Hoc Netw. **81**, 183–196 (2018)
27. David, G., Ferrández, A., Higinio, M.M., Peral, J.: Internet of things: a review of surveys based on context aware intelligent services. IEEE Sens. **16**, 1069–1092 (2016)
28. Perera, C., Zaslavsky, A., Liu, C.H., Compton, M., Christen, P., Georgakopoulos, D.: Sensor search techniques for sensing as a service architecture for the internet of things. IEEE Sens. J. **14**, 406–420 (2014)
29. Yao, L., Sheng, Q.Z., Falkner, N.J.G., Ngu, A.H.H.: ThingsNavi: finding most-related things via multi-dimensional modeling of human-thing interactions. In: Proceedings of the 11th International Conference on Mobile and Ubiquitous Systems: Computing, Networking and Services, London (2014)
30. Ebrahimi, M., ShafieiBavani, E., Wong, R.K., Fong, S., Fiadhi, J.N.: An adaptive meta-heuristic search for the internet of things. Future Gen. Comput. Syst. **12**, 1–9 (2019)
31. Chen, Y., Zhou, J., Guo, M.: A context-aware search system for Internet of Things based on hierarchical context model. Telecommun. Syst. **62**, 77–91 (2016)
32. Samek, W., Montavon, G., Lapuschkin, S., Anders, C.J., Müller, K.R.: Explaining deep neural networks and beyond: a review of methods and applications. Proc. IEEE **109**, 247–278 (2021)
33. Sobecki, A., Szymański, J., Gil, D., Mora, H.: Deep learning in the fog. Int. J. Distrib. Sens. Netw. **15**, 1–19 (2019)
34. Shu, W., Cai K., Xiong, N.N.: A short-term traffic flow prediction model based on an improved gate recurrent unit neural network. IEEE Trans. Intell. Transp. Syst. 1–12 (2021)

35. Greff, K., Srivastava, R.K., Koutník, J., Steunebrink, B.R., Schmidhuber, J.: LSTM: a search space odyssey. IEEE Trans. Neural Netw. Learn. Syst. **28**, 2222–2232 (2017)
36. Intel Lab Data. http://db.csail.mit.edu/labdata/labdata.html. Accessed Oct 2016
37. NOS/CO-OPS (National Ocean Service/Center for Operational Oceanographic Products & Services). NOAA Meteorological Data. https://tidesandcurrents.noaa.gov/gmap3/. Accessed 10 Oct 2020

A Two-Stage Inference Method Based on Graph Neural Network for Wind Farm SCADA Data

Zhanhong Ye, Fan Wu$^{(\boxtimes)}$, Cong Zhang, Wenhao Fan, Bihua Tang, and Yuanan Liu

Beijing University of Posts and Telecommunications, Beijing 100876, China
wufanwww@bupt.edu.cn

Abstract. Wind power generation is a representative of high-quality new energy. Real-time monitoring and accurate prediction of wind turbines are critical to ensure their stable operation. Due to sensor failures, network congestion, and communication errors, wind turbine monitoring data are often accompanied by data losses which affects the performance of the wind power prediction model. To address the challenge, we propose a two-stage method for inferring missing values in wind power data. First, the missing value supplement and selection of variables with high similarity in changes are applied, and the top-k nearest neighbors are employed to construct coarse-grained estimation. Second, we proposed a multi-view graph learning framework to capture the latent representation of wind power data from three views. The missing values will be inferred based on these latent representations. Finally, experiments with real world data demonstrate that our method has better inference accuracy than traditional and deep learning inference methods.

Keywords: wind power data · continuous missing · Graph neural networks · spatio-temporal

1 Introduction

Nowadays, wind energy has become one of the main renewable energy sources accommodated by smart grids. In 2022, 77.6 GW of new wind power capacity was connected to the grid worldwide, with a total installed capacity of 906 GW, representing a 9% increase compared to 2021 [1]. Within this context, accurately predicting wind turbine(WT) power based on existing monitoring data and making timely regulations is crucial for alleviating the pressure on real-time smart grid dispatch. However, due to sensor failures, network congestion, and communication errors, there are varying degree of data loss in the WT Supervisory Control and Data Acquisition (SCADA) system. These data losses pose various obstacles to the operation and maintenance of wind farms, such as fault diagnosis [2], status monitoring, and power generation prediction [3]. On the one

© ICST Institute for Computer Sciences, Social Informatics and Telecommunications Engineering 2025
Published by Springer Nature Switzerland AG 2025. All Rights Reserved
X. Li et al. (Eds.): SmartGift 2024, LNICST 600, pp. 100–111, 2025.
https://doi.org/10.1007/978-3-031-78806-2_6

hand, missing data cannot be directly processed by many data-driven prediction models, which significantly reduces the model's expected performance. On the other hand, the lack of some important monitoring data can directly affect the status adjustment of WTs, potentially leading to more severe failures. Therefore, ensuring the integrity and accuracy of SCADA data has great significance in intelligent regulation of wind power systems.

Existing methods for handling missing data can be divided into two categories: deletion and imputation. In smart grids, SCADA systems can contain values for many attributes, simply discarding entire incomplete records due to a few missing values may not be ideal. These shortcomings limit the popularity of deletion methods in practice. Imputation refers to the application of specific algorithms to fill in missing values and obtain a complete dataset. Compared to deletion methods, imputation methods are widely used but differ in applicability and accuracy.

Imputation methods can be roughly divided into two categories: classical statistical methods and data-driven methods. Interpolation methods [4], nearest neighbors (KNN) [5], k-means, autoregressive integrated moving average models, etc., are effective methods in statistics for recovering missing values. These methods are often based on a series of strict assumptions, such as linearity, normality, and independence and identical distribution. Nevertheless, high-dimensional data frequently deviate from these assumptions owing to their intricate non-linear connections, heteroscedasticity, and correlations. The disadvantages of statistical methods which can not accurately describe the complex structures and patterns in high dimensional wind power data, leading to the efficiency of data imputation significantly decreasing when missing rate increases. As a new powerful method, data-driven methods often achieve better results when applied to the imputation of missing data in wind farms. A new LSTM model has been proposed to interpolate missing data in multivariate time series [6]. A new attention-based architecture has been introduced to reconstruct observations regarding corresponding sensors and their adjacent nodes by leveraging a spatiotemporal propagation architecture consistent with the imputation task [7]. A denoising autoencoder based on a spatiotemporal graph neural network has been developed to perform inference on spatiotemporal sequences of wind power data [8]. Compared with classical statistical methods, data-driven based method fully learned the complex data patterns of different WTs, resulting in higher accuracy and wider application. But these methods consider the physical distance between graph nodes as adjacency matrix which is static, while the wind data between adjacent wind farms exhibits dynamic relationships. Additionally, these methods ignore the feature correlation between different attributes of data in WTs monitoring. Furthermore, missing data are often set to zero as the input of the neural network, which can lead to slow network convergence and affect the extraction of spatiotemporal features when there are a large of missing values.

Given the variability in missing data patterns across different scenarios, the imputation performance of the aforementioned data-driven methods may be different. In many studies [11,12], simulation experiments were conducted by randomly removing parts of the data and generating inferred data to validate the performance of imputation methods. According to the form of missing wind power data, its missing types can be divided into continuous missing and dispersive missing [10,11], as shown in Fig. 1. The former is due to sensor failure of WTs, which usually leads to the loss of a group of related attribute data for a continuous period of time, such as data loss caused by icing of anemometers on WTs [9]. The latter is usually manifested as random missing of multiple feature values on some WTs, which is often caused by communication failure or unexpected errors in the data recording process. Based on the knowledge of on-site experts, the frequency of dispersive missing is relatively low [2].

(a) Dispersive missing   (b) Continuous Missing

Fig. 1. Two types of missing SCADA data.

Therefore, based on the continuous missing mode, this paper proposes a two-stage multi-view data recovery architecture, and its main contributions are as follows:

(1) We design a two-stage inference framework combining traditional inference methods with deep learning algorithms, providing a new perspective for inferring missing wind power data.
(2) A multi-view graph learning framework is proposed to capture spatial relationships within features and correlations between features. In terms of space, dynamic spatial correlation and static geographic correlation are considered.

2   System Model and Problem Formulation

Assuming there are $N = \{1, 2, \ldots, n\}$ WTs in a large wind farm, with a total monitoring time period of $T = \{1, 2, \ldots, t\}$, and data features are $D = \{1, 2, \ldots, d\}$. The monitoring data of the turbine n is denoted as $X_{D,T}^n$. Thus, the dataset of the wind farm $X_{D,T}^N \in \mathbb{R}^{N \times D \times T}$ during monitoring cycles T is denoted as:

$$X_{D,T}^N = \langle X_{D,T}^1, X_{D,T}^2, \ldots, X_{D,T}^n \rangle = \begin{bmatrix} x_{D,1}^1 & \cdots & x_{D,1}^n \\ \vdots & \ddots & \vdots \\ x_{D,t}^1 & \cdots & x_{D,t}^n \end{bmatrix} \quad (1)$$

For each node n in the wind farm, we represent its observed value at times-tamp t as $x_{d,t}^n \in \mathbb{R}$. To describe the pattern of missing data, we suppose a matrix M that has the same size as X, denoted as $M \in \mathbb{R}^{N \times D \times T}$, where $m_{d,t}^n = 0$ if observation $x_{d,t}^n$ is missing, otherwise $m_{d,t}^n = 1$. Thus, the actual collected missing dataset in the wind farm can be represented as:

$$X^M = X \cdot M \tag{2}$$

where $\cdot$ denotes element-wise product. Then, we use the inference algorithm $\Psi()$ to infer missing data within short periods, with X representing the inferred data. ε represents the error between the observed data and the inferred data.

$$\Psi(X^M) = \widetilde{X} \approx X \tag{3}$$

$$\varepsilon(\widetilde{X}, X) = \sum_{k=1}^{d} \sum_{i=1}^{n} \sum_{j=1}^{t} \left| x_{k,j}^i - \widetilde{x}_{k,j}^i \right| \tag{4}$$

Inference of missing SCADA data is defined as a supervised learning task aimed at minimizing the difference between estimated values and actual values. Assuming the values of missing SCADA data are real numbers, the classification of missing data values is treated as a regression problem.

3 Data Inference Model

3.1 Overall Structure

In a wind farm, the SCADA data from different turbines exhibit high correlation, thus we assume a graph structure to model the spatial correlation among SCADA data. Due to the dynamic nature of SCADA data, this paper utilizes a dynamic weighted graph $G = (V, \varepsilon, \hat{A})$ to accurately describe the interaction within a region, where V is the set of N nodes, each corresponding to a turbine, ε is the set of edges, and $\hat{A} = (A_c, A_d)$ represents the adjacency matrix, consisting of a geographically-based static adjacency matrix A_c and a dynamic adjacency matrix A_d based on mutual information (MI).

The calculation of elements in the static adjacency matrix A_c is as follows:

$$a_{i,j}^c = \begin{cases} e^{-\left(\frac{d_{i,j}}{\delta}\right)^2} & \text{if } a_{i,j}^c < \tau_c \\ 0 & \text{otherwise} \end{cases} \tag{5}$$

where $d_{i,j}$ represents the Euclidean distance between node i and j, δ is the distance standard deviation, and τ_c is the distance threshold. In the above equation, τ_c controls the threshold for adjacency matrix distribution and spar-sity. Distance-based adjacency matrices can capture spatial correlations to some extent because data from nearby nodes typically have similar patterns. However, considering that data from distant nodes may also exhibit similar trends, distance should not be the sole indicator for determining spatial correlations. The distance-based static adjacency matrix ignores the dynamic spatial correlation between two nodes. MI can be used to estimate the trend of spatial correlation between two nodes. Based on this, the calculation of the element in the dynamic adjacency matrix A_d is as follows:

$$a_{i,j}^d = \begin{cases} MI(v_i^{t_d}, v_j^{t_d}) & \text{if } a_{i,j}^d < \tau_d \\ 0 & \text{otherwise} \end{cases} \tag{6}$$

where v_i and v_j are two nodes in the graph structure, t_d is the period for computing MI. τ_d is the threshold controlling the distribution and sparsity of the dynamic adjacency matrix. A smaller value of $a_{i,j}^d$ indicates a smaller difference in feature data between the two nodes during the calculation period.

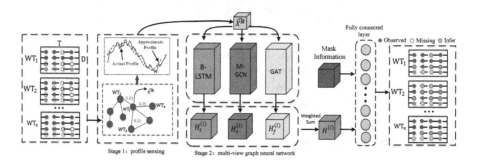

Fig. 2. Overall framework of the proposed methodology

Missing data in deep learning is typically filled with zeros, but these data can somewhat affect feature extraction by neural networks. Therefore, we propose a two-stage method for inferring missing SCADA data. The framework of the proposed method is illustrated in Fig. 2. Firstly, the TS-KNN algorithm is used to fill in missing data at a coarse granularity, giving an approximate profile $\widehat{X^M}$. Then, we use multi-view graph neural networks to extract latent representations aiming at precise prediction of missing data.

3.2 Profile Sensing

We proposed a time series K-nearest neighbors algorithm (TS-KNN) to perform coarse-grained preprocessing of missing data, extracting subsequences $x_{d,[t:t+L]}^u = \{x_{d,t}^u, x_{d,t+1}^u, x_{d,t+2}^u, \dots, x_{d,t+L-1}^u\}$ of length L from $x_{d,T}^u$. For the subsequences $x_{d,[t:t+L]}^u, x_{d,[t:t+L]}^v$ in X, their normalized distance is measured by the statistical Pearson correlation coefficient as follows:

$$d_{u,v} = \sqrt{\frac{2L\,|1 - (\Lambda_{u,v} - L\mu_u\mu_v)|}{L\sigma_u\sigma_v}} \tag{7}$$

where $\Lambda_{u,v}$ represents the dot product of corresponding elements in the two subsequences, μ_u and μ_v represent their means, and σ_u and σ_v represent their variances. We calculate the similarity of data for different WTs over the L time points as the distance measure for KNN. We select the k WTs with the smallest distances and take their average as the coarse-grained inferred value for the missing data.

3.3   Multi-view Graph Network Model

After Profile sensing, we propose a multi-view graph network to learn latent representations for specific nodes and time steps. We then use the weighted latent representations of various features to infer missing values of target features. Depending on the considered feature dimensions, it can be divided into three parts: dynamic spatial correlation, inter-feature and spatial correlation at a specific time, and temporal correlation.

Dynamic Spatial Correlation. The traditional spatial Graph Convolutional Network (GCN) structure typically assumes that the receptive field remains unchanged, focusing only on the directly connected first-order neighboring nodes. On one hand, this overlooks those indirectly connected graph nodes and their influence. In fact, not only do first-order nodes exhibit strong spatial proximity, but also those graph nodes relatively far from the target node also show spatial correlations. We proposed a graph convolutional network based on MI dynamic information (MI-GCN). The input of the graph convolutional network is the hidden layer features of the previous graph convolution, along with the weighted adjacency matrix. Utilizing Chebyshev polynomials to approximate the convolution process in GCN improves the traditional receptive field size extension, not limited to directly connected nodes. The minimal unit computation representation of the spatial GCN is as follows:

$$A = U_{c,d}A_c + (1 - U_{c,d})A_d \tag{8}$$

$$T_k(A) = \begin{cases} 2AT_{k-1}(A) - T_{k-2}(A), & \text{if } k \geq 2 \\ A, & \text{if } k = 1 \\ I, & \text{if } k = 0 \end{cases} \tag{9}$$

$$H_s^l = \sigma(\sum_{k=1}^{K} T_k(A)H_s^{(l-1)}\theta^{(l-1,k)}) \tag{10}$$

where A is the weighted adjacency matrix, l is the number of hidden layers, and $U_{c,d}, W, \theta$ are weight matrices formed by neural network parameters.

Through the above design, not only the relationship between dynamic data and static data in spatial structure can be balanced well, but also the adaptability of the model can be enhanced, thereby it is better to capture deep spatial features.

Inter-Feature and Spatial Correlation at a Specific Time. Different attributes of wind power data may demonstrate Different correlations. For example, wind speed and power often exhibit similar trends, while the trend between power and Nacelle temperature may be different. Although the previous view captured spatial correlations between the same attribute data, It did not model the spatial correlations of different attribute data at specific times. Since the dynamic adjacency matrix A_d obtained from the MI layer is learned from all features, it cannot capture feature-specific correlations between nodes. Therefore, we suggest learning the correlations of different attribute data between nodes from the target time series.

Therefore, we design a Graph Attention Network (GAT) based on static adjacency matrix to capture feature-related correlations. The computational expression is as follows:

$$\alpha_{i,j} = \frac{\exp(\text{LeakyReLU}(A_c))}{\sum_{j \in N} \exp(\text{LeakyReLU}(A_c))} \tag{11}$$

$$h_i^{(l)} = \sigma \left(\sum_{j \in N} \alpha_{i,j} W h_j^{(l-1)} \right) \tag{12}$$

$$H_f^{(l)} = \left[h_1^l, h_2^l, \ldots, h_n^l \right] \tag{13}$$

where $H_f^{(l)}$ represents the overall hidden layer features extracted by the graph attention mechanism, and W denotes the learnable spatial and feature weight matrix. In this way, the graph attention mechanism not only captures feature correlations from a longitudinal perspective but also captures spatial correlations at specific times.

Temporal Correlation. Existing spatiotemporal inference tasks usually use variants of RNN to capture temporal dependence. Through empirical comparisons, we choose bidirectional LSTM(B-LSTM), which achieves relatively good performance in our specific Scenario. We apply B-LSTM separately and identically to each node. At each time step, The B-LSTM network recursively takes X_t as the input vector and aggregates historical and future information into two hidden state vectors $Z_{f,t}$ and $Z_{b,t}$, then integrates the learned features from both directions, using

$$Z_{f,t} = LSTM(X_t, Z_{f,t-1}, C_{f,t-1}) \tag{14}$$

$$Z_{b,t} = LSTM(X_t, Z_{b,t-1}, C_{b,t-1}) \tag{15}$$

$$H_t^{(l)} = W_l[Z_{f,t} : Z_{b,t}] + b_l \tag{16}$$

where $Z_{f,t}$, $C_{f,t}$ are the cell memory state vector and candidate state vector in the forward direction, $Z_{b,t}$, $C_{b,t}$ are state vectors in the backward direction, W_l is the parameter matrix for linear transformation, b_l is the biased term.

We combine the latent representations generated by the three modules mentioned above. Because these representations capture correlations from different perspectives and are defined in different hidden spaces, we integrate feature information from these different dimensions by weighting them and connecting them with some other information, then we infer missing values through a fully connected layer.

$$H^{(l)} = \alpha_1 H_s^{(l)} + \alpha_2 H_t^{(l)} + \alpha_3 H_f^{(l)} \tag{17}$$

$$\widetilde{X} = FC(H^{(l)}||\mathrm{Embedding}(M)) \tag{18}$$

where $\alpha_1, \alpha_2, \alpha_3$ are hyperparameters, $H_t^{(l)}, H_s^{(l)}, H_f^{(l)}$ are features extracted from different dimensions, M is mask matrix, and FC(.) represents a fully connected layer.

Fig. 3. Missing-data distribution of wind power. Other attributes have similar distributions. The white gaps represent the missing values. The bigger the gap, the more missing values exist.

4   Experiments and Analysis

4.1   Dataset and Experiment Setting

The experimental data is collected from the SCADA system of the Penmanshiel Wind Farm in Ireland, which contains a total of 14 WTs. The data cover the period from January 1, 2017, to July 1, 2021, with a time resolution of 10 min. The dataset comprises three different types of feature data: wind speed, wind power, and Nacelle temperature. There are some real missing value in the dataset such as depicted in Fig. 3.

To validate the effectiveness of the method, The missing data is obtained by randomly deleting some time series of length over 50 from the complete data, making the missing pattern more closely resemble real-world scenarios. We choose h = 6 (i.e., 1 h) for the datasets, where h is the length of time for each sample. We use a sliding-window approach on: $[t, t + h), [t + h, t + 2h), [t + 2h, t + 3h)$, etc. Ensuring that there are no duplicate values in different samples.

4.2   Evaluation Metric and Compared Methods

We use the Mean Absolute Percentage Error (MAPE) and the Root Mean Square Error (RMSE) to evaluate our algorithm, which is defined as follows:

$$\text{MAPE} = \frac{1}{dnt} \sum_{k=1}^{d} \sum_{i=1}^{n} \sum_{j=1}^{t} \frac{|x_{k,j}^{i} - \hat{x}_{k,j}^{i}|}{x_{k,j}^{i}} \tag{19}$$

$$\text{RMSE} = \sqrt{\frac{1}{dnt} \sum_{k=1}^{d} \sum_{i=1}^{n} \sum_{j=1}^{t} (x_{k,j}^{i} - \hat{x}_{k,j}^{i})^2} \tag{20}$$

where $x_{k,j}^{i}$ and $\hat{x}_{k,j}^{i}$) represent the true and inferred values of feature k for turbine i at time point j, respectively. In the experiment, both traditional and state-of-the-art imputation methods are used as our comparison methods.

(1) ST-lazy [4]: ST-lazy algorithm is a classic traditional data inference algorithm. It learns to compute the missing values for the nth WT based on the temporal and spatial correlations between other wind turbines.
(2) IGNNK [13]: IGNNK is a data inference algorithm based on diffusion graph convolution. It is used to recover data from unsampled sensors on graph structures and has shown good performance on many datasets.
(3) GNN-LSTM [14]: GNN-LSTM is a classic data-driven spatiotemporal inference algorithm.

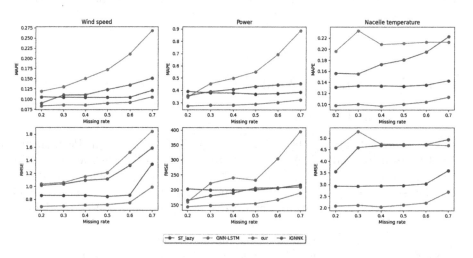

Fig. 4. Imputation error comparison for different methods under different missing rates.

4.3   Imputation Results

Method Performance Under Different Missing Rates. To evaluate the differences in the inference capabilities of our model and the compared method for the task, we use a mask matrix to randomly mask 20%, 30%, 40%, 50%, 60%, and 70% of the values in the SCADA data according to continuous missing patterns. Figure 4 illustrates the performance of our model with three other methods that perform well in the field of missing value imputation. We found that our model outperforms the other contrastive methods across different missing rates. Overall, the ST-lazy algorithm exhibits relatively stable performance across different missing rates and outperforms some deep learning algorithms. This phenomenon may occur because of the relatively strong spatial correlations between nodes, which only impact the ST-lazy algorithm when the missing rate is high. The poor inference performance of the GNN-LSTM algorithm may be attributed to the fact that GNN only performs neighborhood message passing. In wind power fields, spatial relationships are complex and sometimes extend beyond the neighborhood, which GNN fails to capture the changes in global spatial correlations.

The performance of the model may vary across different types of SCADA data. For wind speed and nacelle temperature data, our method still achieved inference errors of 9.21% and 10.42% under a 60% missing rate. across different missing rates, which are significantly better than other algorithms. However, the manual shutdowns of turbines within wind farms, coupled with the occurrence of sudden power fluctuations, generally result in a high inference error of the aforementioned methods for inferring power data.

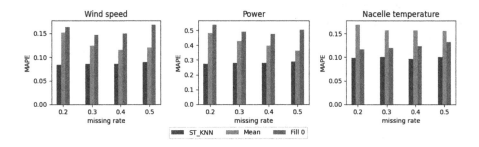

Fig. 5. The impact of different algorithms on the model in profile sense.

Comparison with Different Methods of State1 in Our Method. To better understand the effectiveness of Profile sensing, we adopt different approaches to handle missing values as inputs to the multi-view graph neural network. We observe the performance of the multi-view graph neural network under missing rates of 20%, 30%, 40%, and 50%. As shown in Fig. 5, compared to no filling and mean filling methods, the MAPE estimated by TS-KNN for missing values significantly decreases. This result validates the motivation behind our proposed TS-KNN Profile sensing method. This approach not only achieves coarse-grained data imputation but also facilitates the calculation of dynamic information for multi-view graph neural networks.

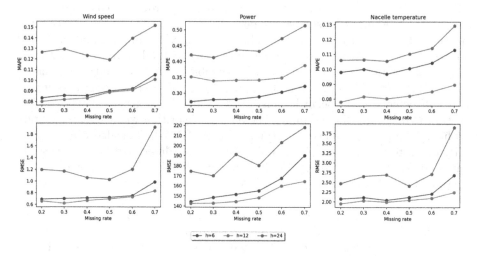

Fig. 6. The impact of different h on method performance.

The Impact of Different Lengths of Time for Sample h on Method Performance. Figure 6 shows the impact of different lengths of time for sample h on our method performance. We used h = 6, 12, and 24, respectively. A large h may lose time dependencies, but a small h might fail to capture the correlations between time steps. In Fig. 6, the inference performance is optimal when h is 12, whereas it significantly deteriorates when h is 24. This suggests that overly large h is adverse to the model from capturing temporal dependencies and bringing noise.

5   Conclusion

The two-stage wind power data inference method proposed in this paper improves the accuracy of inferring missing data from two aspects: 1) a TS-KNN algorithm is used to infer data profile and it is helpful to extract significant features from the multi-view neural network, which improves the effectiveness of data calculation. 2) We proposed a Multi-view Graph Network Model to capture the deep dynamic correlation of time series data from different WTs. Finally, the experimental results show that the method reduces the average inference error RMSE by 19.01% under different missing rates compared with the best comparison algorithm, and the data calculated by the method has high accuracy and stability.

Acknowledgements. This work was supported in part by the Beijing Natural Science Foundation (No. JQ21036), the National Natural Science Foundation of China (No. 62293494, No. 62301078, No. 61821001, No. 62271086), the China Postdoctoral Science Foundation underGrant Number GZB20230086, and the Beijing Key Laboratory of Work SafetyIntelligent Monitoring.

References

1. Global Wind Energy Council. Global Wind Report 2023, Sao Paulo (2023). https://gwec.net/globalwindreport2023
2. Liu, X., Zhang, Z.: A two-stage deep autoencoder-based missing data imputation method for wind farm SCADA data. IEEE Sens. J. **21**, 10933–10945 (2021)
3. Li, Z., et al.: A spatiotemporal directed graph convolution network for ultra-short-term wind power prediction. IEEE Trans. Sustain. Energy **14**, 39–54 (2022)
4. Sun, C., Chen, Y., Cheng, C.: Imputation of missing data from offshore wind farms using spatio-temporal correlation and feature correlation. Energy **229**, 120777 (2021)
5. Poloczek, J., Treiber, N., Kramer, O.: KNN regression as geo-imputation method for spatio-temporal wind data. In: Proceedings of the International Joint Conference SOCO 2014-CISIS 2014-ICEUTE 2014, Bilbao, 25–27 June 2014, pp. 185–193 (2014)
6. Fouladgar, N., Främling, K.: A novel LSTM for multivariate time series with massive missingness. Sensors **20**, 2832 (2020)
7. Marisca, I., Cini, A., Alippi, C.: Learning to reconstruct missing data from spatiotemporal graphs with sparse observations. Adv. Neural. Inf. Process. Syst. **35**, 32069–32082 (2022)
8. Kuppannagari, S., Fu, Y., Chueng, C., Prasanna, V.: Spatio-temporal missing data imputation for smart power grids. In: Proceedings of the Twelfth ACM International Conference on Future Energy Systems, pp. 458–465 (2021)
9. Coville, A., Siddiqui, A., Vogstad, K.: The effect of missing data on wind resource estimation. Energy **36**, 4505–4517 (2011)
10. Li, H., Liu, L., He, Q.: A joint missing power data recovery method based on the spatiotemporal correlation of multiple wind farms. J. Renew. Sustain. Energy **16** (2024)
11. Fan, H., Zhang, X., Mei, S.: Wind power time series missing data imputation based on generative adversarial network. In: 2021 IEEE 4th International Electrical and Energy Conference (CIEEC), pp. 1–6 (2021)
12. Hu, X., Zhan, Z., Ma, D., Zhang, S.: Spatiotemporal generative adversarial imputation networks: an approach to address missing data for wind turbines. IEEE Trans. Instrument. Measur. (2023)
13. Wu, Y., Zhuang, D., Labbe, A., Sun, L.: Inductive graph neural networks for spatiotemporal kriging. Proc. AAAI Conf. Artif. Intell. **35**, 4478–4485 (2021)
14. Li, J., et al.: A nested machine learning approach to short-term PM2. 5 prediction in metropolitan areas using PM2. 5 data from different sensor networks. Sci. Total Environ. **873**, 162336 (2023)

A Comprehensive Evaluation Method for KG-Augmented Large Language Models

Xingyu Chen[1] , Ligang Dong[1(✉)] , and Meng Han[2]

[1] College of Information and Electronic Engineering, Zhejiang Gongshang University, Hangzhou 310018, China
donglg@zjsu.edu.cn
[2] College of Computer Science and Technology, Zhejiang University, Hangzhou 310058, China
mhan@zju.edu.cn

Abstract. Integrating factual information from knowledge graphs (KGs) into large language models (LLMs) has emerged as a promising approach to mitigate hallucination issues inherent in LLMs. This augmentation not only addresses the problem of generating inaccurate or fictional content but also offers avenues for tailoring LLMs to specific domains. Despite the potential benefits, the current body of research lacks a thorough examination of how KG augmentation influences various large language models.

This paper introduces a comprehensive evaluation method specifically designed for assessing the performance of KG-augmented LLMs. By evaluating these frameworks across multiple dimensions, the proposed method aims to provide a nuanced understanding of the strengths and limitations associated with integrating KGs into LLM-based question-answering systems. The systematic evaluation is expected to offer valuable insights, guiding future research endeavors and facilitating enhancements in this emerging field. This approach contributes to advancing the integration of KGs with LLMs and fostering the development of more robust and context-aware language models tailored to specific knowledge domains.

Keywords: Large Language Model · Knowledge Graph · Augmented

1 Introduction

Recently, Large Language Models (LLMs) like GPT-4 [1], Baichuan [2], and ChatGLM [3] have achieved remarkable success in Natural Language Processing (NLP) tasks. LLMs have demonstrated human-level performance across a wide spectrum of NLP tasks, including question answering, translation, and information extraction, among others. Despite their outstanding general capabilities,

© ICST Institute for Computer Sciences, Social Informatics and Telecommunications Engineering 2025
Published by Springer Nature Switzerland AG 2025. All Rights Reserved
X. Li et al. (Eds.): SmartGift 2024, LNICST 600, pp. 112–121, 2025.
https://doi.org/10.1007/978-3-031-78806-2_7

LLMs still suffer significant challenges, including hallucination, a lack of interpretability, and the absence of domain-specific knowledge.

Firstly, hallucinations in LLMs are attributed to the fact that the knowledge embedded in these models relies on pre-trained data, which may contain misinformation and biases. This can result in issues such as missing domain-specific knowledge and reliance on outdated information. Furthermore, the random content generation based on probability in LLMs makes them prone to hallucinations. Secondly, as black box models, the knowledge within LLMs is internalized in the parameters, which cannot explain and verify the knowledge obtained by LLM to produce answers. Finally, the currently available LLMs are designed for general purposes and lack specialization for specific fields. This limitation is particularly critical in applications like medical diagnosis, where an erroneous result poses a significant risk to the health and safety of patients.

To address these issues, researchers have proposed to integrate knowledge graphs (KGs) into LLMs [4]. KGs are structured representation of knowledge, where the fundamental unit is a triplet, i.e., (entity, relationship, entity). KGs play a crucial role in providing explicit knowledge to LLMs, ensuring the generation of interpretable results. Moreover, KGs support the integration of new knowledge, effectively mitigating the problem of knowledge obsolescence. Additionally, there are numerous domain-specific KGs, including those in finance, law, education, etc., which furnish LLMs with precise and reliable domain knowledge. This approach effectively addresses the issue of missing domain knowledge in LLM and eliminates the need for expensive fine-tuning. The framework that combines KGs with LLMs is collectively referred to as KG-LLM in this paper.

As the demand for large models continues to grow in the specific field, researchers have introduced an increasing number of KG-augmented methods. However, a notable gap exists as there is currently no established framework for evaluating the effectiveness of these approaches. To bridge this gap, this paper proposes a comprehensive evaluation method for KG-augmented methods. This method utilizes two KGs from different domains to evaluate the capabilities of the state-of-the-art KG-LLM framework from six perspectives. It reveals limitations in their performance across diverse domains.

2   Related Work

While LLM has demonstrated strong performance in numerous tasks, its performance in knowledge-intensive tasks has been less than satisfactory. For example, in Knowledge Graph Question Answering (KGQA) tasks, LLMs may suffer from hallucinations, inaccurate answers, and outdated knowledge [5]. In recent years, a considerable amount of research has been conducted to enhance LLM's question answering capabilities using KGs. Specifically, the approach involves extracting relevant triplets from the KGs that are related to the given question. These extracted knowledge pieces are then injected into the reasoning process of LLM, serving as prompts to generate more reliable answers.

To tackle the challenge of LLMs' performance in knowledge-intensive tasks, Wu, et al. [6] proposed a KG-To-Text method, which aims to represent the knowledge stored in a knowledge graph (KG) as natural language. By transforming KG knowledge into a textual format, LLMs can leverage this information more effectively to generate accurate and contextually appropriate answers. Beak, et al. [8] proposed a Zero-Shot Knowledge-Augmented language model Prompt-ING (KAPING) framework in which facts retrieved from KGs are added to questions passed to LLM to generate more reliable answers. Wang, et al. [10] proposed a knowledge-based PLM framework KP-PLM that can be combined with any mainstream LLM. Firstly construct a knowledge subgraph from KBs for each context, and then design multiple sequential prompt rules to turn the knowledge subgraph into a natural language prompt to help LM generate more accurate answers. To improve the zero-shot reasoning ability of LLMs on structured data in a uniform way, Jiang, et al. [9] proposed StructGPT, an Iterative Reading-then Reasoning method targeting at structured Data (such as KGs, data table, and database) to support LLMs to reason structured data with the help of external interfaces. Guan, et al. [7] introduced a novel framework called Knowledge Graph-based Retrofitting (KGR) to address the issue of factual hallucination during the reasoning process of LLMs. This framework leverages the factual knowledge stored in knowledge graphs (KGs) to mitigate the problem.

An increasing number of KG-augmented LLM methods have been proposed by researchers, but there lacks a unified framework to evaluate them. In this paper, the framework proposed by us aims to evaluate the performance of KG-enhanced LLM methods from multiple dimensions.

3   Evaluation Criteria

This paper proposes a framework for comparing KG-enhanced LLM Question Answering (QA) systems and defines fundamental criteria across multiple dimensions: answer accuracy, randomness, universality, robustness, reasoning ability on the complex questions, and knowledge updating capability. By evaluating performance along these dimensions, a more comprehensive understanding of the strengths and limitations of KG-enhanced LLM question-answering systems can be obtained, providing guidance for further research and improvement. Here are detailed explanations of the metrics mentioned:

Accuracy: In the KGQA task, the accuracy of the provided answers is an important metric in the framework proposed in this paper. When performing the KGQA task, accuracy is measured by comparing the answers to those contained in the ground truth. However, LLMs, as generative models, produce answers in an uncontrolled format that differs from the generated answers in KGQA, LLMs primarily generate text similar to human language and require semantic understanding to assess the accuracy of the generated answers. This paper compares the answers generated by the LLMs with the vertices from the KGs. To overcome these challenges, the paper performed manual evaluation to ensure fairness. The calculation formula for the accuracy metric is as follows:

$$\text{Accuracy} = \frac{\text{Number of Correctly Answered Questions}}{\text{Total Number of Answered Questions}}$$

Randomness: As generative models, LLMs often exhibit a certain degree of randomness in the answers they generate when faced with the same context and given question. Therefore, assessing the randomness of the KG-LLM framework is also a crucial metric. To account for this factor, this paper employs a method of running each question three times and calculates accuracy based on the best answer obtained. This approach allows for a more comprehensive evaluation of the performance of the KG-LLM framework.

Universality: The universality of the KG-LLM framework refers to its ability to be applied to various knowledge graphs in different domains without retraining the model, while maintaining its ability to answer questions effectively. To evaluate the universality of the framework, this paper conducts experiments on four real-world knowledge graphs from two domains and benchmarks. The datasets includes questions of varying complexity and styles, carefully curated to ensure a wide coverage in evaluating the framework.

Robustness: In LLMs, robustness encompasses their ability to tolerate erroneous inputs, such as questions containing spelling or grammatical errors. These errors are quite common due to the free-form nature of human input. Despite the presence of errors, a well-trained LLM is still capable of generating correct answers. Furthermore, when presented with a question that is related to entities in the KGs but for which the answer does not exist in KGs, LLMs should either refuse to answer the question or provide a response indicating insufficient information.

Complex question reasoning: When tackling KGQA tasks, we often encounter both simple and complex questions. Simple questions refer to those that can be answered using a single relation path without additional reasoning, while complex questions require reasoning through multiple relation paths to arrive at answers. When users pose questions of varying complexity, such as temporal questions or multi-hop questions, evaluating the model's ability for complex question reasoning becomes crucial. LLMs typically encapsulate question understanding within a broader output generation process. For complex questions, we need to observe whether the model can generate accurate answers by combining reasoning and relation paths. By analyzing the model's generated answers, we can assess its ability for complex question reasoning and evaluate its performance.

Knowledge update: KGs are frequently updated by adding, deleting, or modifying facts. For instance, Wikipedia undergoes edits at an astonishing rate every second, which means hundreds of thousands of edits are made in the corresponding Wikidata KG every day. Users typically expect to receive the most up-to-date answers. In our evaluation, we take this criterion into consideration to ensure that our framework can adapt to evolving knowledge and provide the latest answers.

4   Experiment

In this section, we evaluated the performance of various KG-LLM frameworks and analyzed the results to summarize the main challenges currently faced. We conducted extensive testing on these frameworks and considered various metrics. Through an objective analysis of these issues, this paper provides valuable insights for further improvement and development of KG-LLM frameworks.

4.1   Datasets

To evaluate the performance of the KG-LLM framework, this paper has chosen two commonly used Knowledge Graph Question Answering (KGQA) datasets: WebQuestionsSP (WebQSP) [11] and MetaQA [12].

4.2   Main Results

We employed the proposed evaluation method in this paper to assess the performance of four KG-LLM frameworks. Table 1 summarizes the accuracy scores of each participant under various benchmarks. To ensure fairness in the evaluation, each KG-LLM framework utilized LLaMA2-Chat-7B as the LLM backbone. In the experiments presented in this paper, answers were categorized into three groups:

(1) Correct, where the LLM provided an answer semantically consistent with the correct answer;
(2) Incorrect, where the answer provided by the LLM did not align with the semantic meaning of the correct answer;
(3) No Answer, indicating that the LLM concluded the question was unanswerable. Only answers categorized as correct are considered as accurate in this study.

Table 1. Baselines results comparison on WebQSP and CWQ datasets.

Model	WebQSP		CWQ	
	Accuracy	F1	Accuracy	F1
KAPING	59.5	62.1	55.2	54.3
RoG	67.4	70.5	52.4	55.9
RRA	72.4	76.0	68.3	70.4
ChatKBQA	73.6	78.2	72.6	77.3

1. KAPING [8]: A zero-shot framework that forwards knowledge from KG to LLM to generate answers without additional training
2. RoG [13]:RoG initially generates relation paths grounded in KGs as faithful paths. Subsequently, these paths are employed to retrieve valid reasoning paths from the KGs, enabling LLMs to perform faithful reasoning.

3. Retrieve-Rewrite-Answer (RRA) [6]: A KG-to-Text approach is introduced, which is sensitive to answers, aiming to convert knowledge from the KGs into textual descriptions, thereby enhancing the accuracy of LLM answers.
4. ChatKBQA [14]: A generation-retrieval framework based on fine-tuned open source LLMs.

By analyzing the results in Table 1, it is evident that the performance of the four evaluated KG-LLM frameworks on WebQSP surpasses their performance on CWQ. RoG, by generating faithful paths grounded in KGs as reasoning paths, achieves better results than KAPING. RRA employs a KG-to-Text method, converting triples into free-format text, enabling LLMs to better comprehend the provided factual knowledge and thus enhancing their capabilities in KGQA. To ensure experimental fairness, the ChatKBQA framework continues to use an LLM without fine-tuning. The generation-retrieval approach utilized by ChatK-BQA proves superior to the three aforementioned retrieval-generation methods, as the latter may introduce erroneous interference information in the retrieved data, impacting downstream LLM tasks.

In terms of universality, the experimental results indicate that all four KG-LLM frameworks are applicable to different datasets without the need for retraining the models, while maintaining accuracy in answering questions. It's worth noting that both the WebQSP and CWQ datasets encompass complex questions. In the CWQ dataset, specifically in the testset, over half of the questions involve multiple entities, and some questions require intricate reasoning. Importantly, the aforementioned KG-LLM frameworks demonstrate excellent performance in addressing complex questions, maintaining high accuracy even when confronted with intricate reasoning scenarios.

4.3   Randomness Analysis of KG-LLM Framework

In order to assess the randomness of the KG-LLM framework, this section randomly sampled 100 questions from the WebQSP and MetaQA datasets, running each question three times. The results of the runs can be categorized into three scenarios:

1. Consistent Semantics (CS) across all three responses;
2. Consistent Semantics between Two Responses (CSTR), with the third being inconsistent;
3. Inconsistent Semantics (IS) across all three responses.

Analyzing the experimental results in Figs. 1 and 2, it is observed that the four compared KG-LLM frameworks exhibit a high level of determinism with a certain degree of randomness in LLMs. During the experiments, explanations for some answers varied slightly, but the answers remained consistent. In certain cases, questions initially went unanswered but produced correct responses in subsequent iterations. Furthermore, for some questions, the results changed entirely across three attempts. The reason for this phenomenon is that LLMs, as

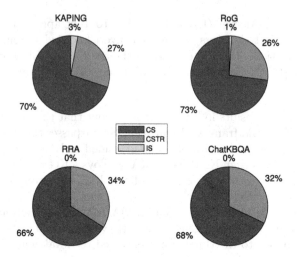

Fig. 1. The performance of KG-LLM frameworks running three times on WebQSP.

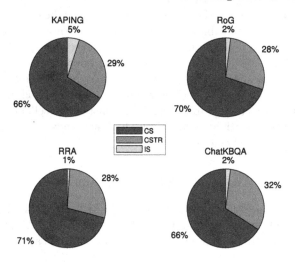

Fig. 2. The performance of KG-LLM frameworks running three times on CWQ.

generative models, rely on probabilistic calculations for each response, introducing inherent randomness into the answering process. Additionally, the process of retrieving knowledge from KGs also involves an element of randomness, making it challenging to ensure consistent results with each retrieval.

4.4   Robustness Analysis of KG-LLM Framework

In order to assess the robustness of the KG-LLM framework, this section initially randomly selected 10 questions from the WebQSP and MetaQA datasets. Four different versions of each question were created by introducing various spelling errors and grammatical errors. There were two types of spelling errors, namely entity misspelling and non-entity misspelling, along with two types of grammar errors. Subsequently, based on the knowledge graph corresponding to the WebQSP and MetaQA datasets, 40 questions were generated. These questions involved entities from the knowledge graph, but the answers were not present in the knowledge graph. For such questions, the model should Reject to Answer (RA).

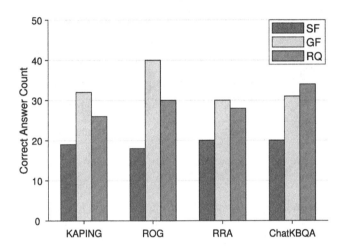

Fig. 3. Robustness analysis of KG-LLM Framework.

SE represents spelling errors, GE represents grammatical errors, and RA represents questions that should be refused to answer. Analysis of the results in Fig. 3 reveals that most spelling errors that the model cannot answer correctly are related to misspelled entities. The inability to correctly locate the right entities and relation paths in KGs due to misspelled entities leads to the generation of incorrect answers. Grammar errors have the least impact on the KG-LLM framework, as the LLM, leveraging its advanced semantic understanding capabilities, can still comprehend questions accurately. For questions that involve entities in KGs but are not present in them, noise is introduced during KG retrieval, increasing the difficulty of LLM reasoning. In general, current KG-LLM frameworks face challenges in effectively handling questions with entity spelling errors.

4.5   Knowledge Update Ability Analysis of KG-LLM Framework

In order to assess the KG-LLM framework's ability to handle new knowledge, this section employed the following approach: in the WebQSP, half of the information in the knowledge graph was removed, leaving only the remaining half. This was done to compare the performance of the KG-LLM framework in answering questions under these conditions.

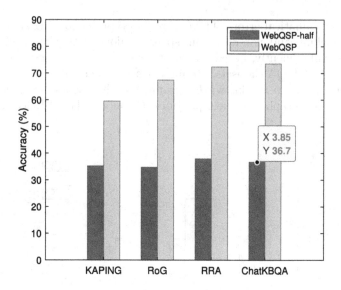

Fig. 4. The knowledge update ability on WebQSP.

Through the analysis of the results in Fig. 4, it is evident that when only half of the information in the knowledge graph remains, the KG-LLM framework often struggles to deduce correct answers through reasoning. This underscores the crucial importance of the adequacy of information within the knowledge graph for the successful inference of the KG-LLM framework. Effective reasoning and obtaining accurate results only occur when the information within the knowledge graph is extended to cover the content of the questions. It is worth noting that the emphasis here goes beyond the quantity of knowledge, encompassing the coverage and quality of knowledge. The evaluated knowledge update capabilities of the four KG-LLM frameworks in this study have been validated.

5 Conclusion

This paper introduces a Comprehensive Evaluation Method for KG-Augmented Methods, aiming to assess the effectiveness of KG-LLM framework from various perspectives. The proposed method defines six metrics for quantitative evaluation, providing a method for comparing KG-LLM frameworks. Extensive experiments conducted on the WebQSP and CWQ datasets reveal that current KG-LLM frameworks still exhibit certain limitations and challenges.

References

1. OPENAI, O.: GPT-4 Technical Report (2023)
2. Yang, A., Xiao, B., et al.: Baichuan 2: open large-scale language models (2023)
3. Zeng, A., Liu, X., et al.: Glm-130b: an open bilingual pre-trained model (2022)

4. Lewis, P., Perez, E., et al.: Retrieval-augmented generation for knowledge-intensive nlp tasks. Adv. Neural. Inf. Process. Syst. **33**, 9459–9474 (2020)
5. Pan, S., Luo, L., et al.: Glm-130b: unifying large language models and knowledge graphs: a Roadmap(2023)
6. Wu, Y., Hu, N., et al.: Retrieve-rewrite-answer: a KG-to-text enhanced LLMs framework for knowledge graph question answering (2023)
7. Guan, X., Liu, Y., et al.: Mitigating large language model hallucinations via autonomous knowledge graph-based retrofitting (2023)
8. Baek, J., Aji, A., et al.: Knowledge-augmented language model prompting for zero-shot knowledge graph question answering (2023)
9. Jiang, J., Zhou, K., et al.: Structgpt: a general framework for large language model to reason over structured data (2023)
10. Wang, J., Huang, W., et al.: Knowledge prompting in pre-trained language model for natural language understanding (2022)
11. Yih, W., Richardson, M.: The value of semantic parse labeling for knowledge base question answering. In: Proceedings of the 54th Annual Meeting of the Association for Computational Linguistics, vol. 2, pp. 201–206 (2016)
12. Zhang, Y., Dai, H.: Variational reasoning for question answering with knowledge graph. In: Proceedings of the AAAI Conference on Artificial Intelligence, vol. 32 (2018)
13. Luo, L., Li, Y., et al.: Reasoning on graphs: faithful and interpretable large language model reasoning (2023)
14. Luo, H., Tang, Z., et al.: Chatkbqa: a generate-then-retrieve framework for knowledge base question answering with fine-tuned large language models (2023)

Security in Wireless Communication

Collaborative-Based Batch Verification Scheme for Event-Driven Messages in Vehicular Ad Hoc Networks

Wenqi Cao[1(✉)], Fan Wu[2], and Cong Zhang[2]

[1] China Asserts Cybersecurity Technology Co., Ltd., Beijing 100041, China
wwenqicao@163.com,wenqicao@bupt.cn
[2] School of Electrical and Electronic Engineering, Beijing University of Posts and Telecommunications, Beijing, China
{wufanwww,cong1126}@bupt.edu.cn

Abstract. To ensure the information security of the Vehicle Ad hoc Networks (VANETs), it is necessary to verify the integrity and identity of safety messages transmitted in the networks. Previous safety message verification schemes mostly focus on basic security messages, which are not appropriate for emergency messages in event-driven scenarios. The generation of emergency messages in the VANETs is often sudden and massive with strict time requirements, which is a great challenge for verification terminals with the limited computation capabilities. To address these issues, a collaborative-based batch verification scheme is proposed in this paper with the goal of maximizing the number of verified safety messages in the system during some time. This solution provides three message verification strategies for the collaborative node to address verification peaks under different scales emergency message broadcasting. Performance evaluation demonstrates that compared to the RSU centralized batch verification scheme, this scheme can significantly reduce the loss rate of safety messages that fail due to untimely verification in VANETs.

Keywords: Vehicular Ad Hoc Networks · Message Batch Verification · Distributed Network

1 Introduction

Vehicle Ad hoc Networks (VANETs) is committed to improving road traffic safety, making an important role in the solution of Intelligent Transportation System (ITS) [1]. In addition, VANETs can provide various applications for road users in areas, including driving assistance and social interaction. The exchange of information among different terminals in VANETs serves as the foundation of various application services. According to the Dedicated Short Range Communication (DSRC) protocol, there are two types of security applications in VANETs: periodic messages and event-driven messages [2]. VANETs adopt periodic broadcast basic safety messages (BSMs) to transmit safety related

© ICST Institute for Computer Sciences, Social Informatics and Telecommunications Engineering 2025
Published by Springer Nature Switzerland AG 2025. All Rights Reserved
X. Li et al. (Eds.): SmartGift 2024, LNICST 600, pp. 125–144, 2025.
https://doi.org/10.1007/978-3-031-78806-2_8

data, such as vehicles' location, speed, direction, etc. The other refers to emergency messages (EMs) that are sent upon detection of a hazardous event, such as engine brakes or vehicle collision warning [3].

Messages in VANETs are transmitted through wireless channels, which are exposed to various attack risks, such as message replay attack, and denial-of-service attack (DoS). Furthermore, to protect the privacy of road users, information transmission in VANETs usually uses pseudonyms [4]. Consequently, it is necessary to verify the source and integrity of a message before further processing. In order to ensure secure communication, current solutions primarily employ symmetric cryptography verification schemes, asymmetric encryption-based verification schemes, and group signature-based verification schemes [5]. While these security schemes guarantee the confidentiality and integrity of messages, the message verification process relies on computationally intensive cryptographic operations, leading to additional processing delays.

In DSRC communication, vehicles driving in the system broadcast basic safety messages every 100–300 ms. Considering a VANET with about 300 vehicles, every vehicle in the system receives no fewer than 1000 basic safety messages every second [6]. Due to the high-speed movement of vehicles, if messages cannot be verified promptly, they may be discarded upon expiration, potentially resulting in accidents. Consequently, many researchers have begun to concentrate on addressing the efficiency issue of message verification.

Considering the limited computing capability of vehicles, He et al. [7] proposed a random verification scheme. The vehicle nodes in the system randomly select messages for verification, which can result in the loss of important safety messages. Hamida et al. [8] utilized distance-based multi-priority queue and K-means algorithm to classify and process received messages, using the received signal strength as the basis.

The priority-based message verification scheme may result in the loss of important security messages, leading to security risks. The message batch verification method enables the simultaneous verification of multiple safety messages, reducing the time required to verify a large number of signatures. Vijayakumar et al. [9] developed a batch security and key exchange scheme to reduce the burden on the verification nodes in the congested areas. Huang et al. [10] proposed a scheme based on anonymous batch verification, which offers a 48% reduction in verification delay compared to ordinary elliptic curve cryptosystem (ECC) method. Tzeng et al. [11] proposed an identity-based batch verification method using the ECC method with less communication delay and message drop rate. Chim et al. [12] proposed a centralized batch verification scheme, in which the roadside unit (RSU) verifies all messages sent by vehicles and then centrally publishes the verification results of each message. Vehicles in the system can query the verification results of messages through RSU after receiving them. Due to the verification of every message only once in the system, this solution can reduce redundant verification and communication delay costs. However, the centralized message verification method brings significant pressure to a single verification node as VANETs become more complex. Even when batch verification is used, it is hard to meet the requirements of secure message delay.

To address the limitation of the message verification overhead on the verification terminals, Yong et al. [13] developed a collaborative verification schemes, in which some assisted vehicles are selected to help RSU verify messages and share the verification results with surrounding vehicles. Hao et al. [14] introduced edge computing into VANETs and proposed three collaborative vehicle selection algorithms in their scheme. The results of experiments showed that this scheme significantly reduces message verification computation and communication overhead, but it does not solve the problem of message duplicate verification. Wu et al. [15] proposed a distributed message verification system architecture, selecting some assisted verification terminals (AVTs) to help RSU batch verify of BSMs, while avoiding redundant message verification. Simulation results show that it can significantly reduce message verification delay in dense vehicle networks. However, it is important to note that the scheme focuses only on the verification of BSMs and does not address the matter of emergency message verification.

Quick and reliable verification of emergency messages is crucial for the security of the vehicle network as timely response to emergency messages can reduce the risk of accidents. P. Kumar et al. [16] proposed a model of a priority-based message batch verification algorithm that prioritizes the verification of messages sent by emergency vehicles to provide response services as soon as possible. Similarly, S. Banani et al. [17] proposed a scheme that divides emergency message priority by region, in which vehicles determine the message priority they receive based on the distance and speed of the sending vehicle.

In conclusion, previous research has demonstrated the efficacy of message batch verification and collaborative distributed network structures in enhancing verification efficiency. On top of this, this paper focuses on event-driven scenarios in VANETs, we propose an efficient collaborative-based batch verification scheme for surged emergency message in VANETs. The contributions of this paper are as follows:

(1) Three verification strategies are designed to adapt to occasional verification peaks under different emergency messages quantity scales, aiming to maximize the number of secure messages verified within a unit of time.

(2) Because emergency messages arrive following a Poisson distribution, the uncertainty in their arrival makes it challenging to establish a precise delay model. In this scheme, we utilize queuing theory as the analytical foundation to model the verification delay and apply this model to the emergency message verification scheme.

The rest of this paper is organized as follows. Section 2 introduces safety-related applications in VANETs, Sect. 3 presents system architecture and message verification process. Section 4 discusses the verification scheme for emergency messages. Section 5 discusses performance analysis of the proposed scheme. Section 6 concludes the paper.

2 Preliminaries

2.1 Safety Applications in VANETs

The safety applications in VANETs can be divided into periodic safety applications and event-driven applications. Based on this, there are two driving modes for vehicles in the VANETs [18]:

(1) Normal mode: In the system where no accidents have occurred, all vehicles are in normal state and exchange safety information periodically through BSMs.
(2) Warning mode: When a vehicle notice an accident situation, it immediately transitions to warning state and broadcast event-driven emergency messages to remind all vehicles exposed to potential danger in the relevant area, which is called the Zone of Relevance (ZoR). Vehicles in other areas of the VANET continue to drive normally without being affected. The generation of EMs is often abrupt and may lead to an exponential growth of messages within the relevant area.

2.2 Message Batch Verification Basics

A typical VANET system is mainly composed of vehicles, a trust authority (TA) and a roadside unit (RSU). Among them, TA is the completely trusted service organization, responsible for generating and publishing security parameters of the VANET. RSU is the main verification center for messages in the system. Vehicles in VANET are equipped with On-board units (OBUs) for direct communication with adjacent vehicles or RSUs. Usually, the communication radius of the RSU is 1Km, and the communication range between vehicles is 300 m. The definitions of symbols used in this article are shown in Table 1.

The message batch verification method is based on the ECC encryption algorithm. The generation and verification process of message packets is briefly described as follows: TA publishes system security parameters during initialization. When a vehicle joins VANETs, the tamper-resistant unit(TPD) of the vehicle loads system parameters from TA. The vehicle first calculates a pseudonym AID_i, then the TPD signs the message M_i and timestamp T_i, and the result is σ_i. The vehicle finally broadcasts the secure message package$\{AID_i, M_i, T_i, \sigma_i\}$. All receiver terminals in the system need to verify the signature upon receiving a safety message. The verification formula for a single message is as follows:

$$\sigma_i P = h(AID_i)P_{pub} + h(M_i\|T_i)AID_{i,1} \tag{1}$$

By aggregating messages and performing batch verification, a verification node can reduce the number of computation operations and thus decreases the verification delay. For n_i message packages, the node selects a random factor v_i, then multiplies the signature σ_i with v_i and combine it with the parameters

Table 1. Symbol Definition

Symbol	Defination
$h(.)$	Hash equation for encryption
BSM	Basic safety message
EM	Emergency message
RSU	Roadside Unit
TA	Trust Authority
ZOR	Zone of Relevance
VE	Vehicles of normal state in the system
CM	Vehicles of warning state in relevant area
CV	Collaborative Vehicle
CH	Collaborative Vehicle in warning state
t_{pro}^j	The process delay on CV_j
t_{comp}^r	The computational batch-verification delay at the RSU
T_{tran}^c	The transmission delay of the message confirmed packets sent by the CH to RSU
T_B	The period of vehicle broadcast BSM
T_M	The period of vehicle broadcast EM
T_k	The delay tolerance of the safety message
t_R	The period of RSU aggregated-bath verification
t_c	The period of aggregated-bath verification at the CH node
λ_n	The arrival rate of EMs in the system
λ_c	The arrival rate of EMs at the CH node
λ_r	The arrival rate of EMs at the RSU
γ_c	The discount factor of computing power between the CH and RSU
μ_0	The verification efficiency of a single EM at the CH node
n_b	The number of ordinary vehicles verified by the RSU
n_c	The number of collaborative vehicles in the system
n_{tol}	The total number of verified messages in the system over a period of time
N_r	The number of messages accumulated on the RSU during a period
N_b^r	The number of accumulated BSMs at the RSU during a period
N_c^r	The number of message confirmed packets sent by CVs during a period
N_m^r	The number of EM confirmed packets sent by the CH node during a period
r	The number of EMs verified in each batch
δ	The EM reassigned-verification ratio

published by TA to verify whether the message signature has been tampered with. The verification formula is as follows:

$$(_{i=1}^{n_i}(v_i s_i))P = (_{i=1}^{n_i} v_i h(AID_i))_{i=1}^{n_i} v_i h(M_i||T_i)AID_{i,1} \qquad (2)$$

To further quantify the delay overhead of verification, the computational costs of encryption operations in ECC can be obtained by referring typical papers [19]. Let the computational overhead of small factor dot product operation, the dot product calculation, the addition operation and hash operation in the message verification Formula (1) be denoted as $T_{ecc-m}, T_{ecc-sm}, T_{ecc-pa}$, and T_h, respectively. The computational overhead for a single message verification can be obtained as follows:

$$t_e = 2T_h + 3T_{ecc} + T_{sm} \tag{3}$$

To simplify the calculation, let $T_{ecc-m} = T_{ecc-m} + T_{ecc-sm} + T_{ecc-pa} + 2T_h$, and $T_{sm} = 2T_{ecc-m}$. According to Formula (2), the computation overhead for batch verification of n messages is shown as follows:

$$t_{comp} = nT_{ecc} + T_{sm} \tag{4}$$

3   Overview

3.1   System Framework of VANETs in Safe Scenarios

The distributed message batch-assisted verification system architecture used in this paper is slightly different from the regular system. In a safe scenario, all vehicles drive in the normal state, and the batch-assisted verification scheme determine the list of collaborative verification vehicles (CVs) with strong computational capabilities to help verify basic safety messages (BSMs) [15]. Every selected collaborative vehicle (CV) is responsible for verifying the messages from vehicles (VEs) within its communication range. Due to the limitation of vehicle communication range, for ordinary vehicles not assigned to CVs, their messages are batch-verified by the RSU. The message verification process is shown in Fig. 1. First, the VEs send BSMs to the CVs. The CVs first batch-verify the messages and then report the message verified confirmation packets to the RSU. The RSU first verifies BSMs from the VEs and then performs the final verification of the message confirmation packets.

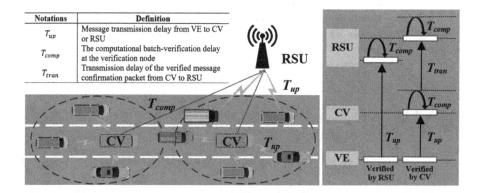

Fig. 1. The process of Message verification

3.2   Message Batch Verification Delay Basics

Message Batch Verification Delay of the Cooperative Vehicle. Assuming the cooperative Vehicle CV_j is responsible for the messages verification of n_j vehicles in the system. First, CV_j batch verifies n_j messages broadcasted by vehicles. Then, CV_j aggregates the authenticated messages pseudonym (AID) and sends it as a confirmed packet to the RSU. Therefore, the process delay t_{pro}^j on CV_j can be calculated as follows:

$$t_{pro}^j = T_{up} + t_{comp}^j + T_{tran}^j \tag{5}$$

To simplify the complexity of the model, the transmission delay of messages to verification nodes is uniformly denoted as T_{up}. Assuming the computing power of RSU is f_r and the computing power of the OBU on CV_j is f_j. Let $\gamma_j = f_j/f_r$. From Formula (4), the computational delay on CV_j for batch-verification is $t_{comp}^j = \gamma_j(n_j T_{ecc} + T_{sm})$. And T_{tran}^j is the transmission delay of the verified messages confirmed packet from CV_j to RSU. For the confirmed packet, the data length of AID is $l_{aid}n_j$, and the length of fixed data is l_0. Assuming the transmission rate of data in the system is donated to B, T_{tran}^j can be calculated as follows:

$$T_{tran}^j = l_{aid}n_j/B + l_0/B \tag{6}$$

Message Batch Verification Delay of RSU. Assuming RSU is responsible for the safety messages verification of n_b vehicles in the system. RSU first batch verifies the safety messages from normal vehicles, and then confirms the verified message packets sent by the CV nodes, which are also verified in batch. For n message packages, the computational delay of batch-verification on the RSU is as follows:

$$t_{comp}^r = T_{ecc}n + T_{sm} \tag{7}$$

3.3   System Framework

In this paper, we consider a densely populated VANETs scenario as shown in the Fig. 2. When a vehicle CM encounters an accident, it immediately switches to warning mode and reminds all other vehicles CMs within the relevant area L_m, triggering them to warning mode and broadcasting emergency messages (EMs) intensively for some time. Normal driving of vehicles in other areas of the system will not be affected. The explosive growth of EM scale can lead to excessive verification delay on the collaborative vehicle (CH) in the relevant area. If selection algorithm for assisted verification terminals is performed in such cases, it would result in additional communication overhead and computational delay for the system. As a result, it is necessary to propose a rapid and dependable emergency message verification solution to the node CH, without adversely affecting the message verification processes of other normal vehicles in the system.

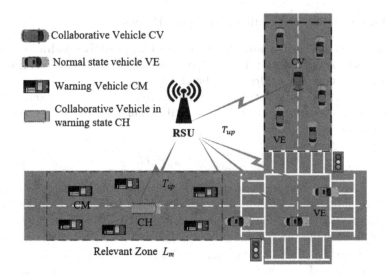

Fig. 2. Emergency messages broadcast scenario of VANETs

4   Collaborative-Based Emergency Message Batch Verification Scheme

The broadcasting frequency of different types of emergency messages varies from 1 Hz to 10 Hz, resulting in varying sizes of message quantities. Our scheme adopts different verification strategies to ensure the success rate of secure message verification in the system. For the batch-verification method, verification nodes first store the secure messages received during the verification period in the message queue, and then the accumulated messages are batch verified at the end of period. Due to the uncertainty of the accident, this scheme constructs different message queuing models on the node CH under different strategies to characterize the average verification delay of EMs. Based on the cooperative message batch verification process, the aggregated verified period on the node CH is derived, which maximizes the number of verified secure messages in the system within a certain period of time, thus reducing the loss rate of message verification in the system.

4.1   Emergency Message Arriving Model

Due to the dense broadcast frequency of emergency messages and the high-speed mobility of vehicles, it is difficult to achieve clock synchronization in the system. The arrival of EMs at the verification terminal can be considered as an asynchronous periodic message stacking process [20], which is usually approximated as a Poisson distribution process [21].

Assuming that there are n warning mode vehicles broadcasting emergency messages in the system, with a broadcasting period of T_M, the arrival rate λ_n

of EM in the system is as follows:

$$\lambda_n = \frac{n}{T_M} \tag{8}$$

Due to the uncertainty of the Poisson distribution, it is difficult to quantify the waiting time of EMs during the aggregation process. Therefore, this paper utilizes queuing theory to the analysis of the EM batch verification process. By optimizing the performance metrics of the queuing system, the verification efficiency of EM can be improved.

4.2   Emergency Messages Single-Verified Strategy on the Collaborative Node

If the EMs are broadcasted at low frequency, it is likely to spend a lot of time waiting for batch-verification. In this case, single sequential by CH node can improve the efficiency of EM verification.

Emergency Messages Single-Verified Queuing Model. For the CH node, the arrival process of EMs follows a Poisson distribution, and the computation time for a single message verification t_e from Formula (3) is fixed. Thus an M/D/1 queuing model can describe the single message verification process of EM on the CH node. In this case, the EM arrival rate on the CH node λ_c is equal to the EM arrival rate in the system, i.e. $\lambda_c = \lambda_n$. The single EM verification rate is $\mu_0 = 1/t_e$. According to the M/D/1 queuing system, the average residence time w_0 of a single EM can be obtained, which is the time from arrival at the CH to departure from the CH node:

$$w_0 = \frac{2\mu_0 - \lambda_c}{2\mu_0(\mu_0 - \lambda_c)} \tag{9}$$

Since the CH node must transmit the verified packets to the RSU for final confirmation, the total verification delay of a single EM on the CH is $t_0^c = w_0 + T_{tran}^c$. Among them, T_{tran}^c is the transmission delay of CH sending packets to RSU, which is $T_{tran}^c = T_{aid} + T_l$.

Emergency Messages Sequential Single-Verified Strategy on the CH Node. In this strategy, the RSU requires a verification period t_R. All the safety messages arriving during a period of t_R are first stored in the message queue, and then the accumulated messages are verified in batch at the end of the period of t_R. The verification tasks of the RSU include n_b BSMs from regular vehicles, the message confirmed packets sent by n_c collaborative vehicles (CVs) and the EM confirmed packets sent by the CH node.

It is assumed that there are n_b vehicles broadcasting BSMs verified by RSU with period of T_B. During a period of t_R, the number of accumulated BSMs at the RSU is denoted as $N_b^r = n_b t_R/T_B$, and the number of message confirmed packets sent by n_c CVs is denoted as $N_c^r = n_c t_R/T_0$. Also, the number of EM confirmed packets sent by the CH node is denoted as $N_m^r = t_R/t_0^c$. Thus, the number of messages accumulated on the RSU during a verification period is $N_r = N_b^r + N_c^r + N_m^r$.

The computational batch-verification delay during a verification period at the RSU can be obtained from Formula (4), where $t_{comp}^r = T_{ecc}N_r + T_{sm}$. In order to improve the efficiency of message verification in the system within a fixed period of time, let Δt represent a longer period of time, during which the number of messages verified at the RSU is as follows:

$$n_{tol} = \frac{\Delta t N_r}{t_R + t_{comp}^r} \tag{10}$$

For an emergency message, the longest delay from generation to completion of verification includes the transmission delay to the CH node T_{up}, the total verification delay at the CH node T_0^c and the batch verification delay at the RSU T_r. The sum of these delays shall not exceed the delay tolerance of the safety message T_k, which is as follows:

$$T_{up} + T_0^c + T_r \leq T_k \tag{11}$$

From the stability requirements of the EM queue on CH, it can be concluded that:

$$\frac{\lambda_n}{\mu_0} < 1 \tag{12}$$

In addition, the verification period t_R needs to be greater than 0, which is as follows:

$$t_R > 0 \tag{13}$$

This strategy modifies the verification period t_R of the RSU based on the actual arrival rate of EMs in the system. The goal is to ensure timely verification of EMs and to maximize the number of verified messages in system over a period of time. The optimization objective function is as follows:

$$max \; n_{tol} = \frac{\Delta t N_r}{t_R + t_{comp}^r} \tag{14}$$

And the objective function is constrained by Formulas (11)–(13).

4.3 Emergency Messages Batch-Verification Strategy on the Collaborative Node

If the arrival rate of EMs in the system λ_n is greater than the verification efficiency at the CH node μ_0, that is, $\lambda_n > \mu_0$, single sequential verification cannot guarantee the stability of the EM queue. To speed up the verification efficiency of EM, the CH node adopts a message batch-verification method. In this case, the CH node needs to set the aggregated-bath verification period t_c for EMs. During the period, the incoming EMs are first queuing in the message queue. At the end of the period the r EMs aggregates accumulated during the period are batch-verified.

Due to the random character of the arrival of EMs at the CH node which makes it difficult to quantify the waiting time, a queuing model can help solve the problem to quantify the batch-verification delay. The total number of verified messages in the system per unit of time can be optimized by determining the period of t_c.

Emergency Message Aggregated-Batch Verification Queuing Model. For the CH node, the aggregated-bath verification period t_c is equivalent to the sum of the average residence time of the EMs at the CH node w_c, and the transmission delay of the message confirmed packets to the RSU. In order to specifically describe the verification delay of EMs, we establishes a queuing model for the message queue on the CH node, and transforms the period t_c into solving the residence time w_c of EMs in the queuing model.

According to Formula (4), the computation overhead for batch verification of x messages on the CH node is donated as $t_{comp}^c(x) = \gamma_c(T_{ecc}x + T_{sm})$, where the γ_c is the discount factor of computing power between the CH and RSU. According to the queuing theory, the average verification rate of EMs at CH node is $\mu_c = 1/(\gamma_c T_{ecc})$. Since the arrival process of EMs at the CH node follows a Poisson distribution with λ_n, and the verification rate μ_c is fixed, the verification process of EMs at the CH node can be modeled as an $M/D^r/1$ queuing system, where r is the number of EMs verified in a single batch.

Emergency Message Aggregated-Batch Verification. The method of establishing an embedded Markov chain is a common approach in queuing theory. In this case, we derive the stationary distribution of the embedded process to obtain the steady-state distribution of message queue length, which make it possible to analyze the batch-verification problem of EMs on the CH node in a more specific manner. Let x_n represent the number of queued EMs at the CH node when the verification of the EMs in the n_{th} batch is completed, $\{x_n, n \geq 0\}$ forms a Markov chain [22]. In order to maintain the stability of the queuing system, the average number of messages received on the CH node during message verification for each batch $\lambda_c d_{(r)}$ should be less than the number of EMs verified in each batch, denoted as r. Therefore, the condition for message queue stability is $\lambda_c d_{(r)} < r$, which is organized as follows:

$$r > \frac{\lambda_c \gamma_c T_{sm}}{1 - \lambda_c \gamma_c T_{ecc}} \tag{15}$$

Figure 3 illustrates the state transition process of the Markov chain x_n. The stationary distribution π_j is defined as $\pi_j = \lim_{n \to \infty} P(x_n = j)\, j = 0, 1, 2...$, subject to the constraint $\sum_{i=0}^{\infty} \pi_j = 1$.

The common method for solving the steady-state distribution of a system is to introduce the generation function $X(z)$ of the queue length to solve. The average queue length $E[x]$ at the steady-state can be obtained by differentiating $X(z)$ with respect to z at $z = 1$ [22]. According to Little's law, we can obtain

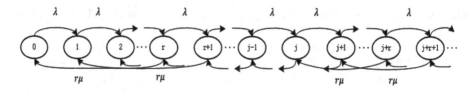

Fig. 3. Markov chain $\{x_n\}$ state transition process

the average residence time w_c of any EM in the n_{th} batch at the CH node, which is the sum of waiting delay and computational verification delay of a EM at the CH node. The average residence time $w_c = E[x]/\lambda_c$.

The aggregated-batch verification period of an EM at the CH node is denoted as t_c, which is composed of the average residence time of the EM w_s, and the transmission delay of the message confirmed packets sent by the CH T_{tran}^c. And t_c can be calculated as follows:

$$t_c = w_s + T_{aid}r = \frac{\gamma_c(T_{ecc} + T_{sm}) - \lambda_c\gamma_c^2 T_{ecc}T_{sm} + r\gamma_c T_{ecc}(1 - \lambda_c\gamma_c T_{ecc})}{2(1 - \lambda_c\gamma_c T_{ecc})}$$

$$+ \frac{\frac{\gamma_c T_{sm}}{2(1-\lambda_c\gamma_c T_{ecc})^2}}{r - \lambda_c\gamma_c T_{sm}/(1 - \lambda_c\gamma_c T_{ecc})} + \frac{1}{\lambda_c}\sum_{n=1}^{r-1}\frac{1}{1 - \delta_n} + T_{aid}r$$

$$(16)$$

According to the Rouche's theorem [23], δ_n represent the roots of the characteristic equation. By analyzing Formula (16), it can be seen that for a CH node with a given EM arrival rate λ_c, the size of the aggregation batch-verification period t_c node is determined by the number of EMs per batch verification r.

Emergency Message Aggregated-Batch Verification Strategy. In this strategy, the CH node first aggregates and verifies r EMs in batch, and then the CH node sends the confirmed package to the RSU. To ensure that EMs can be verified in time, after receiving the EM confirmed package, the RSU immediately batch verifies the accumulated messages within an aggregated-bath verification period t_c.

In this system, the verification tasks on the RSU includes verifying BSMs with the broadcasting period of T_B from n_b ordinary vehicles, and the confirmed message packages sent by n_c CV nodes. During an aggregated-bath verification period t_c, the number of BSMs accumulated on the RSU is donated as $N_b^r = n_b t_c/T_B$, and the number of message confirmed packets sent by n_c CVs is denoted as $N_c^r = n_c t_c/T_B$. In addition, there is a EM confirmed packet sent by the CH node. Thus, the number of messages accumulated within a period of t_c is donated as:

$$N_r = N_b^r + N_c^r + 1 \qquad (17)$$

The computational batch-verification delay during a period of t_c at the RSU is donated as t_{comp}^r, $t_{comp}^r = T_{ecc}N_r + T_{sm}$. During the time period $\Delta t(\Delta t >> T_B)$, the total number of verified messages in the system n_{tol}, includes the sum of the messages verified by RSU, collaborative nodes and CH node, which can be represented as follows:

$$n_{tol} = \frac{\Delta t}{t_c + t^r_{comp}} N_r + \frac{\Delta t}{T_B} \sum_{j=1}^{n_c} \frac{\Delta t}{T_B} n_j + \frac{\Delta t}{t^r_{comp}} r \qquad (18)$$

The sum of all the delays shall not exceed the delay tolerance of the safety message T_k, which is as follows:

$$T_{up} + t_c + t^r_{comp} \leq T_k \qquad (19)$$

The condition for message queue stability is organized as follows:

$$r > \frac{\lambda_c \gamma_c T_{sm}}{1 - \lambda_c \gamma_c T_{ecc}} \qquad (20)$$

In addition, the period of t_c should be greater than 0, which is as follows:

$$t_c > 0 \qquad (21)$$

In this scheme, it is necessary to determine the aggregated-bath verification period t_c of CH node, with the goal of maximizing the total number of verified messages in the system per unit time. The optimization objective is as follows, constrained by Formulas (19)–(21):

$$max \; n_{tol} \qquad (22)$$

4.4   Emergency Messages Reassigned-Verification Strategy

When the broadcast scale of EM messages is large, the number of messages in the system that fail due to untimely verification increases. Due to the limited computing power of the CH node, the aggregated-bath verification strategy still cannot meet the time requirements of large-scale EM verification. At this time, re-election to add collaborative verification nodes will cause the change of network topology, resulting in extra computational and communication delay overhead. Therefore, in order to ensure the message verified in time, this strategy reassigns the EMs verification tasks of warning vehicle CMs which were responsible by the CH node, to both RSU and the CH node. This strategy aims to maximize the number of verified safety messages in the system while ensuring timely message verification.

In this strategy, the CH node still adopts the method of batch-verification for EMs, and the CH node aggregated-bath verification period t_c can be obtained from Formula (16). For the RSU, in order to ensure the timely verification of EMs, upon receiving the message confirmation packet reported by the CH node, the RSU immediately batch verify on the accumulated messages in its message queue over that period of time.

Assuming that the number of warning vehicles (CMs) verified by the CH node is n_c^m, then the arrival rate of the CH node can be obtained as $\lambda_c =$

n_c^m/T_M, where the T_M is the EM broadcasting period. Let the number of warning vehicles(CMs) verified by the RSU be n_r^m, then the arrival rate of EM at the RSU is $\lambda_r = n_r^m/T_M$. Define the EM reassignment ratio as δ, where $\delta = \lambda_c/\lambda_n$, and λ_n is the arrival rate of EMs in the system.

For the RSU, during an aggregated-bath verification period t_c, the number of BSMs accumulated on the RSU is donated as $N_b^r = n_b t_c/T_B$, and the number of message confirmed packets sent by n_c CVs is denoted as $N_c^r = n_c t_c/T_B$. In addition, the number of EMs sent by the CMs can be calculated as $N_m^r = n_r^m t_c/T_M$. Thus, the number of messages accumulated on the RSU within a period of t_c is donated as:

$$N_r = \frac{n_b t_c}{T_B} + \frac{n_c t_c}{T_B} + \frac{n_r^m t_c}{T_M} \tag{23}$$

The verification delay at the RSU is donated as t_{comp}^r, $t_{comp}^r = T_{ecc} N_r + T_{sm}$. Our goal is to maximize the total number of verified messages in the system during the time period $\Delta t(\Delta t \gg T_B)$, which can be represented as follows:

$$max\, n_{tol} = \frac{\Delta t}{t_c + t_{comp}^r} N_r + \frac{\Delta t}{T_B} \sum_{j=1}^{n_c} \frac{\Delta t}{T_B} n_j + \frac{\Delta t}{t_{comp}^r} r \tag{24}$$

The constraints of the total arrival rate of EMs in the system λ_n is given by:

$$\lambda_n = \lambda_c + \lambda_r \tag{25}$$

The sum of all the delays shall not exceed the delay tolerance of the safety message T_k, which is as follows:

$$T_{up} + t_c + t_{comp}^r \leq T_k \tag{26}$$

According to formula (20), the condition for message queue stability is organized as follows:

$$r > \frac{\lambda_c \gamma_c T_{sm}}{1 - \lambda_c \gamma_c T_{ecc}} \tag{27}$$

In addition, the period of t_c should be greater than 0, which is as follows:

$$t_c > 0 \tag{28}$$

In this case, our optimization goal is constrained by Formulas (25)–(28). We need to determine the aggregated-bath verification period t_c of CH node and the EMs reassigned-verification ratio δ.

4.5   Emergency Message Verification Algorithm

For EM verification schemes, different strategies need to be adopted based on different emergency message arrival rates. The following pseudocode describes the specific algorithm.

Algorithm 1. Emergency Messages Verification Algorithm

Input: The total number of vehicles in the system N, the broadcasting frequency of EM f, and the number vehicles in warning state n.

Output: The total number of verified messages in the system over a period of time n_{tol} and the loss of the verification safety messages in the system α.

System Initialization: Determine the number of collaborative vehicles and the CV_lists.

Stage1: Emergency Messages Sequential Single-verified Strategy

1: if $\lambda_n < \mu_0$ then
2:     **Calculate** w_0; // Calculating the Single-verified
3:     $max\ n_{tol} \leftarrow t_c$;
4: **end if**

Stage2: Emergency Messages Batch-Verification Strategy

5: if then$\alpha > 0.15$
6:     **for** $r = 1 : n$ **do**
7:         **for** $i = 1 : (r - 1)$ **do**
8:             Calculate δ_i; // Calculating the roots of the characteristic equation
9:         **end for**
10:         Calculate t_c; // Calculate the period of aggregated-bath verification
11:         Calculate $N_{tol} \leftarrow t_c$;
12:     **end for**
13: **end if**
14: $max\ n_{tol} \leftarrow t_c$;
15: Observing the effect of system safety message loss rate α

Stage3 Emergency Messages Reassigned-Verification Strategy

16: if $\alpha > 0.15$ then;
17:     **for** $\lambda_m = 1 : \lambda_n$ **do**;
18:         **for** $r = 1 : n$ **do**;
19:             Calculate $t_{m,s}^r \leftarrow \delta_i$; // Calculate the period of aggregated-bath
20:         **end for**
21:         Calculate $maxN_{tol}^{\lambda_m} \leftarrow t_c$;
22:     **end for**
23:     $max\ N_{tol} \leftarrow \lambda_m$;
24: **end if**

5   Performance

In order to analyze the performance of proposed scheme, we use SUMO (Simulation of Urban Mobility) to simulate a traffic heavy VANET scenario. The simulation area is set to a vertical intersection of $2000\,m \times 2000\,m$. The wireless communication protocol IEEE 802.11p provides a transmission rate of $12\,Mbit/s$ in the VANETs. Besides, we use the SUMO Traffic Control Interface (TracI) in Python to achieve the interaction and acquisition of vehicle status and data information in the running traffic simulation environment.

Firstly, in a secure system scenario, the list of assisted vehicles can be determined according to batch-assisted verification scheme [15]. Based on this, we evaluate our proposed scheme in an event-driven scenario. The communication

Table 2. Caption

Parameters	Description	Value
N	The number of vehicles in the system	300
n	The number of vehicles of warning state in relevant area	30
λ_n	The arrival rate of EMs in the system (message/ms)	[0.15, 2.7]
n_b	The number of ordinary vehicles verified by the RSU	19
n_c	The number of collaborative vehicles in the system	14
T_k	The delay tolerance of the safety message	100 ms
f_r	The computing power of the RSU	2–3 GHz
f_c	The computing power of the OBU	1.3–1.5 GHz
B	Transmission rate in VANET	12 Mbit/s
l_{BSM}	The length of basic safety message packet	184 bytes
$l_R(n)$	The length of verified comfirmation packets of n messages	$60n+84$ bytes

radius of RSU and Vehicles are set to 1 km and 300 m respectively. The broadcast frequency of different types of EMs is generally between 1 Hz and 10 Hz, and for other vehicles in normal state in the system, they broadcast BSMs at the period of 100ms. The execution time of basic encryption operations can be obtained from MIRACL library [24]. T_{ecc}, $T_{ecc\_sm\_s}$, T_{ecc_pa}, and T_h, are 0.42, 0.0138, 0.0018 and 0.0001 ms, respectively. All the relevant parameters are shown in the Table 2 below.

In this section, we define the total loss rate of safety messages is the ratio of the number of safety messages that fail to be verified within their delay tolerance to the number of safety messages generated in the system. Here, we evaluate the performance of the proposed schemes EM single-verified strategy (CH-SV), EM aggregated-batch verification strategy (CH-ABV) and EM reassigned-verification strategy (CH-RV), and compare them with the traditional scheme, which is the RSU centralized batch-verification algorithm (RCBV). The RCBV scheme centrally verifies all the security messages in the system at the RSU. This scheme aims to maximize the number of verified messages per unit time by establishing a $M/D^r/1$ queuing model.

Figure 4 (a) shows the total loss rate of system safety messages as the arrival rate of EMs in the system λ_m changes under CH-SV strategy, CH-ABV strategy, CH-RV strategy and RCBV strategy. From the figure, it can be seen that the message loss rate of the RCBV algorithm is always around 30%. When λ_m is between [0.1,0.3], the CH-SV strategy results in the lowest total loss rate of messages, which is basically zero, while the other three strategies, due to batch verification, result in long waiting delay for EMs. When λ_m is between [0.15, 0.75], adopting the CH-ABV strategy can ensure that the total loss rate of system security messages is controlled below 15%. When λ_m is greater than 1.05, the safety message loss rate of the CH-ABV strategy is much smaller than that of the CH-ABV strategy due to the limitation of the computing power on

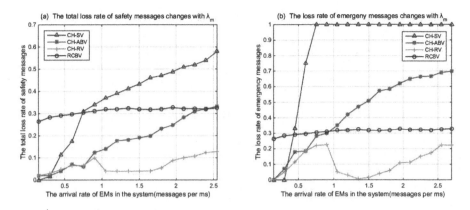

Fig. 4. The loss rate of messages changes with the arrival rate of emergency messages in the system

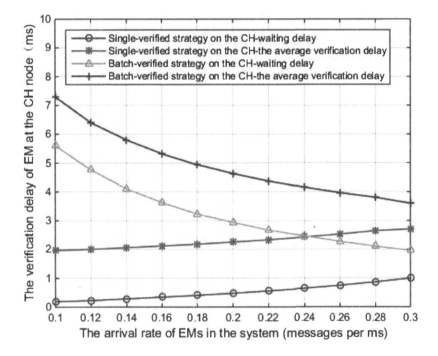

Fig. 5. The verification delay of the emergency messages at the CH node changes with the arrival rate of emergency messages in the system

the CH node. Even if the arrival rate of EMs in the system is 2.7 messages per ms, which corresponds to the maximum broadcast frequency of EMs at 10 Hz, the message loss rate of the RABV strategy can be kept within 15%. The system can choose an appropriate scheme based on the different sizes of EMs to reduce the total loss rate of system safety messages.

Figure 4 (b) shows the loss rate of EMs as the arrival rate of EMs in the system λ_m changes under four strategies. The trend of the loss rate of EMs under four strategies is similar to that of the total loss rate of safety messages in the system. The CH-SV strategy can ensure that the loss rate of EMs in the system is basically 0 when λ_m is between [0,0.3], which is much less than the other three strategies. Due to the limitation of the computing power of the CH node, when the EM arrival rate increases, the CH-ABV strategy has a significant advantage in EM loss rate among the four strategies.

According to Fig. 4 , when the EM arrival rate is less than 0.3, the EM single-verified strategy on the CH node is adopted to decrease verification delay. Figure 5 shows the average waiting time and average verification time for EMs under the EM single-verified strategy and batch-verified strategy on the CH node within the [0.1,0.3] range of EMs arrival rates of the system. When the arrival rate of the system is less than 0.3, batch verification would require some time for message aggregation, causing an increase in the waiting and verification delay. When a CH node adopts EM single-verified strategy, its verification process corresponds to a $M/D/1$ queuing system, and the average verification time of EMs increases with the arrival rate. When CH nodes adopt batch verification strategy, their verification process corresponds to a $M/D^r/1$ queuing system. The

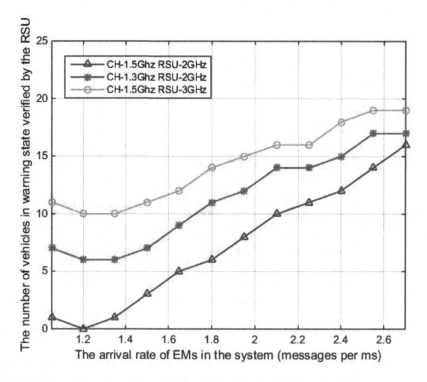

Fig. 6. The number of warning vehicles verified by the RSU under different computing power of RSU and CH node

waiting delay and average verification delay of EMs decrease with the increase of message arrival rate. Therefore, adopting batch verification strategy is more effective when the arrival rate is high.

When the arrival rate of EMs is greater 1.05 messages per ms, the system adopts the CH-ABV strategy. Figure 6 shows the relationship between the number of warning vehicles (CM) verified by the RSU and the EMs arrival rate under the CH-ABV strategy with different computing power of RSU and the CH vehicle. It can be seen that the CH-ABV strategy tends to assign more EMs to the RSU to be verified. This strategy optimizes the success rate of safety message verification by adjusting the allocation ratio of EM verification tasks between the RSU and CH nodes at different EM broadcast frequencies.

6   Conclusion

This paper is based on the system structure of collaborative distributed message batch verification. It considers the scenario of accidents in VANETs and addresses the situation where there is a surge of emergency messages in a specific area due to sudden accidents. It proposes a message collaborative verification scheme to ensure timely verification of all safety messages in the system.

Simulation results demonstrate that compared to the RSU centralized batch verification scheme, this scheme can significantly reduce the loss rate of safety messages in the system caused by untimely verification under different message scales.

Acknowledgements. This work is supported by the National Natural Science Foundation of China under Grant 62301078 and the China Postdoctoral Science Foundation under Grant Number GZB20230086.

References

1. Mchergui, A., Moulahi, T., Zeadally, S.: Survey on artificial intelligence (AI) techniques for vehicular ad-hoc networks (Vanets). Vehicul. Commun. **34**, 100403 (2022)
2. St. Amour, B., Jaekel, A.: Data rate selection strategies for periodic transmission of safety messages in Vanet. Electronics **12**(18) (2023)
3. Zhou, H., Shouzhi, X., Ren, D., Huang, C., Zhang, H.: Analysis of event-driven warning message propagation in vehicular ad hoc networks. Ad Hoc Netw. **55**, 87–96 (2017)
4. Jan, S.A., Amin, N.U., Othman, M., Ali, M., Umar, A.I., Basir, A.: A survey on privacy-preserving authentication schemes in Vanets: attacks, challenges and open issues. IEEE Access **9**, 153701–153726 (2021)
5. Al-Shareeda, M.A., Anbar, M., Hasbullah, I.H., Manickam, S.: Survey of authentication and privacy schemes in vehicular ad hoc networks. IEEE Sens. J. **21**(2), 2422–2433 (2021)
6. Jiangwei, X., Wang, L., Wen, M., Yu, L., Chen, K.: DPB-MA: low-latency message authentication scheme based on distributed verification and priority in vehicular ad hoc network. IEEE Trans. Veh. Technol. **72**(4), 5152–5166 (2023)

7. He, D., Zeadally, S., Baowen, X., Huang, X.: An efficient identity-based conditional privacy-preserving authentication scheme for vehicular ad hoc networks. IEEE Trans. Inf. Forensics Secur. **10**(12), 2681–2691 (2015)
8. Ben Hamida, E., Javed, M.A.: Channel-aware ECDSA signature verification of basic safety messages with k-means clustering in Vanets. In: 2016 IEEE 30th International Conference on Advanced Information Networking and Applications (AINA), pp. 603–610 (2016)
9. Vijayakumar, P., Azees, M., Kozlov, S.A., Rodrigues, J.J.P.C.: An anonymous batch authentication and key exchange protocols for 6g enabled Vanets. IEEE Trans. Intell. Transp. Syst. **23**(2), 1630–1638 (2022)
10. Huang, J.-L., Yeh, L.-Y., Chien, H.-Y.: Abaka: an anonymous batch authenticated and key agreement scheme for value-added services in vehicular ad hoc networks. IEEE Trans. Veh. Technol. **60**(1), 248–262 (2011)
11. Tzeng, S.-F., Horng, S.-J., Li, T., Wang, X., Huang, P.-H., Khan, M.K.: Enhancing security and privacy for identity-based batch verification scheme in Vanets. IEEE Trans. Veh. Technol. **66**(4), 3235–3248 (2017)
12. Chim, T.W., Yiu, S.M., Hui, L.C.K., Li, V.O.K.: Specs: secure and privacy enhancing communications schemes for Vanets. Ad Hoc Netw. **9**(2), 189–203 (2011). Advances in Ad Hoc Networks (I)
13. Yong Hao, Yu., Cheng, C.Z., Song, W.: A distributed key management framework with cooperative message authentication in Vanets. IEEE J. Sel. Areas Commun. **29**(3), 616–629 (2011)
14. Yong Hao, Yu., Cheng, C.Z., Song, W.: A distributed key management framework with cooperative message authentication in vanets. IEEE J. Sel. Areas Commun. **29**(3), 616–629 (2011)
15. Fan, W., Zhang, X., Zhang, C., Chen, X., Fan, W., Liu, Y.: Batch-assisted verification scheme for reducing message verification delay of the vehicular ad hoc networks. IEEE Internet Things J. **7**(9), 8144–8156 (2020)
16. Vinoth Kumar, P., Maheshwari, M.: Prevention of sybil attack and priority batch verification in Vanets. In: International Conference on Information Communication and Embedded Systems (ICICES2014), pp. 1–5 (2014)
17. Banani, S., Gordon, S.: Selecting basic safety messages to verify in Vanets using zone priority. In: The 20th Asia-Pacific Conference on Communication (APCC2014), pp. 423–428 (2014)
18. Sanguesa, J.A., et al.: A survey and comparative study of broadcast warning message dissemination schemes for Vanets. Mobile Inf. Syst. **2016** (2016)
19. Zhong, H., Huang, B., Cui, J., Yan, X., Liu, L.: Conditional privacy-preserving authentication using registration list in vehicular ad hoc networks. IEEE Access **6**, 2241–2250 (2018)
20. Kan, W.: Classification of queueing models for a workstation with interruptions: a review. Int. J. Prod. Res. **52**(3), 902–917 (2014)
21. Hafeez, K.A., Zhao, L., Mark, J.W., Shen, X., Niu, Z.: Distributed multichannel and mobility-aware cluster-based mac protocol for vehicular ad hoc networks. IEEE Trans. Veh. Technol. **62**(8), 3886–3902 (2013)
22. Chaudhry, M.L., Templeton, J.G.C.: A first course in bulk queues. (No Title) (1983)
23. Gabrel, V., Murat, C., Thiele, A.: Recent advances in robust optimization: an overview. Eur. J. Oper. Res. **235**(3), 471–483 (2014)
24. Lo, N.-W., Tsai, J.-L.: An efficient conditional privacy-preserving authentication scheme for vehicular sensor networks without pairings. IEEE Trans. Intell. Transp. Syst. **17**(5), 1319–1328 (2016)

Enhancing Mobile Communication System Security via Neural Cryptography Applications

Lela Mirtskhulava[1]([✉]) [ID], Nana Gulua[2] [ID], and Khatuna Putkaradze[2] [ID]

[1] Ivane Javakhishvili Tbilisi State University, 0186 Tbilisi, Georgia
lela.mirtskhulava@tsu.ge
[2] Sokhumi State University, 0186 Tbilisi, Georgia
{ngulua,khatuna-putkaradze}@sou.edu.ge

Abstract. The given paper aims to understand how the emerging technologies of 5G and Beyond, and artificial intelligence could affect the security of mobile communication systems and to explore ways to mitigate any potential risks. We analyze the vulnerabilities of 5G and beyond systems to attacks and the potential risks associated with the use of AI in these systems. We optimise a security protocol and systems that can withstand the power of quantum computing and enhance the security of IoT and "5G and beyond" systems. We identify potential areas of regulatory intervention and ensure that AI is used responsibly and transparently in 5G and beyond systems. The proposed method is novel - implementing a type of synchronization mechanism between two Tree Parity Machines (TPMs) using feedback. A feedback mechanism helps to adjust the weights of one TPM based on the outputs of both TPMs on the same input. This is different from traditional methods of training neural networks, which usually involve minimizing a cost function or optimizing weights using some form of gradient descent. The use of TPMs instead of traditional neural networks is also somewhat novel as TPMs are a type of recurrent neural network that has been proposed for use in cognitive modeling. In the training phase of TPMs, the Hebbian learning rule is employed to adjust connection weights between perceptrons.

Keywords: 5G and beyond · TPMs · synchronization · security · neural cryptography

1 Introduction

In the evolving landscape of mobile communication systems, safeguarding sensitive information and ensuring secure data transmission has become paramount. The growing utilization of mobile devices continues unabated, and the need for robust security mechanisms becomes more critical than ever. We offer an innovative approach gaining prominence to address the security challenges is integrating neural cryptography applications into mobile communication systems [1].

Neural cryptography - a branch of artificial intelligence and cryptography, leverages the power of neural networks to secure communication channels against unauthorized access and cyber threats. This cutting-edge methodology goes beyond traditional

X. Li et al. (Eds.): SmartGift 2024, LNICST 600, pp. 145–156, 2025.
https://doi.org/10.1007/978-3-031-78806-2_9

encryption techniques providing a dynamic and adaptive security framework tailored to the unique challenges posed by mobile communications.

Neural cryptography uses adaptive encryption protocols capable of dynamically adjusting to the changing nature of communication patterns. Via leveraging neural networks, these protocols can continuously learn and optimize encryption strategies based on real-time data, securing them and making them more resilient against emerging threats. Neural cryptography can detect anomalies in communication systems by integrating behavioral analysis. Then the system can identify deviations from typical usage, triggering alerts and responses to potential security breaches [2].

Classical authentication methods often face challenges caused by sophisticated cyber attacks. Neural cryptography can enhance security by using self-learning authentication mechanisms that continuously adapt to evolving patterns and reduce the risk of unauthorized access. On the other hand, with advancing quantum computing capabilities, classical cryptographic methods are becoming susceptible to new vulnerabilities. Neural cryptography applications provide quantum-resistant security measures and ensure the long-term viability of mobile communication system security.

Neural cryptography applications provide robust key management systems, securing cryptographic keys against various attack vectors. By implementing neural networks, these systems enhance the randomness and complexity of generated keys, making them more resistant to brute-force attacks. The integration of neural cryptography enables mobile communication systems' real-time threat detection and response mechanisms enable the system to adapt its security measures dynamically. Neural cryptography applications ensure the development of end-to-end encryption mechanisms with minimal latency.

The intersection of quantum AI (Artificial Intelligence), 5 G (Fifth Generation), and beyond telecommunications is a rapidly evolving field that has the potential to revolutionize various industries. However, as with any new technology, it also poses significant security challenges. The novelty of using a detailed analysis of the impact of quantum AI on the security of IoT and 5 G lies in the fact that it addresses a critical gap in current research. Traditional cryptographic methods used in IoT and 5 G systems may not be sufficient to protect against attacks from quantum computers. Therefore, understanding the potential impact of quantum AI on the security of these systems is crucial to developing effective countermeasures [3].

Long-term usage of public-key algorithms showed the necessity to explore new methods of public and private key generations. GSMA organization announced that the security of wireless networks (5 G/LTE/3 G/2 G) and user equipment (UE), is essential to providing secure services since 5 G evolving brings new security threats. 5 G wireless networks are still in the process of deploying across the world where the transition from 4 G to 5 G addresses many challenges such as addressing the threats faced in 2 G/3 G/4 G networks. In 5 G and beyond, the implementation of new technologies introduces new potential threats in the industry [4].

5G and beyond standard security techniques are based on classical cryptography and unfortunately do not take into account the threats or issues that can be potentially caused by quantum computing. The development of quantum computers (QC) is going rapidly and promising to solve computing problems that cannot be solved by traditional computers. Moreover, they can generate new threats at a very high speed. They can break traditional encryption algorithms like the RSA and ECC in seconds using quantum algorithms such as Shor's algorithm. It is necessary to shift to the world of quantum cryptography [5, 6].

AI is expected to be widely used to mitigate previous undetected and AI-driven attacks in 5 G networks in real time and benefit security. Leveraging Machine Learning AI techniques will automate threat detection. AI is particularly relevant to be used in generating the volumes of data in 5 G networks. The wide employment of AI in 5 G networks will enhance 5 G security.

The 3rd Generation Partnership Project (3 GPP) offered a standard for 5 G networks. It contains the identity protection scheme, which addresses the important privacy problem of permanent subscriber-identity disclosure. This offer contains two stages: the identification stage, which provides the security context between service providers and mobile subscribers using the authenticated key agreement with the symmetric key. 3 GPP offers to protect the identification stage using a public-key scheme. They offer to use the Elliptic Curve Integrated Encryption Scheme (ECIES). The offered scheme is not secure against the attacks of quantum computers. It is important to integrate the quantum-resistant scheme into 5 G networks and beyond.

This motivation drove our exploration into the Neural Key Exchange concept, involving the utilization of AI algorithms to generate secret keys for authenticated users. To accomplish this goal, we employ the components of tree parity machines. This paper delves into the workings of tree parity machines and outlines the adaptations we have devised to enhance the algorithm's resilience against quantum attacks. Our methodology aims to fortify both the algorithm and its structure, ensuring increased robustness while preserving the desired balance between computational cost and speed.

The implemented code incorporates a synchronization mechanism between two Temporal Product Machines (TPMs) through feedback. This approach stands out due to its novelty, employing a feedback mechanism to fine-tune the weights of one TPM based on the outputs of both TPMs for the same input. This diverges from conventional neural network training methods, which typically center around minimizing a cost function or optimizing weights through gradient descent. Furthermore, the use of TPMs, instead of traditional neural networks, adds to the novelty, given that TPMs are a subtype of recurrent neural networks suggested for cognitive modeling.

2 Related Work

Tree parity machines (TPMs) have a longstanding history, with numerous studies exploring the integration of AI logic for key generation. Revankar, P [7], for instance, employed TPMs with a single hidden layer to generate public keys and demonstrated mathematically that breaking the key through brute force is nearly impossible given today's computational capabilities. Kinzel and Kanter [8, 9] established that increasing the synaptic depth of the network makes it progressively more challenging for attackers to compromise the key, resulting in an exponential rise in computational cost.

In a similar vein, Dorokhin and Fuertes [10] conducted experiments revealing that not only does the depth influence the security of a TPM network, but also the use of a large number of neurons in hidden layers enhances its security. Dolecki and Kozera [11] explored the impact of weight initialization in the network, comparing random allocation with Gaussian distribution. Their findings suggested that Gaussian distribution outperforms random initialization, facilitating faster synchronization even with an increasing depth. However, caution is advised, as using Gaussian distribution may inadvertently provide more information to potential attackers attempting to synchronize their weights with authorized hosts, potentially compromising security.

Mirtskhulava et al. [12] proposed a systematic approach is essential for monitoring and mitigating all potential threats to IoT security. Encryption stands out as a primary requirement to establish secure communication within the IoT framework. Key exchange is pivotal in securing information exchange across the IoT network. Neural networks present an effective strategy through the synchronization process, employing the Hebbian learning rule to balance weights. This synchronization in neural networks provides a cryptographic key-exchange protocol. A significant advantage of this process is the extended time required for an attacker to guess the generated key.

Mirtskhulava et al. [13] proposed an analysis of NTRU (Nth Degree Truncated Polynomial Ring Units), which stands out as the first lattice-based public key cryptosystem, primarily due to its notable advantages, such as the absence of an established install base and resilience against long-term cryptanalysis. NTRU's cryptosystem demonstrates significantly higher speed compared to algorithms like RSA or ECC. Employing one-off keys, NTRU allows for key changes within seconds of use.

This characteristic imposes a formidable challenge for potential attackers, as they would need to obtain hundreds or thousands of keys instead of just one to crack the encryption on video files. The Internet of Things (IoT) represents a vast network comprising thousands of interconnected smart devices, including cars, smart medical equipment, industrial control systems, smart grids, and more. The escalating use of connected vulnerable devices poses serious security threats, leading to an increased risk of security breaches.

Through these vulnerable devices, attackers can potentially gain access to sensitive information, compromising enterprise networks. The proliferation of malwares, botnets, and other security threats exacerbates the challenges associated with the security of IoT networks.

Shishniashvili, Mamisaishvili, and Mirtskhulava [14] introduced an innovative approach to constructing a feedforward neural network with multiple hidden layers by incorporating elements from Tree Parity Machines. With the exponential increase in the permutations of weights within these layers, it becomes highly challenging for an attacker to replicate the key. Simulations, involving 10,000 attacker machines attempting to imitate the key, substantiate this claim. Balancing security considerations and the complexity of structures, the proposed algorithm maintains time efficiency for real-time applications. Simulations executed on an Intel Core processor demonstrate that key generation takes less than 1 s. Given the evolving landscape of asymmetric cryptographic algorithms, exploring and testing novel methods for generating both public and private keys is imperative in the modern era.

Mirtskhulava et al. [15] explored the lattice-based open-source NTRU cryptosystem designed for public-key encryption, specifically applicable in the context of the Internet of Things (IoT). Given that IoT encompasses individuals' sensitive data and various aspects of personal lives, it necessitates a specialized level of protection. The security of IoT involves safeguarding both the network and the connected devices. Cryptographic technologies emerge as optimal solutions to counter communication attacks.

Mirtskhulava et al. [16] proposed an approach for securing the Mobile Internet of Things (MIoT) ecosystem in the era of rapidly advancing mobile internet (5G and 6G) involves the adoption of post-quantum digital signature-based blockchain. This method is deemed suitable as the MIoT ecosystem gains significance due to the expanding accessibility and higher speeds of mobile internet.

In contrast to existing approaches, we propose a three-layer TPM with random initialization and provide evidence that, without sacrificing efficiency, it offers a heightened level of security.

3   Tree Parity Machine Architecture

3.1   TPM with Three-Layered Perceptron

We offer a Tree Parity Machine (TPM) with a three-layered perceptron architecture (Fig. 1) consisting of three layers of perceptrons organised in a tree-like structure. In the given architecture, the first layer of the perceptron is connected to the input vector, where the second layer is connected to the first layer, and the third layer represents the output layer.

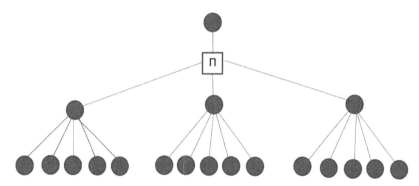

Fig. 1. The structure of the Tree Parity machine.

Each perceptron has binary weights in the network, where the weights are randomly initialized. The perceptrons have the same number of inputs in each layer, which is dimensionality equal to the input vector. The outputs of the first-layer perceptrons are connected to the inputs of the second-layer perceptrons, and the outputs of the second-layer perceptrons are connected to the inputs of the third-layer perceptrons [17].

Mathematically, the output of a TPM with a three-layered perceptron architecture can be represented as follows:

$$y = sign(W_3 \cdot g(W_2 \cdot g(W_1 \cdot x)))$$ (1)

where:

- x is the input vector
- W_1 is the weight matrix between the input layer and the first hidden layer
- W_2 is the weight matrix between the first and second hidden layers
- W_3 is the weight vector between the second hidden layer and the output layer
- $g()$ is the activation function
- $sign()$ is the sign function mapping positive values to $+1$ and negative values to -1

In the TPM, the weights of the perceptrons are updated through a learning process called training. During training, the TPM is presented with a set of input patterns and their corresponding labels. The weights are adjusted based on the difference between the actual output and the desired output, using a learning rule such as the perceptron learning rule or the backpropagation algorithm.

The goal of training a TPM is to learn a set of weights that can correctly classify input patterns into their respective categories. Once the TPM is trained, it can be used to classify new input patterns by computing the output of the network and comparing it to a threshold value. If the output is above the threshold, the input is classified as belonging to one category, and if it is below the threshold, the input is classified as belonging to another category.

3.2   TPM Key Agreement Protocol

The TPM key agreement protocol is a method of exchanging a secure key between two parties based on the output of a TPM. The protocol comprises the following three steps: initialization, key generation, and key agreement.

1st step -Initialization: both parties agree on the number of input bits, the number of layers, and perceptrons in the TPM. They also agree on a shared seed value, which is used to initialize the weights of the TPM.

2nd step – Key Generation: both parties generate random input bit vectors and use them as inputs to their respective TPMs. The TPMs produce output vectors that are sent over a secure channel to the other party. The parties then compute the dot product of their output vector with the received output vector, and if the result is positive, they set the corresponding bit in a shared secret key to 1. Otherwise, they set it to 0. This process is repeated for a predetermined number of iterations to generate a shared secret key.

3rd step – Key Agreement: both parties compare their generated secret keys to ensure that they are identical. If the keys match, they can use them as shared secret keys for symmetric encryption or other cryptographic applications.

The security of the TPM key agreement protocol is based on the difficulty of computing the dot product of the output vectors of the TPMs. The weights of the TPMs are initialized randomly and kept secret, and the output vectors are highly sensitive to changes in the input vectors. Therefore, an attacker would need to know the weights of the TPMs to compute the dot product, which is computationally infeasible in most cases.

The train_tpm function applies this rule to each perceptron's output for every input pattern, facilitating weight updates. Widely utilized in various neural network architectures such as Hopfield networks, Boltzmann machines, and self-organizing maps, the Hebbian learning rule proves to be a straightforward yet effective mechanism for learning.

4   Security of TPMs

The security of TPMs lies in their ability to perform non-linear classification and their resistance to certain types of attacks. However, like any cryptographic algorithm, TPMs are not completely secure, and their security depends on various factors such as the size of the network, the quality of the seed used to initialize the weights, and the number of training iterations.

One of the primary advantages of TPMs is their ability to perform non-linear classification, which makes them resistant to linear attacks. In contrast to linear classifiers, TPMs can learn complex decision boundaries between input patterns, which makes them more difficult to attack. Additionally, TPMs are highly sensitive to changes in the input, and small changes in the input can cause large changes in the output, which makes them resistant to certain types of attacks such as gradient-based attacks.

However, TPMs are vulnerable to certain types of attacks such as brute force attacks and adversarial attacks. Brute force attacks involve guessing the weights of the TPM through trial and error, and the security of the TPM depends on the size of the network and the quality of the seed used to initialize the weights. Adversarial attacks involve modifying the input to the TPM to cause it to misclassify the input. While TPMs are resistant to certain types of adversarial attacks, they are not completely immune, and recent research has shown that it is possible to construct adversarial examples that can fool the TPM.

In addition to the above, TPMs can also be vulnerable to side-channel attacks, where an attacker gains information about the network by analyzing its behavior or the physical environment in which it is located. For example, an attacker might be able to learn the weights of the TPM by analyzing the electromagnetic radiation emitted by the network.

It is imperative to address the susceptibility of TPMs to side-channel attacks, which pose a significant threat to the security of mobile communication systems. Side-channel attacks exploit unintended information leakage from the system's physical implementation rather than directly targeting cryptographic algorithms. When it comes to electromagnetic radiation analysis, an attacker can intercept and analyze the emitted radiation from the TPM network to gain crucial information, such as the weights of the TPMs. Moreover, attackers can potentially compromise the security of the communication system by discerning these weights, undermining the confidentiality and integrity of transmitted data.

The above-mentioned vulnerability underscores the importance of enhancing the resilience of synchronized TPMs against side-channel attacks. It requires the implementation of robust countermeasures, such as noise injection to mitigate information leakage and prevent adversaries from exploiting these vulnerabilities. Comprehensive security protocols will play a crusial role to detect and respond to potential side-channel attacks effectively, thereby enhancing the level of security of mobile communication systems employing synchronized TPMs.

Addressing these vulnerabilities and implementing effective countermeasures are essential steps towards strengthening the security of mobile communication systems against sophisticated adversaries aiming to exploit side-channel weaknesses in synchronized TPMs. Mitigating these risks, we can ensure the integrity, confidentiality, and reliability of communication channels in real-world deployment processes.

5   Synchronization Time of TPMs with Differentiated Input Vectors

The synchronization time of Tree Parity Machines (TPMs) with differentiated input vectors refers to the amount of time it takes for two or more TPMs to synchronize their output vectors given different input vectors. The synchronization time is an important metric for assessing the performance of TPMs in tasks such as key agreement, where two parties need to synchronize their TPMs to generate a shared secret key.

The synchronization time of TPMs with differentiated input vectors depends on several factors such as the size of the network, the number of layers and perceptrons, and the quality of the seed used to initialize the weights. Generally, the synchronization time is longer for larger networks and networks with more layers and perceptrons, as there are more parameters to synchronize. Additionally, the synchronization time can be affected by the quality of the seed used to initialize the weights, as poor initialization can lead to longer convergence times.

One way to reduce the synchronization time of TPMs with differentiated input vectors is to use a pre-synchronization phase, where the TPMs are trained with the same input vectors for a few iterations before being used with differentiated input vectors. This pre-synchronization phase can help to align the output vectors of the TPMs, which can reduce the amount of time needed for synchronization when different input vectors are used.

Another way to reduce the synchronization time of TPMs is to use a smaller number of layers and perceptrons, which reduces the number of parameters that need to be synchronized. However, reducing the number of layers and perceptrons can also reduce the complexity of the decision boundary learned by the TPM, which can affect its ability to perform non-linear classification.

6   Hebbian Learning Rule

The Hebbian learning rule is a simple unsupervised learning rule that reinforces connections between neurons that are active at the same time. The rule can be expressed mathematically as:

$$\Delta w_{ij} = \eta \cdot x_i \cdot x_j \tag{2}$$

where Δw_{ij} is the change in weight between neuron i and neuron j, η is the learning rate, x_i and x_j are the binary states of neuron i and neuron j, respectively. This means that the weight between two neurons is increased when both neurons are active ($x_i = 1, x_j = 1$), and is decreased when both neurons are inactive ($x_i = -1, x_j = -1$). If only one neuron is active, the weight remains unchanged.

The Hebbian learning rule is used to update the weights of the connections between the perceptrons in the TPMs during the training phase. The train_tpm function applies the Hebbian learning rule to the output of each perceptron in the TPM for each input pattern and updates the weights accordingly. The Hebbian learning rule is a simple but powerful mechanism for learning in neural networks and has been used in many different types of neural networks, including Hopfield networks, Boltzmann machines, and self-organizing maps.

7   Simulation Results and Discussions

In this section, we discuss the results of the simulation by generating the code in Python. This code defines two TPMs, tpm1 and tpm2, each with num_layers layers of size layer_size and num_bits input bits. The initial weights for the TPMs are randomly generated using the *np.random.randint* function with values of -1, 0, and 1. The feedback function takes the two TPMs and an input vector as arguments, and returns the output vectors of the TPMs after processing the input, as well as updates the weights of the second TPM if there is a difference in output with the first TPM.

The synchronization loop runs for 100 iterations, where in each iteration, a new input vector is generated randomly using the *np.random.randint* function. The feedback function is called with the two TPMs and the input vector, which produces the output vectors of the TPMs and updates the weights of the second TPM if needed (See Table 1).

The outputs of the TPMs and the updated weights of the second TPM are printed after each iteration. However, the way the function updates the weights of tpm2 based on the diff variable and input vector is incorrect and will not produce the desired results.

The above code does not use a traditional training algorithm like backpropagation to adjust the weights of the TPMs. Instead, it uses a feedback mechanism to synchronize the weights of two separate TPMs.

During each iteration of the loop, the code generates a random input vector and applies it to both TPMs using the feedback function. The feedback function calculates the output vectors of both TPMs for the input vector and compares them. If the output vectors differ, it calculates the difference and adjusts the weights of the second TPM accordingly. The loop continues until the output vectors of both TPMs are identical.

Table 1. TP1 and TPM 2 outputs for some iterations

Iteration 57	Iteration 58	Iteration 59	Iteration 82	Iteration 99
TPM 1 output: [1 1 1]	TPM 1 output: [-1 -1 -1]	TPM 1 output: [1 1 1]	TPM 1 output: [0 0 0]	TPM 1 output: [1 0 -1]
TPM 2 output: [1 1 1]	TPM 2 output: [-1 -1 -1]	TPM 2 output: [1 1 1]	TPM 2 output: [0 0 0]	TPM 2 output: [1 1 -1]
TPM 2 weights after feedback: [[[3 3 -2] [3 4 -3] [3 3 -2] [4 5 -2] [3 4 -1]] [[0 1 -3] [2 2 -3] [2 1 -4] [0 1 -3] [2 2 -5]] [[4 -2 0] [2 -2 -1] [4 -1 0] [3 -3 -1] [4 -1 1]]]	TPM 2 weights after feedback: [[[3 3 -2] [3 4 -3] [3 3 -2] [4 5 -2] [3 4 -1]] [[0 1 -3] [2 2 -3] [2 1 -4] [0 1 -3] [2 2 -5]] [[4 -2 0] [2 -2 -1] [4 -1 0] [3 -3 -1] [4 -1 1]]]	TPM 2 weights after feedback: [[[3 3 -2] [3 4 -3] [3 3 -2] [4 5 -2] [3 4 -1]] [[0 1 -3] [2 2 -3] [2 1 -4] [0 1 -3] [2 2 -5]] [[4 -2 0] [2 -2 -1] [4 -1 0] [3 -3 -1] [4 -1 1]]]	TPM 2 weights after feedback: [[[2 3 -3] [2 4 -4] [2 3 -3] [3 5 -3] [2 4 -2]] [[0 1 -3] [2 2 -3] [2 1 -4] [0 1 -3] [2 2 -5]] [[4 -2 1] [2 -2 0] [4 -1 1] [3 -3 0] [4 -1 2]]]	TPM 2 weights after feedback: [[[2 3 -3] [2 4 -4] [2 3 -3] [3 5 -3] [2 4 -2]] [[1 0 -3] [3 1 -3] [3 0 -4] [1 0 -3] [3 1 -5]] [[4 -2 0] [2 -2 -1] [4 -1 0] [3 -3 -1] [4 -1 1]]]

This method of synchronization is based on the principle that the weights of two TPMs that produce the same output for the same input must be identical. By applying the same input to both TPMs and adjusting the weights of the second TPM to match the output of the first TPM, the two TPMs become synchronized and have identical weights.

This method of synchronization can be thought of as a form of unsupervised learning, where the TPMs learn to produce the same output for the same input without being explicitly told what the correct output should be. It is important to note, however, that this method of synchronization may not work in all cases and may require careful tuning of the parameters to achieve good results.

```
1  # Initialize TPMs with random weights
2  num_layers = 3
3  layer_size = 5
4  num_bits = 3
5  tpm1 = random_weights(num_layers, layer_size, num_bits)
6  tpm2 = random_weights(num_layers, layer_size, num_bits)
7
8  # Feedback function
9  def feedback(tpm1, tpm2, input):
10     output1 = compute_output(tpm1, input)
11     output2 = compute_output(tpm2, input)
12     error = compute_error(output1, output2)
13
14     if has_error(error):
15         diff = compute_difference(output1, output2)
16         adjust_weights(tpm2, input, diff)
17
18     return output1, output2
19
20 # Synchronize TPMs using feedback
21 for i in range(100):
22     input = random_input(num_bits)
23     output1, output2 = feedback(tpm1, tpm2, input)
24
25     print("Iteration", i)
26     print("TPM 1 output:", output1)
27     print("TPM 2 output:", output2)
28     print("TPM 2 weights after feedback:", tpm2)
29
30 # Display results
31 display_results()
```

Algorithm: Pseudocode of implementing a key exchange
mechanism using TPMs

8 Conclusion

We provided the code in Python that diverged from conventional training algorithms
such as backpropagation for adjusting the weights of the Tree Parity Machines (TPMs).
Instead, it employs a feedback mechanism for the synchronization of weights between
two distinct TPMs. In each iteration of the loop, the code generates a random input vector
and utilizes the feedback function to apply it to both TPMs. This feedback function
computes the output vectors of both TPMs for the given input and compares them. If
discrepancies arise in the output vectors, the function calculates the disparity and adjusts
the weights of the second TPM accordingly. The loop runs until the output vectors of
both TPMs achieve identical states.

This synchronization approach operates on the principle that two TPMs yielding
the same output for identical inputs must possess identical weights. By subjecting both
TPMs to the same input and adjusting the weights of the second TPM to align with
the output of the first TPM, synchronization occurs, resulting in identical weights. This

synchronization method can be conceptualized as a form of unsupervised learning, where the TPMs learn to produce identical outputs for the same inputs without explicit guidance on the correct output.

The TPM-based key agreement protocol is an efficient method for secure key exchange between two parties. However, it is important to ensure that the TPMs are initialized with sufficiently large weights and that the number of iterations is appropriate to ensure the security of the generated key.

References

1. https://www.gsma.com/security/network-equipment-security-assurance-scheme/
2. Chakraborty, S., Dalal, J., Sarkar, B. and Mukherjee, D.: Neural Synchronization based secret key exchange over public channels: a survey. Arxiv.org. (2015). https://arxiv.org/ftp/arxiv/pap ers/1502/1502.05153.pdf
3. https://www.gsma.com/security/securing-the-5g-era/
4. https://www.gsma.com/security/5g-cybersecurity-knowledge-base/
5. Rivest, R.: The RC4 encryption algorithm, RSA Data Security (1992)
6. Zhou, X., Tang, X.: Research and Implementation of RSA Algorithm For Encryption And Decryption - IEEE Conference Publication. Ieeexplore.ieee.org. (2011). https://ieeexplore. ieee.org/abstract/document/6021216
7. Revankar, P., Gandhare, W., Rathod, D.: Private inputs to tree parity machine. Pdfs.semanticscholar.org. (2010). https://pdfs.semanticscholar.org/dfbc/7fde64f2b55d876 7daa50e9ea2130bf6db69.pdf
8. Kinzel, W., Kanter, I.: Neural cryptography. In: Proceedings of the 9th International Conference on Neural Information Processing. ICONIP 2002, vol. 3, pp. 1351–1354. Singapore (2002). https://doi.org/10.1109/ICONIP.2002.1202841
9. Kinzel, W., Kanter, I.: Interacting neural networks and cryptography. Adv. Solid State Phys. 383–391 (2003)
10. Salguero Dorokhin, É., Fuertes, W., Lascano, E.: On the development of an optimal structure of tree parity machine for the establishment of a cryptographic key. Secur. Commun. Networks 1–10 (2019)
11. Dolecki, M., Kozera, R.: The impact of the TPM weights distribution on network synchronization time. Comput. Inform. Syst. Indust. Manage. 451–460 (2015)
12. L. Mirtskhulava, N., Gulua, N., Meshveliani: Iot security analysis using neural key exchange. GESJ: Computer Science and Telecommunications |No.2 (57) (2019)
13. L. Mirtskhulava, N., Gulua, N., Meshveliani.: Ntru cryptosystem analysis for securing IoT. GESJ: Computer Science and Telecommunications |No.1 (56) (2019)
14. Shishniashvili, E., Mamisashvili, L., Mirtskhulava, L.: Enhancing IoT security using multi-layer feedforward neural network with tree parity machine elements. Int. J. Simul. Syst. Sci. Technol. 21(2), 371–383 (2020). https://doi.org/10.5013/ijssst.a.21.02.37
15. Mirtskhulava L.N. Meshveliani, N., Gulua, Globa, L.: Cryptanalysis of Internet of Things (IoT) wireless technology. In: IEEE International Conference on Information and Telecommunication Technologies and Radio Electronics – UkrMicO. Odessa, Ukraine (2019)
16. Mirtskhulava, L., GlobaL, L., Gulua, N., Meshveliani N.: Complex approach in cryptanalysis of Internet of Things (IoT) using blockchain technology and lattice-based cryptosystem. In: Ilchenko, M., Uryvsky, L., Globa, L. (eds.) Advances in Information and Communication Technology and Systems. MCT 2019. NNS, vol. 152. Springer, Cham (2021). https://doi.org/ 10.1007/978-3-030-58359-0_4
17. Klimov, A., Mityagin A., Shamir: Analysis of Neural Cryptography, Springer.com (2002). https://doi.org/10.1007/3-540-36178-2_18

System Design for Smart Grid and IoT

EcoIntegrity: AI-Augmented Blockchain Framework for Carbon Footprint Tracking and Incentives in IoT

Liyuan Liu[1] and Meng Han[2]([✉])

[1] Saint Joseph's University, Philadelphia, PA 19131, USA
lliu@sju.edu
[2] Zhejiang University, Hangzhou 310027, Zhejiang, China
mhan@zju.edu.cn

Abstract. The accelerating demands for environmental sustainability necessitate the development of robust systems capable of meticulous carbon footprint tracking. This paper introduces "EcoIntegrity," an AI-augmented blockchain framework tailored for IoT environments to ensure transparent and accurate carbon footprint monitoring. Our comprehensive approach involves a three-phase solution that combines advanced AI algorithms, immutable blockchain technology, and an equitable incentive mechanism. The first phase harnesses IoT devices for data acquisition, emphasizing the need for precise and reliable data collection. This sets the foundation for the second phase, where AI, particularly recurrent neural networks and Local Outlier Factor algorithms, come into play. These algorithms are adept at predicting anomalous activities and emissions, thereby bolstering data integrity. The subsequent phase leverages the blockchain's secure ledger system to store the verified data, thereby fortifying the framework against potential breaches and ensuring data immutability. Furthermore, recognizing the collaborative nature of IoT networks in environmental monitoring, the framework integrates the Shapley value from cooperative game theory. This ensures a fair distribution of incentives among the IoT devices, encouraging accurate data reporting and collaboration. Our results demonstrate that "EcoIntegrity" not only streamlines carbon tracking but also significantly contributes to sustainable environmental management. Our proposed framework pioneers an intelligent framework for IoT-based carbon monitoring advances AI applications for integrity assurance, promotes blockchain for secure data storage, and fosters fairness through strategic reward distribution. The practical implications of our work extend to improved environmental reporting, regulatory adherence, and the promotion of sustainable practices within IoT networks.

Keywords: carbon footprint · artificial intelligence · blockchain · IoT · incentive mechanism

© ICST Institute for Computer Sciences, Social Informatics and Telecommunications Engineering 2025
Published by Springer Nature Switzerland AG 2025. All Rights Reserved
X. Li et al. (Eds.): SmartGift 2024, LNICST 600, pp. 159–181, 2025.
https://doi.org/10.1007/978-3-031-78806-2_10

1   Introduction

As global awareness of sustainability issues intensifies, the significance of carbon footprint tracking has escalated, drawing widespread attention across various sectors. This growing concern is underpinned by alarming environmental data: according to the Global Carbon Project, global CO_2 emissions soared to approximately 36.4 gigatonnes in 2021, underscoring the critical need for effective monitoring and reduction strategies [1]. These emissions not only degrade the quality of human life but also contribute to overarching global problems, particularly climate change. In this context, the Intergovernmental Panel on Climate Change (IPCC) stresses the necessity of curtailing CO_2 emissions to limit global warming to 1.5°C, highlighting the vital role of carbon footprint tracking in evaluating progress towards these climatic objectives [2]. The repercussions of climate change pose a threat to all life on Earth, propelling individuals and organizations alike to assume responsibility for environmental stewardship. Numerous corporations, for instance, are adopting ambitious sustainability targets, such as Microsoft's commitment to achieving carbon negativity by 2030 [3]. Precise carbon footprint measurement is crucial for these entities to assess and disclose their advancements accurately.

Beyond corporate initiatives, consumer attitudes are also shifting. A Nielsen report in 2020 revealed that 73% of global consumers are willing to alter their consumption patterns to lessen environmental impacts, underscoring the demand for transparent carbon footprint tracking [4]. In tandem with these societal changes, governmental bodies are instituting regulations to aid in carbon management. The European Union's Emissions Trading System (EU ETS), for example, plays a fundamental role in regulating emissions from key industrial sectors [5]. Moreover, carbon footprint tracking serves as a tool for enhancing energy efficiency. The industrial sector in the United States, accounting for 32% of the nation's total energy consumption in 2020, stands to benefit from such data-driven strategies [6]. Additionally, urban centers are leveraging smart technologies for carbon management. Copenhagen's goal to achieve carbon neutrality by 2025 exemplifies the use of carbon footprint data in steering urban development policies [7].

The Internet of Things (IoT) is a rapidly growing technology widely used in various fields, including smart homes, smart grids, and smart cities. Its widespread use has led to innovative applications, such as tracking and monitoring carbon footprints in different sectors. Research by Chakravarthi et al. [8] and Faize et al. [9] shows that smart grids can use IoT sensors and smart meters to monitor electricity use in real-time. This information is essential for calculating the carbon footprint from energy use, especially when it involves high carbon-emitting sources. Studies by Kokare et al. [10] and Ionescu et al. [11] focus on monitoring and controlling power consumption in real-time, highlighting the increasing range of IoT applications in energy management. Recent developments include IoT devices that can report carbon emissions directly. For instance, Hamidu et al. [12] developed a low-cost IoT sensor for monitoring greenhouse gases in industrial areas, emphasizing the accuracy and importance of IoT in environmental protection. However, there are concerns about the reliability of these IoT-based carbon tracking systems. Security issues, like those exposed by the Mirai malware attack that infected networked IoT devices and created a controllable network of bots [13], show the vulnerabilities in IoT. Additionally, smart grids, which rely heavily on IoT technologies, have faced data breaches. In the energy sector, there have been cases of smart meters or energy consumption data being manipulated for inaccurate billing. The concerns surrounding data security and privacy in IoT devices have highlighted potential integrity issues in their use for tracking and monitoring carbon footprints in real-world scenarios. Moreover, when multiple IoT devices collaborate to monitor a single piece of equipment, the complexity increases. Therefore, it becomes crucial to design an effective incentive mechanism that encourages collaborative work among these diverse devices. This approach not only ensures the accurate collection of data but also fosters a cooperative environment among various IoT components involved in carbon footprint tracking. According to the integrity challenges we faced, we proposed the research questions below:

- How can advanced anomaly detection algorithms be integrated into IoT systems to enhance the integrity of carbon footprint tracking and monitoring?
- What are the most secure database architectures or technologies suitable for mitigating risks of hacking and data breaches in IoT networks focused on environmental monitoring?
- In the context of collaborative IoT systems working on unified tasks, what incentive models, based on principles of fairness and efficiency, can be effectively implemented to ensure fair reward distribution among participating devices?

Therefore, in this study, we have developed "EcoIntegrity," an AI-augmented blockchain framework with integrated incentive mechanisms for tracking and monitoring carbon footprints in IoT environments. This framework is specifically designed to address the research questions we have proposed. EcoIntegrity presents a groundbreaking AI-augmented blockchain framework, revolutionizing carbon footprint tracking in the IoT landscape. This paper explores EcoIntegrity's multifaceted approach to automate carbon reporting. The framework commences by utilizing IoT devices for comprehensive data collection, focusing on historical and behavioral aspects essential for accurate carbon footprint analysis. The next phase involves the deployment of AI algorithms for meticulous data scrutiny, targeting fraud detection to uphold reporting integrity. Subsequently, EcoIntegrity incorporates blockchain technology to securely record verified carbon data, enhancing transparency and trust in the process. Another novel aspect of EcoIntegrity is its incentive mechanism, employing the Shapley value method to equitably reward the collaborative efforts of IoT devices. This strategy aims to foster honest and precise data reporting. By integrating these advanced technologies, EcoIntegrity not only optimizes carbon footprint tracking but also signifies a significant stride towards sustainable environmental practices. Our main contribution can be concluded below:

- We developed EcoIntegrity, a three-phase intelligent framework designed to ensure the integrity of IoT-based carbon footprint tracking and monitoring. This framework uniquely integrates AI algorithms, blockchain technology, and an incentive mechanism, providing a comprehensive solution for environmental data integrity.
- Our approach utilizes recurrent neural networks and Local Outlier Factor (LoF) algorithms for the advanced prediction of anomalous activities and carbon emission prediction. This application of AI enhances the system's ability to detect and address data integrity issues effectively.
- We employ blockchain technology for the secure storage of carbon emission and energy consumption data. This not only ensures the safety and reliability of the data but also enhances transparency and traceability within the framework.
- Addressing the collaborative nature of IoT devices in environmental monitoring, we implement the Shapley value-a concept from game theory-to distribute rewards fairly among participating devices. This ensures equitable compensation based on each device's contribution to the task.
- Lastly, the real-world benefits of the EcoIntegrity framework are substantial. It offers a scalable, secure, and efficient solution for carbon footprint tracking, potentially leading to more accurate environmental reporting, enhanced regulatory compliance, and fostering a culture of sustainability and accountability in IoT networks.

The structure of the remainder of this paper is as follows: Sect. 2 presents the related works pertinent to this study. Section 3 details the three phases of the EcoIntegrity framework, elaborating on its design and functionality. Section 5 describes the experimental setup and discusses the results obtained from applying the EcoIntegrity framework. Finally, Sect. 6 concludes the paper, addressing its limitations and outlining potential directions for future research.

2   Related Works

2.1   Advanced Anomaly Detection and Prediction in IoT for Sustainability

This section delves into advanced anomaly detection techniques within the IoT framework, emphasizing their significance for sustainability. Numerous researchers have been developing various algorithms, including those for anomaly detection in IoT, aimed at enhancing sustainability. For instance, Gomez et al. [14] introduced a deep learning-based framework to combat the increasing threat of cyberattacks in industrial sectors, which threaten sustainability efforts. By creating precise anomaly detectors for industrial systems and implementing them in a water treatment facility, they achieved notable recall and precision rates, surpassing previous methods in identifying cyberattacks that affect sustainability. Mohamudally et al. [15] tackled the complexities of implementing Anomaly Detection Engines (ADE) within IoT networks. They assessed various

time series models for instantaneous anomaly detection to boost predictive maintenance and cybersecurity, ultimately favoring unsupervised machine learning as
the most flexible and effective approach for IoT analytics. Singh et al. [16] proposed an adaptive machine learning framework utilizing Principal Component
Analysis (PCA) for anomaly detection in the Oil and Gas industry. This method
significantly reduced carbon emissions by accurately forecasting and analyzing
shutdown events, aiding in achieving climate goals by improving system reliability and operational efficiency. Malik et al. [17] investigated an IoT-based system
for the remote monitoring and control of photovoltaic (PV) installations. They
underscored the integration of AI for anomaly detection and optimization to
boost energy efficiency and reduce carbon emissions in the renewable energy
sector.

Focusing on specific models for anomaly detection, supervised learning models such as Decision Trees, Support Vector Machines (SVM), and Neural Networks are commonly used. These models require labeled data to learn and predict
anomalies. Alloghani [18] reviewed supervised deep learning techniques in IoT
security, particularly assessing their effectiveness in intrusion detection within
smart environments like agriculture, homes, and cities. Due to the occasional
scarcity of labeled data, unsupervised models are also employed in anomaly
detection within IoT. These include Clustering (e.g., K-Means, DBSCAN) and
PCA, suitable for identifying outliers in data without labeled instances. For
example, Habeeb et al. [19] developed a clustering-based algorithm named
Streaming Sliding Window Local Outlier Factor Coreset Clustering Algorithms
(SSWLOFCC) for anomaly detection in IoT technology. Deep neural networks
and recurrent neural networks are effective for analyzing spatial data and time-
series data, common in IoT devices, for predicting and detecting anomalies. Bao-
jao et al. [20] reviewed threat detection algorithms in IoT, focusing on three models: Convolutional Neural Network (CNN), Long Short-Term Memory (LSTM),
and Gated Recurrent Unit (GRU). Also, some researchers employed Generative
Adversarial Networks (GANs) models to identify the anomalies in IoT devices.
For example, Ullah et al. [21] developed a framework that utilizes conditional
GANs (cGANs) to detect anomalies in IoT networks by generating realistic
distributions for given feature sets to address data imbalance issues. This approach used a single class cGAN (ocGAN) to learn minority data classes and a
binary class cGAN (bcGAN) for binary balance dataset augmentation, showing
improved performance in anomaly detection metrics across several IoT datasets.

In reviewing the literature on anomaly detection within IoT systems, it
becomes clear that there is a gap in the application of hybrid algorithms for
enhancing the integrity of carbon footprint records in IoT devices. While considerable work has been done in applying artificial intelligence and machine
learning for anomaly detection, the specific use of hybrid algorithms to improve
the accuracy of carbon footprint data has not been extensively explored.
This gap suggests an opportunity for developing a hybrid model that combines the strengths of multiple algorithms to better monitor and verify carbon
emission data from IoT devices. Addressing this gap is crucial for improving

sustainability efforts and ensuring the accuracy of environmental impact assessments in the IoT domain, which in turn could lead to more effective carbon management strategies.

2.2 Blockchain for IoT Security

In the context of utilizing IoT devices for carbon footprint tracking, as mentioned in some studies [22], the issue of data security within these devices is a persistent challenge. IoT devices are known to collect a vast array of sensitive personal data critical for monitoring carbon footprints. A prime real-world application is smart energy meters, widely used in homes and businesses, which play a key role in monitoring energy consumption and carbon footprint. However, their data security is a pressing issue. Research from Oregon State University revealed that these devices could be hacked to cause power grid instability [23], underscoring the risk of sensitive data exposure that could reveal personal habits and occupancy.

Addressing IoT security challenges, current research increasingly explores the integration of blockchain technology into IoT devices. Blockchain, known for its decentralization, transparency, and immutability, offers a robust solution to enhance data security within IoT ecosystems. Such integration aims to preserve data integrity, providing a secure and transparent framework for data storage and management amidst evolving threats. Yu et al. [24] investigated blockchain's potential to resolve IoT security and privacy concerns, proposing a framework that combines blockchain with IoT to ensure data security and enable features like authentication and decentralized transactions, showcasing blockchain's applicability through practical instances. Tahir et al. [25] developed a blockchain-empowered IoT network tailored for healthcare, introducing a lightweight framework for authentication and authorization that employs random numbers and joint conditional probability to secure IoT device connections. Zhang et al. [26] proposed a blockchain-based security architecture for IoT, aimed at establishing a mutual trust environment among devices to facilitate reliable data exchange, addressing the critical need for a secure communication infrastructure within IoT networks. Moreover, blockchain's application extends to carbon footprint data tracking within IoT. Luo et al. [27] explored IoT's role in the food sector, particularly in reducing carbon emissions through enhanced supply chain transparency, notably in high-impact areas like meat production. Liu et al. [28] introduced a novel framework that combines carbon footprint calculation with blockchain technology, utilizing blockchain as a tool for transparent and secure carbon emission management. Niya et al. [29] presented a distributed system, powered by IoT and blockchain, for automated water and air quality monitoring, employing blockchain to securely store sensor data, thus ensuring the integrity of environmental monitoring data.

While the integration of blockchain technology into IoT devices has been increasingly explored to enhance data security and integrity, the specific focus on employing blockchain to ensure the integrity of carbon footprint tracking in IoT devices presents a notable research gap. This gap is particularly evident when considering the potential for combining blockchain with game theory algorithms and AI to bolster the accuracy and reliability of carbon footprint data. Such an approach would not only address security vulnerabilities but also significantly contribute to the transparency and accuracy of carbon emissions tracking. This innovative combination could provide a robust framework for environmental monitoring and sustainability efforts, offering a new dimension to IoT applications in carbon footprint management.

2.3   Incentive Models in Collaborative IoT Systems

Collaborative IoT systems are pivotal in the realm of carbon footprint tracking, leveraging the interconnectedness of devices to offer a multifaceted view of emissions data. For instance, in smart cities, IoT sensors across transportation, residential, and industrial sectors can collectively monitor and analyze emissions, providing a holistic understanding of the city's environmental impact [30]. Similarly, in agriculture, the collaboration between IoT devices monitoring soil conditions, crop health, and equipment usage can optimize farming practices, reducing unnecessary resource consumption and associated carbon emissions [31–33]. This collaborative approach not only enhances the accuracy of carbon footprint assessments but also fosters targeted and effective sustainability measures, illustrating the critical role of inter-device cooperation in environmental conservation efforts.

However, in collaborative IoT systems aimed at environmental monitoring, ensuring consistent participation is challenging due to diverse stakeholders and technological variability. Incentives are essential here to motivate participants to share data [34], aligning individual contributions with collective environmental objectives and overcoming collaboration barriers, thereby enhancing the system's efficacy in carbon footprint reduction efforts. Several studies have developed incentive mechanisms within collaborative IoT systems to promote fairness and integrity in data sharing, ensuring that contributions are both recognized and secure. Lim et al. [35] proposed a federated learning-based approach with a hierarchical incentive mechanism to address incentive mismatches in mobile crowdsensing, facilitating collaborative machine learning among IoT devices without compromising data privacy. Ferreira et al. [36] developed a collaborative approach using IoT for parking control in cities, employing Bluetooth Low Energy (BLE) beacons and a reward mechanism to incentivize user participation. Yu et al. [37] introduced intelligent algorithms incorporating learning-enabled incentives and coalitional games to encourage resource sharing among IoT devices in 5G networks. Cheng et al. [38] presented a reverse auction-based incentive mechanism integrated with blockchain to motivate IoT managers to collaborate, aiming to minimize and stabilize incentive costs while ensuring privacy. Liu et al. [39,40] introduced a blockchain-based system for verifying education, employment, and skill information, employing a two-stage process with a game-based incentive mechanism to ensure accuracy and participation.

Yin et al. [41] introduced a collaborative sensing model for IoV, utilizing bidding and blockchain for enhanced participation and secure data exchange.

Collaborative IoT systems employ monetary and non-monetary incentives, leveraging game theory algorithms such as Vickrey-Clarke-Groves (VCG) [42], Stackelberg games, second-price auctions, and Shapley values to promote fair and secure data sharing. The VCG mechanism is often applied to maximize social welfare by encouraging truthful bidding [43], while Stackelberg games model the strategic interaction between leaders and followers in the system [44]. Second-price auctions are used to determine the optimal pricing strategy without overcharging [45], and Shapley values are employed to fairly distribute rewards among contributors based on their individual contributions to the collaborative effort [34]. These algorithms play a crucial role in aligning individual incentives with the collective goals of the IoT ecosystem, ensuring equitable participation and contribution.

The integration of IoT in environmental monitoring, especially in carbon footprint tracking, has progressed but faces a significant gap in data integrity and reliability. Current systems often miss a cohesive strategy that merges advanced analytics, secure data handling, and incentives for active engagement and accurate data collection. EcoIntegrity tackles this issue with an innovative framework that blends AI and blockchain, enhanced by a well-designed incentive scheme. AI, with a focus on deep learning and LoF algorithms, bolsters anomaly detection and data integrity, while blockchain provides data security and transparency. EcoIntegrity also introduces a fair incentive model using game theory's Shapley value, addressing the need for cooperative IoT environments in sustainability efforts. EcoIntegrity represents a major step forward in creating scalable, secure IoT systems for carbon tracking, enhancing reporting accuracy, and promoting sustainability within IoT networks.

3   Introduction to EcoIntegrity

The EcoIntegrity framework is structured around three distinct phases, each meticulously crafted to ensure fairness and integrity in monitoring carbon footprints using IoT devices. As illustrated in Fig. 1, the framework begins with the phase of data collection and anomaly detection, followed by the phase where data is stored securely using Blockchain and smart contracts. The final phase involves the distribution of rewards based on incentives, completing the comprehensive approach to environmental monitoring.

Phase 1: The initial stage of the EcoIntegrity framework is devoted to the meticulous acquisition and analysis of carbon emission data from IoT devices. Aimed at constructing an extensive and varied dataset, this phase intricately reflects the operational behaviors and environmental impact of these devices. The strategy for data collection is comprehensive, incorporating an array of sensors and techniques that extend from direct emission measurements to indirect evaluations based on usage patterns and energy consumption. Following data collection, the EcoIntegrity framework employs LOF algorithms to discern anomalies within the dataset-data points that markedly diverge from established patterns. Such outliers may reveal operational inefficiencies, like heightened energy usage

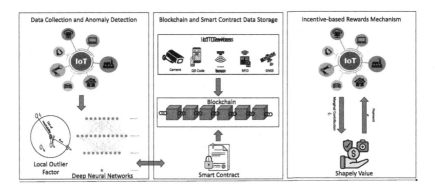

Fig. 1. Overview of EcoIntegrity

or irregular usage patterns, or suggest possible device malfunctions that could erroneously elevate reported emissions. In tandem, RNNs, such as LSTM, recognized for their proficiency in processing sequential and time-series data, are utilized for behavior analysis of IoT devices. LSTM is particularly effective for predicting future emissions based on historical patterns, thereby contributing to a deeper understanding of device behavior over time. This dual-analytic approach serves not only to identify irregularities in emission reporting but also to bolster the cybersecurity aspects of the framework. Through the continuous analysis of data, LSTM aids in detecting signs of security compromises or unauthorized intrusions, enhancing the protective measures of the system, and ensuring the integrity of the data collection phase.

Phase 2: In the transition to the second phase, the EcoIntegrity framework shifts its focus from the initial collection of data to its strategic management and storage, leveraging the core attributes of blockchain technology: decentralization, transparency, and immutability. This phase is fundamentally about securing the integrity and accessibility of the carbon emission data and the insights gleaned during the anomaly detection stage. The decentralized nature of blockchain eliminates central points of failure, thereby enhancing the resilience and reliability of the data storage system. The transparency inherent in blockchain technology allows for every transaction and data entry to be visible to all participants in the network, subject to privacy controls. The immutability of blockchain ensures that once data or a transaction has been recorded, it cannot be altered retroactively. Smart contracts play a pivotal role in this phase, acting as self-executing contracts with the terms of the agreement directly written into lines of code. These contracts autonomously enforce and execute the predefined rules and operations, such as data storage protocols and access permissions. In the context of EcoIntegrity, smart contracts are used to store not only the raw and analyzed emission data but also the algorithms and parameters defining baseline behaviors and operational norms. This codification into the blockchain ensures that the methodologies used for emission monitoring and anomaly detection are transparent, consistent, and tamper-proof. IoT devices first register with the central authority, undergoing authentication via asymmetric cryptography to ensure secure communication. Following registration, devices either directly report carbon emissions using onboard sensors or estimate emissions based on operational data. This emission information is then encrypted using the device's private key for authenticity. For secure and private storage on the blockchain, emission data is hashed and accompanied by a zero-knowledge proof (ZKP), allowing devices to prove data validity without revealing the actual data. This process ensures that emission reporting and storage are both secure and privacy-preserving, leveraging cryptographic techniques to maintain data integrity and confidentiality within the blockchain-based EcoIntegrity framework.

Phase 3: EcoIntegrity's final phase embodies the essence of the platform's commitment to environmental integrity by leveraging the Shapley value, a sophisticated concept from cooperative game theory, to establish a transparent and equitable reward mechanism. This meticulous approach evaluates the contributions of IoT devices towards reducing the carbon footprint, taking into account not only direct emission reductions but also efficiency improvements and the implementation of sustainable operational practices. Each device's contribution is quantitatively assessed, ensuring that rewards are allocated in a manner that accurately reflects the device's impact on environmental sustainability. The integrity of the EcoIntegrity system is further upheld by the transparent application of the Shapley value, which ensures that the reward distribution is not only fair but also based on a clear and logical assessment of each device's marginal contribution to the collective goal of carbon footprint reduction. This methodical approach to reward allocation underlines the system's dedication to fairness, encouraging broader adoption of sustainable practices among IoT device operators. By integrating the Shapley value, EcoIntegrity not only incentivizes eco-friendly behavior but also establishes a framework where the integrity of contributions and rewards is paramount. This fosters trust among participants, ensuring that the system remains robust, transparent, and focused on its core mission of promoting environmental sustainability through technological innovation.

4   Formulation of EcoIntegrity

In the foundational phase of the EcoIntegrity framework, the dataset D is constructed from data points d_i, where $i = 1, 2, \ldots, n$, and n represents the total number of data points collected from IoT devices. Each data point d_i can be represented as a tuple containing emissions data, usage patterns, and power consumption metrics, denoted as $d_i = (e_i, u_i, p_i)$. The data collection integrates a range of sensors S and methodologies M, leading to a comprehensive dataset:

$$D = \bigcup_{j=1}^{s} S_j \cup \bigcup_{k=1}^{m} M_k$$

where s is the number of sensors and m is the number of methodologies employed. Upon aggregation, the dataset D undergoes analysis through LoF algorithms and

LSTM models. The LoF algorithm identifies anomalies by calculating the local density deviation of a given data point d_i with respect to its neighbors. The anomaly score, $A(d_i)$, for each data point is given by:

$$A(d_i) = \text{LoF}(d_i, \text{Neighbors}(d_i))$$

where $\text{Neighbors}(d_i)$ represents the neighboring data points of d_i. Parallelly, LSTM models are employed to uncover complex patterns within the dataset D. The function f_{LSTM} represents the LSTM model that maps input data points to an output space that highlights intricate patterns and correlations:

$$f_{LSTM} : d_i \mapsto o_i.$$

where o_i represents the output indicating patterns, correlations, or features identified by the LSTM model from data point d_i. This dual-layered analytical approach ensures a robust examination of the IoT devices' emissions data, enhancing the framework's ability to detect deviations and potential cybersecurity threats within the dataset D. The LOF-LSTM model within EcoIntegrity, outlined in Algorithm 1, serves dual functions: it detects anomalies in IoT carbon emissions data and predicts irregular activities. Initially, LOF identifies outliers by assessing local density variations, highlighting potential inefficiencies. Then, the LSTM component, proficient in handling time-series data, predicts future anomalies by learning from both standard and atypical patterns. This combination enhances EcoIntegrity's ability to proactively manage environmental impacts, improving the sustainability of IoT devices.

Transitioning into Phase 2, the EcoIntegrity framework shifts its focus towards the strategic management and secure storage of carbon emission data, leveraging the inherent strengths of blockchain technology such as decentralization, transparency, and immutability. This phase is characterized by a series of key formalizations, each building upon the last to create a robust and secure data management system. At the heart of Phase 2 lies the seamless integration of blockchain technology, signified by:

- A blockchain $B = \{b_1, b_2, \ldots, b_n\}$, with each block b_i serving as a repository for a set of transactions T_i.
- Transactions $t \in T_i$, each encapsulating vital emission data or insights, are meticulously structured as $t = \{\text{data}, \text{signature}, \text{timestamp}\}$, ensuring clarity and traceability.

Building on the foundation of blockchain integration, the framework enhances $\text{Visibility}(t) \forall t \in T_i$ within each block $b_i \in B$, promoting unparalleled transparency and accessibility to all network participants. A cornerstone of blockchain technology, immutability, is rigorously enforced through:

$$\text{Hash}(b_i) = \text{Hash}(\text{PrevHash}(b_{i-1}) + \text{Hash}(T_i) + \text{Nonce}), \tag{1}$$

ensuring that once data is recorded, it becomes an immutable part of the blockchain. Further fortifying Phase 2 are smart contracts, denoted as SC, which

Algorithm 1. Advanced Integrated LOF-LSTM Model for Anomaly Detection and Carbon Emission Prediction

1: **Input:** Time-series dataset $D = \{d_1, d_2, \ldots, d_n\}$, where $d_i = (e_i, u_i, p_i)$ represents emissions, usage, and power data
2: **Output:** Anomaly scores $\text{LOF}_k(d_i)$ and LSTM-based insights
3: **procedure** ENHANCEDLOF(D, k)
4:     **for** $i = 1$ to n **do**
5:         Compute k-distance: $d_k(d_i) = \min\{d(d_i, d_j)|d_j \in N_k(d_i) \setminus \{d_i\}\}$
6:         **for** each $d_j \in N_k(d_i)$ **do**
7:             Compute reachability distance: $rd_k(d_i, d_j) = \max\{d_k(d_j), d(d_i, d_j)\}$
8:         **end for**
9:         Compute LRD: $\text{LRD}_k(d_i) = \left(\frac{1}{|N_k(d_i)|} \sum_{d_j \in N_k(d_i)} rd_k(d_i, d_j)\right)^{-1}$
10:         Compute LOF score: $\text{LOF}_k(d_i) = \frac{1}{|N_k(d_i)|} \sum_{d_j \in N_k(d_i)} \frac{\text{LRD}_k(d_j)}{\text{LRD}_k(d_i)}$
11:     **end for**
12: **end procedure**
13: **procedure** ADVANCEDLSTM(D)
14:     Initialize LSTM parameters Θ
15:     **for** each time step $t = 1$ to T **do**
16:         Compute the forget gate: $f_t = \sigma(W_f \cdot [h_{t-1}, d_t] + b_f)$
17:         Compute the input gate: $i_t = \sigma(W_i \cdot [h_{t-1}, d_t] + b_i)$
18:         Compute the cell candidate: $\tilde{C}_t = \tanh(W_C \cdot [h_{t-1}, d_t] + b_C)$
19:         Compute the cell state: $C_t = f_t * C_{t-1} + i_t * \tilde{C}_t$
20:         Compute the output gate: $o_t = \sigma(W_o \cdot [h_{t-1}, d_t] + b_o)$
21:         Compute the new hidden state: $h_t = o_t * \tanh(C_t)$
22:     **end for**
23:     **return** Hidden states h_t and cell states C_t as LSTM-based insights for each time step
24: **end procedure**
25: **Combine** insights from ENHANCEDLOF and ADVANCEDLSTM for a comprehensive environmental impact analysis

act as self-executing contracts with predefined rules and operations, encapsulating data storage protocols and access permissions within immutable lines of code. A pivotal aspect of Phase 2 involves:

$$\text{DeviceKeyPair} = (\text{PublicKey}, \text{PrivateKey}), \tag{2}$$

facilitating secure communication and authentication of IoT devices within the framework.

$$\text{Signature} = \text{Sign}(\text{PrivateKey}, \text{Data}), \tag{3}$$

ensuring the authenticity and integrity of the transmitted data. To round off Phase 2, the framework employs advanced cryptographic techniques to ensure data privacy and security, including:

$$\text{EncryptedData} = \text{Encrypt}(\text{PublicKey}, \text{Data}) \tag{4}$$

These interconnected formalizations coalesce to ensure that Phase 2 of the EcoIntegrity framework not only adheres to the principles of blockchain technology but also advances the framework's mission to secure the integrity and confidentiality of carbon emission data through sophisticated cryptographic techniques.

In the final phase of the EcoIntegrity framework, the essence of the platform's commitment to environmental integrity is captured through the application of the Shapley value, a concept derived from cooperative game theory. This phase is characterized by the following formulation: Given a set of IoT devices $N = \{1, 2, \ldots, n\}$ and a characteristic function $v : 2^N \to \mathbb{R}$ that assigns a total value to each coalition of devices, the Shapley value for device i is given by:

$$\psi_i(M) = \sum_{S \subseteq N \setminus \{i\}} \frac{|S|!(n - |S| - 1)!}{n!} (M(S \cup \{i\}) - M(S)) \tag{5}$$

where:

- S is a subset of N not containing device i.
- $|S|$ denotes the number of devices in subset S.
- $M(S \cup \{i\}) - M(S)$ represents the incremental contribution of device i to the monitoring and tracking effectiveness of the coalition S.

This formulation ensures that the reward for each IoT device is proportional to its marginal contribution to the collective goal of reducing the carbon footprint, considering both direct emission reductions and efficiency improvements.

The effectiveness of each IoT device in monitoring and tracking carbon footprint is quantitatively evaluated based on a blend of emission data accuracy, operational efficiency, and adherence to data reporting standards, formalized as:

$$M_i = \alpha A_i + \beta(1 - O_i) + \gamma R_i \tag{6}$$

where:

- M_i is the monitoring effectiveness score of device i.
- A_i quantifies the accuracy of the emission data captured by device i.
- O_i is the operational downtime rate of device i, with $1 - O_i$ indicating operational efficiency.
- R_i denotes the device's adherence to reporting standards and frequency for device i.
- α, β, γ are weighting coefficients that signify the relative importance of each aspect in the overall effectiveness.

The integration of the Shapley value ensures that the EcoIntegrity framework not only incentivizes eco-friendly behavior but also establishes a fair and transparent system for rewarding contributions, thereby fostering trust and encouraging the broader adoption of sustainable practices. Algorithm 2 illustrates how the Shapley Value algorithm strengthens EcoIntegrity by ensuring each IoT device's contributions to carbon tracking are assessed fairly and transparently. It deters data manipulation by evaluating each device's impact in different network setups, thus enhancing collective data reliability. This method fosters trust and cooperation within the IoT ecosystem by quantitatively acknowledging contributions to improved monitoring, aligning with the framework's goal of precise environmental data oversight.

Algorithm 2. Shapley Value Calculation for IoT Payments

1: **Input:** Set $N = \{1, \dots, n\}$, Effectiveness M
2: **Output:** Shapley ψ_i for each $i \in N$
3: **procedure** SHAPLEYVALUES(N, M)
4:     **for** $i \in N$ **do**
5:         $\psi_i \leftarrow 0$
6:         **for all** $S \subseteq N \setminus \{i\}$ **do**
7:            $MC \leftarrow M(S \cup \{i\}) - M(S)$
8:            $\psi_i \leftarrow \psi_i + \frac{|S|! \cdot (n-|S|-1)!}{n!} \cdot MC$
9:         **end for**
10:    **end for**
11:    **return** $\{\psi_i\}_{i=1}^{n}$
12: **end procedure**

We present a mathematical proof to demonstrate that the Shapley value serves as an effective incentive mechanism ensuring fairness and integrity in the context of IoT devices monitoring and tracking carbon footprints. The Shapley value is defined by four key properties, as outlined below [34]:

Property 1 (Efficiency). Efficiency in Shapley value allocation ensures that the total effectiveness is fully distributed:

$$\sum_{i \in N} \psi_i = M(N)$$

Property 2 (Symmetry). It ensures equal rewards for equal contributions. If $M(S \cup \{i\}) = M(S \cup \{j\})$ for any $S \subseteq N \setminus \{i, j\}$, then $\psi_i = \psi_j$.

Property 3 (Dummy Player). A device i with no marginal contributions ($M(S \cup \{i\}) = M(S)$ for all $S \subseteq N \setminus \{i\}$) receives $\psi_i = 0$, ensuring integrity by not rewarding non-contributory devices.

Property 4 (Additivity). For any two effectiveness functions M_1 and M_2, the Shapley value satisfies $\psi_i(M_1 + M_2) = \psi_i(M_1) + \psi_i(M_2)$ for all $i \in N$. This property ensures that the Shapley value behaves consistently across different monitoring scenarios or combined effectiveness measures, reinforcing the integrity of the incentive mechanism.

Theorem 1. *Shapley values ψ_i ensure fairness and integrity in distributing rewards among IoT devices in N based on their contributions to the network's effectiveness M.*

Proof. The properties of efficiency, symmetry, dummy player, and additivity ensure that rewards are distributed fairly and in proportion to the actual contributions, maintaining fairness and integrity in the reward system.

5   Experiments and Results

5.1   Anomaly Detection and Carbon Emission Prediction

For Phase 1, our experimental design aims to demonstrate the advantages of the hybrid model, particularly in enhancing anomaly detection and the performance of carbon emission predictions through the integration of LOF algorithms.

Dataset Description: The dataset utilized is the publicly available Environmental Sensor Telemetry Dataset, sourced from Kaggle.com [46]. The dataset under examination was generated by an intricate network of three identical, custom-engineered sensor arrays, each linked to a Raspberry Pi device. These arrays, embodying the essence of IoT technology, were strategically positioned across diverse environmental settings to capture a broad spectrum of data. Specifically, the deployment locations included an area characterized by stable, cooler, and more humid conditions, a second locale subject to highly fluctuating temperature and humidity levels, and a third setting known for its consistently warmer and drier atmosphere. The IoT devices, were distinguishable by three unique devices and meticulously recorded seven distinct types of sensor data, encompassing temperature, humidity, carbon monoxide (CO), liquid petroleum gas (LPG), smoke, light, and motion metrics. The comprehensive dataset, spanning a week from July 12, 2020, to July 19, 2020, encompasses a total of 405,184 data entries. Each data record was meticulously timestamped and transmitted as a single MQTT message payload, adhering to the ISO-standardized Message Queuing Telemetry Transport (MQTT) network protocol.

Experiments Design and Discussion: In our first experiment of Phase 1, we embarked on a detailed investigation of environmental sensor data, leveraging the LOF algorithm to identify anomalies across three IoT devices. In our analysis, the LOF algorithm was meticulously configured with specific parameters to optimize its performance for detecting anomalies within the IoT sensor data. The parameter "$n_{neighbors}$" set at 20, was chosen to define the number of neighboring points considered when calculating the local density deviation of a given data point, thus balancing sensitivity to local anomalies against the broader data context. Additionally, the "contamination" parameter was set to 0.1, indicating an estimated proportion of outliers in the data, guiding the LOF algorithm in thresholding anomaly scores. This careful parameterization of the LOF model was pivotal in tailoring the anomaly detection process to the nuanced characteristics of the environmental sensor dataset, ensuring both precision and reliability in identifying data points that deviated significantly from established patterns.

Figures 2a, 2b, and 2c show the anomalies and normal activities for each IoT device, delineating normal data points in green, symbolizing standard environmental readings, and anomalies in red, highlighting deviations from the norm.

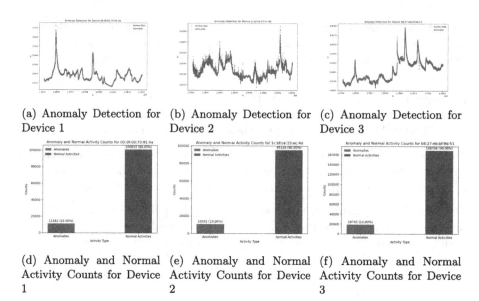

(a) Anomaly Detection for Device 1   (b) Anomaly Detection for Device 2   (c) Anomaly Detection for Device 3

(d) Anomaly and Normal Activity Counts for Device 1   (e) Anomaly and Normal Activity Counts for Device 2   (f) Anomaly and Normal Activity Counts for Device 3

Fig. 2. Anomaly detection results and activity counts for three devices (Color figure online)

These visualizations provided an intuitive understanding of the data's distribution and the LOF algorithm's effectiveness in isolating outliers. From these figures, we found that Device 1, situated in stable, cooler, and more humid conditions, shows distinct peaks where anomalies were detected. Device 2, exposed to highly variable temperatures and humidity, presents a more frequent occurrence of anomalies, reflecting the unstable environmental conditions. Device b8:27:eb:bf:9d:51, operating in warmer and drier conditions, shows fewer anomalies than Device 3, indicating more stable conditions but still with noticeable deviations at specific instances. Figures 2d, 2e, and 2f show the count of normal and anomalous readings captured over the experimental period. Each device shows a consistent pattern where approximately 90% of the data is classified as normal and 10% as anomalies. This consistency underlines the LOF algorithm's ability to discern and maintain a proportionate detection rate across varying environments. The findings suggest that the LOF algorithm is effectively identifying deviations in sensor data that could potentially skew the accuracy of subsequent CO emission predictions.

To verify the hybrid model is better than using LSTM to predict the carbon emission directly, we conducted our second experiment in Phase 1. Our experimental design was meticulously crafted to assess the performance of an LSTM neural network in predicting CO emissions from IoT devices, both before and after the application of the LOF anomaly detection. The dataset was normalized using MinMaxScaler to scale the features, including humidity, light, LPG, motion, smoke, temperature, and CO levels, to a uniform range between 0 and

1, enhancing the model's ability to learn from the data effectively. For the LSTM architecture, we employed a sequential model with two LSTM layers, each consisting of 50 units. The first LSTM layer was designed to return sequences, setting the stage for the second LSTM layer to capture long-term dependencies. This design choice was pivotal in recognizing patterns over sequences of 10-time steps, reflective of the temporal nature of environmental data. The model was compiled with the Adam optimizer and mean squared error loss function, indicative of the emphasis on minimizing prediction errors. Figure 4a illustrates the comparative analysis of Root Mean Square Error (RMSE) values for three distinct IoT devices before and after the application of the LOF for anomaly detection. Prior to implementing LOF, the RMSE values for the devices were significantly higher, indicating a less accurate model for CO emissions prediction. Specifically, Device 1 exhibited an RMSE of 4.56, Device 2 was at 5.54, and Device 3 showed a value of 2.66, reflecting considerable prediction error. Post-LOF application, a substantial decrease in RMSE values across all devices was observed, suggesting a notable enhancement in the predictive accuracy of the LSTM model. This substantial reduction in RMSE underscores the effectiveness of integrating LOF as a preprocessing step to eliminate outliers that can potentially skew the predictive performance of machine learning models.

5.2   Blockchain and Smart Contract Data Storage

In this Phase, the dataset we used is simulated. We use Python to simulate a local blockchain environment. The object of the first experiment in this Phase is to evaluate the efficiency of blockchain storage for IoT carbon footprint data and the integrity of the data once it's stored on the blockchain. For our simulation, we deployed a custom class representing the smart contract and another encapsulating the blockchain's functionality. We simulated IoT devices transmitting data in varying sizes, ranging from 10 to 100 individual readings per transaction, to mimic the variable loads expected in a real-world scenario. Each "transaction" consisted of randomly generated data representing carbon emissions readings. The LOF was configured with 20 neighbors and a contamination factor of 0.1 to filter out anomalies before storage, representing pre-validation efforts. We tracked the latency from data transmission to confirmation on the blockchain, the transaction throughput to determine the system's capacity, and the simulated gas costs for each transaction to estimate operational expenses.

Figure 3a depicts a linear increase in gas costs with the transaction size, indicating that as the volume of data in a single transaction increases, so does the cost of processing that transaction. This is expected in blockchain networks where larger data payloads require more computational resources to validate and record. Figure 3b shows an upward trend in transaction latency as the size of the transaction grows. This suggests that larger transactions take longer to be confirmed on the blockchain, which is consistent with the need for more extensive validation processes that come with increased data size. Figure 3c presents a decrease in transaction throughput as the transaction size increases. This inverse relationship highlights the trade-off between data granularity and system performance; while larger packets of data provide more detailed information per transaction, they also slow down the overall rate at which the system can process transactions. These findings collectively provide valuable insights into the scalability and cost-effectiveness of blockchain solutions for IoT environmental data management. They underscore the need for optimizing the balance between transaction size, cost, and latency to ensure a sustainable and efficient blockchain framework for large-scale IoT data integration.

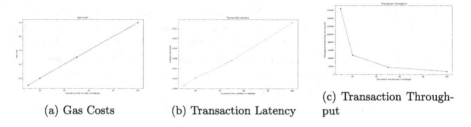

(a) Gas Costs   (b) Transaction Latency   (c) Transaction Through-put

Fig. 3. Blockchain performance metrics: Gas costs, latency, and throughput

5.3   Shapley Value-Based Rewards Distribution

In this phase, the experiment is meticulously crafted to demonstrate the equity of the Shapley Value mechanism. The core objective is to validate Shapley Value as an equitable incentive model that motivates IoT devices to contribute effectively to carbon footprint monitoring within our proposed framework. The initial experiment is structured to evaluate the monitoring efficacy of three distinct IoT devices, each with unique operational characteristics. The devices were chosen based on their diverse performance metrics to simulate real-world scenarios. This experimental setup allows us to explore the nuances of how the Shapley Value can serve as a fair and incentivizing tool for IoT devices engaged in environmental sustainability efforts. The effectiveness score for each device, denoted as M_i, is calculated using the formula:

$$M_i = \alpha A_i + \beta(1 - O_i) + \gamma R_i$$

where A_i represents the accuracy of emission data, O_i denotes operational downtime, and R_i signifies adherence to reporting standards. The coefficients α, β, and γ are set to 1, indicating equal importance of all factors. The devices were characterized as follows to reflect realistic operational conditions:

- **Device 1:** Exhibited high accuracy ($A_i \approx 1.0$), minimal downtime ($O_i \approx 0$), and strong adherence to reporting standards ($R_i \approx 1.0$), making it highly effective in environmental monitoring.

– **Device 2:** Demonstrated moderate levels across all parameters $(A_i, 1 - O_i, R_i \approx 0.9)$, indicating average effectiveness.
– **Device 3:** Showed lower accuracy $(A_i \approx 0.8)$, higher downtime $(O_i \approx 0.2)$, and reduced adherence to reporting standards $(R_i \approx 0.8)$, marking it as the least effective among the three.

This structured approach allows for a comprehensive comparison of the devices' capabilities in monitoring environmental data, which is visually represented through effectiveness scores in the results section. Figure 4b illustrates the monitoring effectiveness scores for these three distinct IoT devices. Device 1's highest effectiveness score of 3.0 can be attributed to its high data accuracy, almost negligible downtime, and strong adherence to reporting standards. These characteristics render Device 1 exceptionally reliable and efficient in environmental monitoring tasks, underlining its suitability for scenarios where precision and continuous operation are critical. Device 2 with an effectiveness score of 2.7, presents a case of balanced operational parameters. Its moderate accuracy, downtime, and adherence to reporting standards (all parameters approximately 0.9) suggest that the effectiveness score is slightly lower than Device 1. Device 3, which scored 2.4 is the lowest among the three devices. Secondly, we explored the allocation of a fixed budget across three IoT devices engaged in carbon footprint tracking, employing three distinct distribution methods: Shapley Value, Equal Distribution, and Random Distribution. The Shapley Value method allocates the budget based on each device's marginal contribution to the collective effort, ensuring a fair distribution that acknowledges individual contributions. Equal Distribution, in contrast, divides the budget equally among all devices, disregarding their individual contributions. The Random Distribution method introduces an element of unpredictability by allocating the budget in random proportions to each device, without consideration for their contributions, ensuring only that the total allocation does not exceed the predefined budget. The experiment's objective was to compare these methods in terms of how they distribute limited resources among participating entities, illustrating the implications of each method on fairness, efficiency, and incentive mechanisms within a collaborative IoT environment. The total budget for this experiment was set at 8.1 units, chosen to demonstrate the allocation dynamics under a constrained resource scenario. Figure 4c displays the budget allocation across three distribution methods. Under the Shapley Value method, the distribution appears fair, reflecting the marginal contributions of each device with allocations of 3.00, 2.70, and 2.40 respectively. This aligns with the principle of Shapley Value, which ensures that each player (device) is rewarded according to their contribution to the total effectiveness. Equal Distribution method allocates an identical budget of 2.70 to each device, disregarding their individual contributions. This approach, while simple, does not account for the differences in the devices' performances or their contributions to monitoring effectiveness. Random Distribution introduces an element of variability, allocating budgets of 2.66, 2.33, and 3.11 to the devices. This method, as indicated by the name, does not follow a predictable

pattern and can result in allocations that may not correspond to the devices'
effectiveness or contributions.

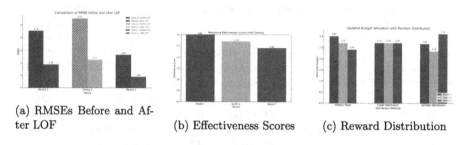

(a) RMSEs Before and Af-
ter LOF

(b) Effectiveness Scores   (c) Reward Distribution

Fig. 4. Experiments Results among Three Random Devices

6   Conclusion

In our research, we introduce "EcoIntegrity," an AI-enhanced blockchain framework tailored for tracking the carbon footprint within an IoT ecosystem. This
innovative framework unfolds in three distinct but cohesive phases, each designed
to harness the capabilities of IoT devices for reliable and accurate carbon footprint monitoring. The first phase leverages artificial intelligence, utilizing LoF
algorithms and recurrent neural networks to detect anomalous behavior in IoT
device activity. Concurrently, LSTM is applied to predict behavioral patterns of
IoT devices, such as carbon emissions, ensuring a proactive approach to environmental impact assessment. In the second phase, we integrate blockchain technology and smart contracts to ensure that the recorded carbon footprint data
are preserved in an immutable, transparent, and secure ledger. This phase is
pivotal in maintaining the credibility of the data by preventing alterations and
providing a clear audit trail. The final phase focuses on incentivization. Recognizing the necessity for IoT devices to engage in carbon footprint reporting
actively, we incorporate an incentive mechanism. Here, the Shapley Value, a
concept derived from game theory, is utilized to ensure equitable and integrity-
driven distribution of rewards. This approach not only stimulates participation
but also upholds fairness and integrity in the recognition of each device's contribution to the network. "EcoIntegrity" stands out as a robust application that
empowers IoT devices to track their environmental impact, embodying principles
of truthfulness and integrity throughout the process.

    One limitation of our current research lies in the utilization of simulated
and public data for the experimental phases. While simulations provide valuable insights and a controlled environment to test our hypotheses, they cannot
fully replicate the intricacies and unpredictable nature of real-world data. Consequently, the findings and efficacy of the "EcoIntegrity" framework, as they
stand, are provisional and subject to the variances that actual IoT device data

would present. To bridge this gap, future work will involve deploying our framework in a real-world setting, where data from physical IoT devices will be used to further validate and refine our model. This progression will allow us to confront practical challenges, adapt to real-time data complexities, and evaluate the framework's performance in a live environment, ultimately enhancing its reliability and applicability.

Funding. This research was funded by the National Key Research and Development Program of China under Grant No. 2023YFB2704400.

References

1. Codur, A.-M., Harris, J.M., Feriz, M.B.: Forests and climate: Economics and policy issues
2. Intergovernmental Panel on Climate Change. Climate change 2021: The physical science basis (2021). https://www.ipcc.ch/report/ar6/wg1/
3. Microsoft. Microsoft's sustainability commitment (2021). https://www.microsoft.com/en-us/sustainability
4. Nielsen: Sustainable shoppers buy the change they wish to see in the world. Nielsen Insights (2020). https://www.nielsen.com/insights
5. Ellerman, A.D., Marcantonini, C., Zaklan, A.: The European union emissions trading system: ten years and counting. Rev. Environ. Econ. Policy (2016)
6. International Energy Agency. Global energy review 2020 (2020). https://www.iea.org/reports/global-energy-review-2020
7. Pedersen, J.L., Bey, N., Friis Gerholt, S., Rohde, R.: The road towards carbon neutrality in the different Nordic countries. Nordic Council of Ministers (2020)
8. Chakravarthi, P.K., Yuvaraj, D., Venkataramanan, V.: Iot-based smart energy meter for smart grids. In: 6th International Conference on Devices, Circuits and Systems (ICDCS). IEEE vol. 2022, pp. 360–363 (2022)
9. Faize, Y., Crenne, J., Hanusse, N., Jego, C.: An energy efficient and scalable node architecture for sensor network. In: 19th IEEE International New Circuits and Systems Conference (NEWCAS), vol. 2021, pp. 1–4. IEEE (2021)
10. M. P. Kokare and S. Pawar, "Energy monitoring system in electric grids: the role of advanced intelligent and iot for future electric grid," in *2020 International Conference on Emerging Trends in Information Technology and Engineering (ic-ETITE)*. IEEE, 2020, pp. 1–4
11. Ionescu, L., Mazare, A., Ionescu, N., Lita, A.: Energy consumption monitoring using private blockchain network based on ethereum smart contracts. In: IEEE 28th International Symposium for Design and Technology in Electronic Packaging (SIITME), vol. 2022, pp. 132–135. IEEE (2022)
12. Hamidu, I., Afotey, B., Ayatul-Lahi, Z.: Design and development of a low-cost sensor IoT computing device for greenhouse gas Momitor from selected industry locations. Scalable Comput. Pract. Experien. **23**(4), 363–376 (2022)
13. Kambourakis, G., Kolias, C., Stavrou, A.: The MIRAI botnet and the IoT zombie armies. In: MILCOM 2017-2017 IEEE Military Communications Conference (MILCOM), pp. 267–272. IEEE (2017)
14. Gómez, Á.L.P., Maimó, L.F., Celdrán, A.H., Clemente, F.J.G.: Susan: a deep learning based anomaly detection framework for sustainable industry. Sustain. Comput. Inform. Syst. **37**, 100842 (2023)

15. Mohamudally, N., Peermamode-Mohaboob, M.: Building an anomaly detection engine (ADE) for IoT smart applications. Procedia Comput. Sci. **134**, 10–17 (2018)
16. Singh, A., Miller, S., Brinkley, M.: Lowering carbon foot-print by increasing operational efficiency using adaptive machine learning. In: SPE Annual Technical Conference and Exhibition? SPE, p. D031S057R005 (2022)
17. Malik, A., Haque, A., Kurukuru, V.B.: IoT-based monitoring and management for photovoltaic system. In: Fault Analysis and its Impact on Grid-connected Photovoltaic Systems Performance, pp. 291–318 (2022)
18. Alloghani, M.A.: Anomaly detection of energy consumption in cloud computing and buildings using artificial intelligence as a tool of sustainability: a systematic review of current trends, applications, and challenges. In: Artificial Intelligence and Sustainability, pp. 177–210 (2023)
19. Ariyaluran Habeeb, R.A., et al.: Clustering-based real-time anomaly detection— a breakthrough in big data technologies. Trans. Emerging Telecommun. Technol. **33**(8), e3647 (2022)
20. Bajao, N.A., Sarucam, J.-A.: Threats detection in the internet of things using convolutional neural networks, long short-term memory, and gated recurrent units. Mesopotamian J. Cybersecur. **2023**, 22–29 (2023)
21. Ullah, I., Mahmoud, Q.H.: A framework for anomaly detection in IoT networks using conditional generative adversarial networks. IEEE Access **9**, 165 907-165 931 (2021)
22. Popli, S., Jha, R.K., Jain, S.: A survey on energy efficient narrowband internet of things (nbiot): architecture, application and challenges. IEEE Access **7**, 16 739-16 776 (2018)
23. Alanazi, F., Kim, J., Cotilla-Sanchez, E.: Load oscillating attacks of smart grids: vulnerability analysis. IEEE Access (2023)
24. Yu, Y., Li, Y., Tian, J., Liu, J.: Blockchain-based solutions to security and privacy issues in the internet of things. IEEE Wirel. Commun. **25**, 12–18 (2018)
25. Tahir, M., Sardaraz, M., Muhammad, S., Khan, M.S.: A lightweight authentication and authorization framework for blockchain-enabled IoT network in health-informatics. Sustainability **12**, 6960 (2020)
26. Zhang, H., Lang, W., Liu, C., Zhang, B.: A blockchain-based security approach architecture for the internet of things. In: 2020 IEEE 4th Information Technology, Networking. Electronic and Automation Control Conference (ITNEC), vol. 1, pp. 310–313 (2020)
27. Luo, Z., et al.: Application of the IoT in the food supply chain: from the perspective of carbon mitigation. Environ. Sci. Technol. **56**(15), 10 567-10 576 (2022)
28. Liu, K.-H., Chang, S.-F., Huang, W.-H., Lu, I.-C.: The framework of the integration of carbon footprint and blockchain: using blockchain as a carbon emission management tool. In: Hu, A.H., Matsumoto, M., Kuo, T.C., Smith, S. (eds.) Technologies and Eco-innovation towards Sustainability I, pp. 15–22. Springer, Singapore (2019). https://doi.org/10.1007/978-981-13-1181-9_2
29. Niya, S.R., Jha, S.S., Bocek, T., Stiller, B.: Design and implementation of an automated and decentralized pollution monitoring system with blockchains, smart contracts, and Lorawan. In: NOMS 2018 - 2018 IEEE/IFIP Network Operations and Management Symposium, pp. 1–4 (2018)
30. Alsamhi, S., Ma, O., Ansari, M.S., Almalki, F.A.: Survey on collaborative smart drones and internet of things for improving smartness of smart cities. IEEE Access **7**, 128 125-128 152 (2019)

31. Mahalakshmi, J., Kuppusamy, K., Kaleeswari, C., Maheswari, P.: IoT sensor-based smart agricultural system. In: Subramanian, B., Chen, S.-S., Reddy, K.R. (eds.) Emerging Technologies for Agriculture and Environment. LNMIE, pp. 39–52. Springer, Singapore (2020). https://doi.org/10.1007/978-981-13-7968-0_4

32. Elijah, O., Rahman, T.A., Orikumhi, I., Leow, C., Hindia, M.N.: An overview of internet of things (IoT) and data analytics in agriculture: benefits and challenges. IEEE Internet Things J. **5**, 3758–3773 (2018)

33. Liu, L., Han, M.: Weatherpon: a weather and machine learning-based coupon recommendation mechanism in digital marketing. In: 2023 IEEE 3rd International Conference on Software Engineering and Artificial Intelligence (SEAI), pp. 28–32. IEEE (2023)

34. Liu, L., Kong, Y., Li, G., Han, M.: Fairshare: an incentive-based fairness-aware data sharing framework for federated learning. In: Yang, H., et al. (eds.) ICIRA 2023. LNCS, vol. 14268, pp. 115–126. Springer, Singapore (2023). https://doi.org/10.1007/978-981-99-6486-4_10

35. Lim, W.Y.B., et al.: Hierarchical incentive mechanism design for federated machine learning in mobile networks. IEEE Internet Things J. **7**, 9575–9588 (2020)

36. Ferreira, J., Martins, A.: Ad hoc IoT approach for monitoring parking control process, pp. 113–121, (2017)

37. Yu, L., Li, Z., Liu, J., Zhou, R.: Resources sharing in 5g networks: learning-enabled incentives and coalitional games. IEEE Syst. J. **15**, 226–237 (2021)

38. Cheng, G., Deng, S., Xiang, Z., Chen, Y., Yin, J.: An auction-based incentive mechanism with blockchain for IoT collaboration. In: 2020 IEEE International Conference on Web Services (ICWS), pp. 17–26 (2020)

39. Liu, L., Han, M., Zhou, Y., Parizi, R.M., Korayem, M.: Blockchain-based certification for education, employment, and skill with incentive mechanism. In: Choo, K.-K.R., Dehghantanha, A., Parizi, R.M. (eds.) Blockchain Cybersecurity, Trust and Privacy. AIS, vol. 79, pp. 269–290. Springer, Cham (2020). https://doi.org/10.1007/978-3-030-38181-3_14

40. Liu, L., Han, M., Zhou, Y., Parizi, R.: E 2 c-chain: a two-stage incentive education employment and skill certification blockchain. In: 2019 IEEE International Conference on Blockchain (Blockchain), pp. 140–147. IEEE (2019)

41. Yin, B., Wu, Y., Hu, T., Dong, J., Jiang, Z.: An efficient collaboration and incentive mechanism for internet of vehicles (IoV) with secured information exchange based on blockchains. IEEE Internet Things J. **7**, 1582–1593 (2020)

42. Liu, L., Ma, Z., Zhou, Y., Fan, M., Han, M.: Trust in ESG reporting: the intelligent Veri-green solution for incentivized verification. Blockchain: Res. Appl. 100189 (2024)

43. Nix, R., Kantarciouglu, M.: Incentive compatible privacy-preserving distributed classification. IEEE Trans. Dependable Secure Comput. **9**(4), 451–462 (2011)

44. Zeng, R., Zeng, C., Wang, X., Li, B., Chu, X.: Incentive mechanisms in federated learning and a game-theoretical approach. IEEE Network **36**(6), 229–235 (2022)

45. Cheng, G., Deng, S., Xiang, Z., Chen, Y., Yin, J.: An auction-based incentive mechanism with blockchain for IoT collaboration. In: 2020 IEEE International Conference on Web Services (ICWS), pp. 17–26. IEEE (2020)

46. Stafford, G.: Environmental sensor data 132k. kaggle dataset (2023). https://www.kaggle.com/datasets/garystafford/environmental-sensor-data-132k

Development Pitfalls: A Case Study in Developing a Smart Grid Co-simulation Platform Based on HELICS

Jeremy Frandon[1], Jun Yan[1(✉)], and Emmanuel Thepie-Fapi[2]

[1] Concordia Institute for Information Systems Engineering, Concordia University, Montréal, Canada
{jeremy.frandon,jun.yan}@concordia.ca
[2] Global AI Accelerator - AI-Hub Canada, Ericsson, Montréal, Canada
emmanuel.thepie.fapi@ericsson.com

Abstract. The recent transformation of the smart grid has led to a complex and heterogeneous cyber-physical system (CPS). The modernizing electric power infrastructure is equipped with multiple systems for sensing, communicating, controlling, and processing an extensive volume of data, for which a platform or a testbed mapping various components of a smart grid is extremely useful for R&D purposes. To this end, a testbed featuring one simulator will not fully characterize the functionalities of such a complex infrastructure. A Co-simulation testbed that federates loosely coupled standalone sub-simulators is appropriate and will accurately represent a Smart Grid. This paper will investigate the process and pitfalls observed in the re-development of ASGARDS-H at Concordia University, Montréal, a co-simulator based on the Hierarchical Engine for Large-scale Infrastructure Co-Simulation (HELICS) for 5G-based smart grid security. The paper will reveal the designs and modifications of the testbed under a microservice architecture via containerization. New tools and code refactorings are proposed and discussed to decouple the simulation logic from the time and value synchronization of the co-simulation. Beyond the final platform that offers improved simulation capacities and functionalities from ASGARDS-H capabilities, the paper also aims to share lessons learned and notable pitfalls that can help smart grid security researchers more effectively and efficiently develop flexible, reliable, and scalable co-simulation testbeds.

Keywords: co-simulation · testbed · smart grid · software engineering

1 Introduction

The traditional electricity grid was designed for a one-way flow of electricity from centralized power plants to customers. However, with the rise of renewable energy sources, distributed energy resources, and electric vehicles, the grid must adapt to become more flexible, reliable, and efficient. This is where the Smart Grid comes into play.

© ICST Institute for Computer Sciences, Social Informatics and Telecommunications Engineering 2025
Published by Springer Nature Switzerland AG 2025. All Rights Reserved
X. Li et al. (Eds.): SmartGift 2024, LNICST 600, pp. 182–195, 2025.
https://doi.org/10.1007/978-3-031-78806-2_11

The Smart Grid refers to an advanced electricity network that integrates digital technology, communication, and sensors to improve the management, monitoring, and control of the electricity system [1]. It enables two-way communication between the grid and its users, allowing for more efficient and effective use of energy resources.

The smart grid presents many benefits, including automated fault recovery, renewable energy integration, and demand-side management. An Automated fault recovery enables the grid to quickly detect and isolate problems, minimizing downtime and improving overall system reliability. By integrating renewable energy sources like solar and wind power, the smart grid promotes sustainability and reduces greenhouse gas emissions, helping combat climate change. Additionally, demand-side management allows for more efficient electricity consumption by providing consumers with real-time data and incentives to adjust their usage during peak and off-peak hours, optimizing energy distribution and reducing costs. These advantages make the smart grid a pivotal technology in creating a more resilient, environmentally friendly, and cost-effective energy infrastructure.

However, as the smart grid becomes more complex and interconnected, it becomes increasingly difficult to model and evaluate the performance and security of the entire system accurately. Co-simulation has been proposed as a solution to this modeling problem.

Co-simulation is a method of simulation that pools domain-specific simulators to interact together and offer a coordinated and connected simulation requirement [2]. In the context of Smart Grid systems, co-simulation enables the testing and evaluating of interactions between different system domains: power flow, network communication, operational logic, and business logic.

A well-implemented co-simulation testbed can provide a more accurate representation of the Smart Grid system [3]. By incorporating real-time data and feedback from the physical system, co-simulation can simulate the system's behavior under different conditions and scenarios. This enables researchers and engineers to identify potential problems and improve the system design before implementation. Advanced co-simulation also allows for evaluating the system's performance in real time. By simulating the system's behavior under different conditions, e.g., load changes or renewable integration, co-simulation can help identify potential bottlenecks, weaknesses, or areas for improvement in the system.

This workshop paper adopts a distinctive approach by focusing on providing valuable insights into the development process of co-simulation testbeds, and it shall serve as a supplement to the existing literature discussing the existing and developed approaches. Through the analysis of a case study, this paper aims to shed light on the intricate process of creating co-simulation testbeds, delving into the underlying methodologies, challenges faced, and best practices employed during their development. By emphasizing the development process, this paper seeks to complement the understanding and knowledge base of researchers, practitioners, and developers, ultimately facilitating the creation of more robust and efficient co-simulation testbeds.

1.1   Related Works

A literature survey [3] outlined the current research trends in the smart grid co-simulation litterature and found that most published research uses purpose-built co-simulators to answer their research questions. The authors compiled a short list of simulators, co-simulation platforms, and simulation architectures. However, there appears to be no consensus about how to select the proper tools and architectures for each co-simulation project. This lack of consensus indicates the existence of major trade-offs made by different research groups during the development of any co-simulation testbed.

For example, co-simulation testbeds like [4], evaluating electric vehicle charging and smart grid security, need to implement the entire ecosystem they want to simulate. The researchers emulated the cars' mobile applications, the smart charging cloud management system, the charging stations' firmware, the human-machine interface, and the car demand for power over time while choosing not to emulate the network communication infrastructure in their design. To the contrary, testbeds like [5] put the focus on accurately simulating data transmission to evaluate the resiliency of the smart grid to cyberattacks but often fail to simulate practical applications that could be targeted by cyber-physical attacks.

On the contrary, projects using the HELICS [6] co-simulation platform seek to capture a holistic and fine-grained view of the smart grid systems they evaluate. For example, [7] extends the Transactive Energy Simulation Platform [8] to evaluate packetized energy management to coordinate energy consumption and supply balance; [9] federates an ns-3 network model with a MATLAB-based power system model to evaluate the impact of non-ideal communication network performance on a proposed Generalized Power System Stabilizer architecture; [10] synchronizes GridLAB-D and Python-based controllers to model an inverter-based microgrid, allowing them to verify a Leader-Follower Consensus (LFC) Architecture for Grid-Forming and Grid-Following Inverter Coordination.

Industry case studies in other fields of CPS discuss the implications of the co-simulation architecture on the development and deployment processes. For example, [11] finds that implementing a microservice-based architecture for DevOps enables continuous deployment, monitoring, and validation of the CPSs they studied (elevator dispatching algorithms). This microservice-based architecture is similar to the one we introduce in this paper. Their findings, which focus on DevOps and continuous deployment, provide yet another insight into CPS testbed developments.

This paper presents ASGARDS-H [12], the co-simulation platform we are building upon. We discuss its design limitations and how they impacted the development of new features. We then present how we overcome those limitations by redesigning and refactoring specific components. We conclude by generalizing our findings based on known software engineering principles and recommending adopting emerging tools for smart-grid co-simulation.

2   Case Study: ASGARDS-H Testbed

ASGARDS-H [12] is a co-simulation platform developed to enable advanced smart grid cyber-physical attacks, risk, and data studies. It aims to provide a modular, complete, and scalable solution for generating standardized datasets for research and development in smart distribution grid security. The platform utilizes the HELICS [6] co-simulation framework and offers capabilities for generating realistic scenarios, including instabilities, faults, and cyber-physical attacks. The generated datasets can be used to develop data-driven approaches and advanced machine learning techniques for enhancing smart grid security. ASGARDS-H is designed to be user-friendly and allows for the customization and extension of its capabilities. It is being developed by a research team at the Concordia Institute for Information Systems Engineering as part of the Ericsson GAIA program and holds potential for future studies on cyber-physical attacks in smart grids.

We chose ASGARDS-H because, compared to other platforms, it is a recently developed platform, its source code was available to us, and [12] commented heavily on its modularity and extensibility. Our team decided to do some development work on top of ASGARDS-H to increase its capabilities and remedy some of its initial design limitations. In this section, we present our understanding of ASGARDS-H design considerations and limitations. In Sect. 3 we present the software engineering challenges encountered when working on ASGARDS-H and how they relate to documented problems in the Evidence-Based Software Engineering literature. In Sect. 4, we document our project-specific solution. This paper aims to provide insight into the development process of a co-simulation testbed by outlining pitfalls to avoid, and possible solutions.

2.1   Design Considerations

The main design consideration was to create a usable testbed capable of generating truthful data about how a smart grid would react under different cyberattacks. Much thought was put into the usability of the testbed configuration system, with a well-integrated project-generation graphical user interface and both a visual and machine-readable output interface.

ASGARDS-H used the capabilities of its federated simulators, GridLAB–D [13] and OMNeT++ [14] to simulate scenarios that include power grid faults, manual cyberattacks, manual physical attacks, configurable cyber-physical attacks, weather events, and network events. The capacities were built by leveraging the integration between HELICS and GridLAB-D and implementing OpenADR [15] and phase measurement unit communication over an LTE network in OMNeT++. The supporting interfaces and API layers for attack generation and testing were written in Python.

2.2   Design Limitations

In its first development cycle, ASGARDS-H accumulated two elements of technical debt that would hinder its development progress. The first one was that the project depended on specific software libraries, which are only available for some Linux distributions. The development team shall work on and deploy ASGARDS-H as a virtual machine. Increasing the development overhead.

The other element of technical debt was the highly coupled code structure. Where the project generator would generate OMNeT++ .ned files and GridLAB–D .glm files with hard-coded values that would be depended on by HELICS and the other Python modules, this breach of the separation of concerns principle makes it difficult for the development team to modify one part of the code without having to attend to all other parts.

3   Software Engineering Challenges

As part of its development lifecycle, our efforts with ASGARDS-H faced multiple challenges that are well-documented in the software engineering literature. The first one was a change in requirements to support new features. This kind of requirement change (adding or changing the scope of the work) is the most common type of requirement change [16].

The second development challenge was turnover-induced knowledge loss. As the main developer in our team left the project in 2021, the new developer onboarded to continue the project had to recover that knowledge using various techniques. The new developer relied on the available documentation, interviewed colleagues who had contributed to the project, and attempted to recreate the knowledge from the codebase. Those techniques are consistent with how most teams deal with turnover-induced knowledge loss [17].

3.1   Change in Requirements

The change in requirement was extending the scope of capabilities of the co-simulation platform to include the ability to simulate a new smart grid capability, such as feeder automation or a 5G cellular network. This new scope requires additional capabilities that should be supported by the power and network simulators: feeder switches and relays, fault-current detection, GOOSE messaging, and 5G user-plane communication.

However, some of those capabilities were not supported by the previous deployment. As the most up-to-date 5G simulator, Simu5G [18] was only compatible with a newer version of OMNeT++. The team had difficulties getting millisecond-level transient values from GridLAB-D for the fault-current detection. The change in requirement, therefore, necessitated a major update to multiple components of ASGARDS-H.

Moreover, the tight coupling of the different pieces of code made it difficult to upgrade ASGARDS-H incrementally. Extensive03260997f refactoring and integration efforts were required to accommodate the new capabilities and ensure seamless communication between the power and network simulators. The team had to carefully design and implement the necessary changes to prevent any adverse effects on the overall performance and stability of the co-simulation platform.

3.2   Turnover-Induced Knowledge Loss

Within the development of ASGARDS-H, a significant hurdle was encountered as the main developer departed, accompanied by changes in project requirements, which created difficulties in adapting and delivering the new features. For a large-scale multi-year co-simulator development project, similar key personnel changes are often inevitable. They can cause substantial consequences, as they disrupt the continuity of knowledge keeping/transfer and hampers the understanding of the intricacies involved in implementing complex functionalities [19]. In the case of ASGARDS-H, replacing the main developer resulted in a knowledge gap that posed challenges to the team's ability to comprehend and modify the existing codebase to meet the evolving requirements. The subsequent change in project requirements further compounded the predicament, as the team faced the daunting task of reconciling the new specifications with the existing codebase, leading to delays and potential design compromises. The departure of the main developer and the subsequent change in requirements highlight the criticality of maintaining a robust development team and implementing efficient knowledge transfer processes, ensuring the continuity of project goals and minimizing disruptions during the development lifecycle.

With the arrival of a new main developer, the development team had to rebuild the knowledge loss and generate an upgrade plan for ASGARDS-H. After understanding the technical debt, as defined by [20], of the project and the major components change needed, the team decided to use this opportunity to update the architecture of ASGARDS-H to address the modularity and dependencies issues. This update first took the form of a refactor. The implementation would change, but the user interface should remain the same. Then, the team would upgrade the different modules incrementally.

4   Project-Specific Solutions

The tightly coupled structure of ASGARDS-H was a main obstacle to updating each module incrementally, therefore the primary focus of the refactor in ASGARDS-H was to reduce coupling between the co-simulation federates by making each federate run in a separate container and within its codebase using modular programming principles.

Once each federate was properly decoupled, a concerted effort was made to refactor the existing code using modular programming techniques. The codebase became more cohesive, maintainable, and extensible by breaking down monolithic components into smaller, self-contained modules. This refactoring approach reduced the interdependencies between different parts of the code, allowing for more granular updates and modifications.

Finally, we updated the co-simulator toolchain, in our case a co-simulation scenario generator, to work with this more decoupled design, and to increase the number of scenarios that can be generated. The combined efforts of containerization and refactoring using modular programming principles were instrumental in achieving a less coupled architecture both between the co-simulation federates

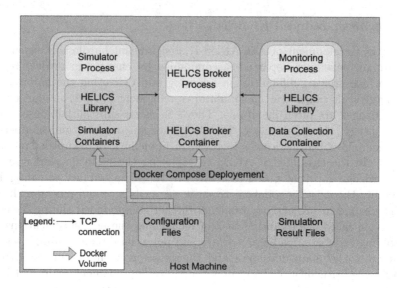

Fig. 1. Containerization architecture.

and within their own codebase, enhancing the overall flexibility, maintainability, and extensibility of the ASGARDS-H co-simulation platform.

4.1 Decoupling the Federates

Containerization is the process of packaging software code with only the operating system libraries and dependencies required to run the code. This creates a single lightweight executable called a container. Containerization was employed to encapsulate each co-simulation federate within a separate container, enabling them to operate independently while communicating through well-defined interfaces. This approach not only enhanced the scalability and portability of the platform but also reduced the dependencies and coupling between the federates, promoting flexibility and ease of integration.

The first step in the refactor was to decouple the various simulators from each other by isolating them in different containers. The separation went as such: the HELICS broker, the user interface, and each of the GridLAB-D, OMNeT++, controller, and attacker simulators were each encapsulated in a Docker [21] container, which allowed a strict separation of the project files for each simulator, as well as enforcing the HELICS broker to be the sole communication interface between the different federates.

Figure 1 shows the containerization architecture. In this architecture, the different federates can then be configured separately. As long as they use the HELICS library to declare the values they need to interface with, the federates can be started together using the Docker management engine and will behave correctly. To create the Docker containers, Dockerfiles are created for both the Broker and the federates. Docker-compose files are created to declare each federate as a service.

For example the HELICS broker Dockerfile reads as such:

```
FROM ubuntu:22.04
LABEL Name=helics:main Version=0.0.1

SHELL [ "/bin/bash", "--login", "-c" ]
ENV DEBIAN_FRONTEND=noninteractive DEBCONF_NONINTERACTIVE_SEEN=true
ENV TZ="US/NY/New York"


RUN apt update && apt install -y #[Dependecies Truncated]

# Clones Helics
WORKDIR /root/develop
RUN git clone \url{https://github.com/GMLC-TDC/HELICS.git} helics
WORKDIR /root/develop/helics/build

#Compile Helics
RUN cmake -DCMAKE_INSTALL_PREFIX=/helics ..
RUN make -j8 && make install

#Export Shared libaries
ENV LD_LIBRARY_PATH="/helics/lib:${LD_LIBRARY_PATH}"
ENV PATH="/helics/bin:${PATH}"
ENV CPATH="/helics/include:${CPATH}"
RUN cp -r /helics /usr/local/
RUN cp /helics/lib/libhelics.so /usr/lib/

ENV PYTHONPATH /usr/local/python
# Python must be installed after the PYTHONPATH is set above for it to
# recognize and import libhelics.so.
RUN apt install -y --no-install-recommends python3-dev \
  && rm -rf /var/lib/apt/lists/*

#Install python requirements
RUN apt-get update
RUN apt install -y openmpi-bin libopenmpi-dev libpcap-dev python3-pip
RUN pip install  numpy scipy pandas matplotlib posix_ipc virtualenv helics
RUN pip install git+https://github.com/GMLC-TDC/helics-cli.git@main
```

The HELICS Dockerfile can be taken as an example for the other federates as it shows the containerization procedure for both C/C++ federates with a compilation step, and python federates with the pip install step.

To see how HELICS is integrated as a service, see the following excerpt from the docker-compose file:

```
broker:
  build:
    context: ./generic
    dockerfile: ./Dockerfile_helics
  expose:
    - "23404"
  volumes:
    - "./generic/broker.sh:/root/broker.sh"
    - "./generic/helics_simplified:/usr/local/python/helics_simplified"
  command: ./broker.sh 2
  networks:
    - cosim
```

The build section points to the Dockerfile we just described; the expose section indicates that the other containers are expected to reach this service on port 23404. The volumes section mounts some scripts and libraries the service will use, in our case `broker.sh` is the startus script for the HELICS Broker, and `helics_simplified` is the federate-level middleware library that we present in the next section. The command section indicates that the broker expects two connections. The network provides separation between co-simulation services and any additional services one may use in conjunction with ASGARDS–H.

The other federates follow a similar structure, mounting libraries or configuration files as volumes.

4.2   Refactoring the Federates

The next step in the refactor efforts was to decouple the simulation logic from synchronizing time and values during co-simulation. The different simulators integrated into ASGARDS-H use various programming languages. For example, OMNeT++ uses C++, and the attacker and controller simulators use Python. To be integrated into the co-simulation, the simulators that do not originally support HELICS need to use the C-style HELICS library. Using the library as-is in the simulator logic code led to a mixed level of abstraction and lack of separation of concern anti-patterns, as defined by [22]. Moreover, the programming idioms of the C-style HELICS library often conflicted with the native programming idioms of the simulators, such as dynamic typing and iterators for the Python-based simulators and the message passing semantic of OMNeT++.

To address this issue during the refactor, Python and OMNeT++ middleware modules called HELICS-simplified were created. These modules introduced an abstraction layer through iterator synchronization and Class-based publication and subscription interfaces, offering object-oriented capabilities to Python. Similarly, the OMNeT++ module provided an abstraction via an OMNeT++ simple module. These modules allowed each simulator to query the simulation time and values from other simulators using idiomatic code without concern for

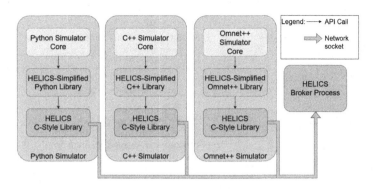

Fig. 2. HELICS-simplified middleware architecture.

the HELICS library semantics. Those modules then use the C-style HELICS library to synchronize time and value among the simulators. The decoupled and middleware-based architecture is illustrated in Fig. 2.

4.3   Updating the Co-simulation Tooling

The original design of ASGARDS-H included a project generator that took a GridLAB-D file as input and produced the necessary configurations for the OMNeT++ simulation, Controller simulator, and HELICS co-simulation framework. This aspect of the project posed challenges from both a compiler theory and toolchain design perspective. The goal of the project generator was to transform simulator specifications (initially obtained from a Graphical User Interface) into a set of configuration files that ensured a coherent co-simulation. However, this tool introduced rigidity in the types of scenarios that could be simulated. After the refactor, we designed a simpler project-generation tool that took as input the scenario files of each simulator (.ini file for OMNeT++ and .glm file for GridLAB-D), as well as the values each simulator expects to exchange through HELICS. The new project-generation tool checks the consistency of the scenario and configures the inter-simulator interfaces before starting a co-simulation. Figure 3 illustrates the overall interaction between the project generator and the co-simulation system.

Table 1. Progress brought by the refactor

ASGARDS-H Property	Before	After
Portability	○	●
Modularity	◑	●
Maintainability	○	●
Versatility	◑	●

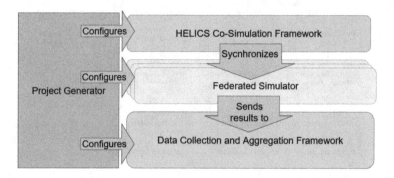

Fig. 3. Co-simulation tooling architecture

By systematically addressing each aspect of the ASGARD-H co-simulation project, the refactoring effort achieved improved modularity and abstraction. Table 1 summarizes the impact of the changes described to the portability, modularity, maintainability, and versatility of ASGARDS-H. The use of docker containers, the introduction of HELICS-simplified modules, the application of the inner dispatch pattern, and the enhancement of the project generator significantly contributed to the overall effectiveness and coherence of the platform.

5 Discussions

As software projects, co-simulation testbeds encounter software development and engineering challenges similar to the ones faced in the industry. As many challenges have been thoroughly documented in the software engineering literature, heeding some of their advice would prevent some of the most common pitfalls for smart grid security researchers.

5.1 Software Engineering Lessons Learned

Adopting evidence-based software engineering practices could have potentially mitigated the shortcomings encountered in the ASGARDS-H co-simulation platform development. By utilizing empirical evidence and best practices to inform decision-making and guide development, several key issues could have been addressed proactively.

Firstly, a systematic approach to software development, including standardized development environments and tools, could have been employed from the outset. This would have ensured greater portability and reduced the ad-hoc nature of the Linux environment, making the platform more accessible and adaptable to different operating systems. Additionally, utilizing established version control systems and documenting the development process would have facilitated knowledge transfer and minimized disruptions caused by the departure of the main developer.

Furthermore, evidence-based practices encourage modular design and code decoupling. By prioritizing modularity and encapsulation during the initial development phase, the platform's maintainability and extensibility could have been improved. Implementing well-defined interfaces between components would have facilitated the integration of control systems and the customization of communication protocols, enabling smoother adaptation to changing requirements.

Moreover, conducting thorough requirements analysis and continuously engaging stakeholders would have reduced the likelihood of significant changes in project specifications. Regular communication with end-users and incorporating feedback into the development process would have ensured that the implemented features aligned with their evolving needs, reducing the need for extensive codebase refactoring.

Finally, adopting rigorous software testing practices, including unit testing, integration testing, and regression testing, would have helped identify and address issues early in the development lifecycle. This would have minimized the impact of bugs and enabled faster iterations, ensuring a more stable and reliable platform.

In conclusion, leveraging evidence-based software engineering practices such as standardized development environments, modular design, thorough requirement analysis, continuous stakeholder engagement, and rigorous testing could have mitigated the shortcomings encountered in the ASGARDS-H co-simulation platform. Embracing these practices fosters a more systematic, adaptable, and reliable development approach, reducing the likelihood of maintainability challenges and facilitating the delivery of robust and feature-rich solutions.

5.2   Advancements in Co-simulation with Functional Mock-Up Interface

The Functional Mock-up Interface [23] (FMI) is a standard for exchanging simulation models between different simulation tools. The last update to the FMI standard, 3.0, released in 2022, includes new features that make it well-suited for creating co-simulation testbeds and digital twins for smart grids.

The Functional Mock-up Interface uses a common interface definition to simulate parts of complex systems encapsulated in Functional Mock-up Units (FMUs). The FMI Application Programming Interface (API) is defined in Common Concepts and allows computations triggered by standardized C functions from the importer into the FMU. Using C as the programming language enables portability and compatibility with all embedded control systems.

Additionally, the FMI Description Schema, defined in XML format, specifies the structure and content of a model description file (modelDescription.xml), containing the definition of all exposed variables, their interdependencies, and capability flags of the FMU. This XML-based approach allows importers to access and store variable definitions with their own representation without the overhead of standardized access functions. The FMU Distribution is done as a single ZIP file, including the modelDescription.xml, the binaries and libraries required for executing FMI functions (.dll or .so files), and the sources of the

FMI functions, with documentation and other data used by the FMU, such as tables or maps.

In the new update to the standard, released after our refactoring efforts, FMI introduces FMI for Co-Simulation, providing a standardized interface for executing simulation models in a co-simulation environment. Unlike FMI for Model Exchange, Co-Simulation FMUs include both the model algorithm and the required solution method. Communication between FMUs is limited to discrete communication points, and the subsystem inside an FMU is solved independently. A co-simulation framework, such as HELICS, should be selected by the researchers to control data exchange and synchronization between FMUs.

As a new standard, FMI for Co-Simulation still needs further investigation. However, it addresses most of the modularity and reusability concerns raised in this paper. A move towards standards like it would foster more flexible and adaptable co-simulation frameworks for the smart grid and CPS research community.

6 Conclusion

In this paper, we discussed the development process and challenges faced in creating a co-simulation testbed for smart grid security. Through the case study of ASGARDS-H, based on the HELICS platform, we highlighted the importance of addressing technical debt, turnover-induced knowledge loss, and other software engineering challenges. We emphasized the need for modularity, maintainability, and versatility in co-simulation platforms to ensure effective and efficient development. By sharing lessons learned and best practices, this paper aims to facilitate the creation of more robust and efficient co-simulation testbeds for smart grid security research.

Acknowledgement. This work is supported in part by the Natural Sciences and Engineering Research Council of Canada (NSERC), RGPIN-2018-06724.

References

1. Bayindir, R., Colak, I., Demirtas, G.K.: Smart grid technologies and applications. Renew. Sustain. Energy Rev. **66**, 499–516 (2016)
2. Gomes, C., Thule, C., Broman, D., Larsen, P.G., Vangheluwe, H.: Cosimulation: a survey. ACM Comput. Surv. **51**(3), 49:1–49:33 (2018)
3. Mihal, P., Schvarcbacher, M., Rossi, B., Pitner, T.: Smart grids cosimulations: Survey & research directions. Sustain. Comput. Inf. Syst. **35**, 100726 (2022)
4. Sarieddine, K., Sayed, M.A., Jafarigiv, D., Atallah, R., Debbabi, M., Assi, C.: A real-time cosimulation testbed for electric vehicle charging and smart grid security. In: IEEE Security & Privacy, pp. 2–11 (2023)
5. Hammad, E., Ezeme, M., Farraj, A.: Implementation and development of an offline co-simulation testbed for studies of power systems cyber security and control verification. Int. J. Electric. Power Energy Syst. **104**, 817–826 (2019)

6. Palmintier, B., Krishnamurthy, D., Top, P., Smith, S., Daily, J., Fuller, J.: Design of the HELICS high-performance transmission-distribution-communication market co-simulation framework. In: 2017 Workshop on Modeling and Simulation of Cyber-Physical Energy Systems (MSCPES), pp. 1–6. (2017)
7. Li, Y., Hou, L., Du, H., et al.: PEMT-CoSim: a co-simulation platform for packetized energy management and trading in distributed energy systems. In: 2022 IEEE International Conference on Communications, Control, and Computing Technologies for Smart Grids (SmartGridComm), pp. 96–102 (2022)
8. McDermott, T., Pelton, M., Hardy, T., et al.: Transactive energy simulation platform. (2017). https://doi.org/10.11578/dc.20171025.1920. https://www.osti.gov/biblio/1898731
9. Elliott, R.T., Arabshahi, P., Kirschen, D.S.: A generalized PSS architecture for balancing transient and small-signal response. IEEE Trans. Power Syst. **35**(2), 1446–1456 (2020)
10. Singhal, A., Vu, T.L., Du, W.: Consensus control for coordinating gridforming and grid-following inverters in microgrids. IEEE Trans. Smart Grid **13**(5), 4123–4133 (2022)
11. Aldalur, I., Arrieta, A., Agirre, A., Sagardui, G., Arratibel, M.: A microservice-based framework for multi-level testing of cyber-physical systems. Softw. Quality J. (2023)
12. Lardier, W.: ASGARDS-h: Enabling advanced smart grid cyber-physical attacks, risk and data studies with HELICS, masters, 181p. Concordia University (2020)
13. Battelle Memorial Institute. GridLAB-d simulation software. (2023). [Online]. https://www.gridlabd.org/. Accessed 17 Aug 2023
14. OpenSim Ltd. OMNeT++ discrete event simulator (2019). [Online]. https://omnetpp.org/. Accessed 17 Aug 2023
15. OpenADR Alliance. OpenADR home. (2012).[Online]. https://www.openadr.org/. Accessed 17 Aug 2023
16. Janes, A., Remencius, T., Sillitti, A., Succi, G.: Managing changes in requirements: aempirical investigation. J. Softw. Evol. Process **25**(12), 1273–1283 (2013)
17. Robillard, M.P.: Turnover-induced knowledge loss in practice. In: Proceedings of the 29th ACM Joint Meeting on European Software Engineering Conference and Symposium on the Foundations of Software Engineering, New York, pp. 1292–1302 (2021)
18. Nardini, G., Stea, G., Virdis, A., Sabella, D.: Simu5g: a system-level simulator for 5g networks. Presented at the 10th International
19. Schneider, K.: Fundamental concepts of knowledge management. In: Schneider, K. (ed.) Experience and Knowledge Management in Software Engineering, pp. 29–66. Springer, Heidelberg (2009)
20. Kruchten, P., Nord, R.L., Ozkaya, I.: Technical debt: from metaphor to theory and practice. IEEE Softw. **29**(6), 18–21 (2012)
21. Docker Inc. Docker: accelerated container application development (May 10, 2022). [Online]. https://www.docker.com/. Accessed 17 Aug 2023
22. Brown, W.H., Malveau, R.C., McCormick, H.W., Mowbray, T.J.: AntiPatterns: Refactoring Software, Architectures, and Projects in Crisis, 1st edn. Wiley, New York (1998)
23. Modelica Association. Functional mock-up interface specification. (May 2022). [Online]. https://fmi-standard.org/docs/3.0/. Accessed 17 Aug 2023

Author Index

© ICST Institute for Computer Sciences, Social Informatics and Telecommunications Engineering 2025
Published by Springer Nature Switzerland AG 2025. All Rights Reserved
X. Li et al. (Eds.): SmartGift 2024, LNICST 600, p. 197, 2025.
https://doi.org/10.1007/978-3-031-78806-2

Printed in the United States
by Baker & Taylor Publisher Services